D1457402

FAULKNER'S
Intruder
in the Dust

FAULKNER'S

Intruder in the Dust

NOVEL INTO FILM

THE SCREENPLAY BY BEN MADDOW

AS ADAPTED FOR FILM BY

CLARENCE BROWN

Regina K. Fadiman

THE UNIVERSITY OF TENNESSEE PRESS

KNOXVILLE

*The illustrations are used through the courtesy of the
Clarence Brown Collection, Special Collections, University of Tennessee Library.*

LIBRARY OF CONGRESS CATALOGING IN PUBLICATION
DATA
Fadiman, Regina K
    Faulkner's Intruder in the dust.
    "Ben Maddow bibliography and filmography": p.
    Includes index.
    I.   Maddow, Ben, 1909–   II.   Faulkner,
William, 1897–1962. Intruder in the dust.
III.   Intruder in the dust.   [Motion picture]
IV.   Title.
PN1997.I518   791.43'7   77–8417
ISBN 0-87049-214-4

To my chicks:
STEPHEN LESSER,
of whom I am very proud,
and
JOHN LESSER,
whose memory I cherish.

PREFACE

OVER THE CENTURIES and long before the invention of the camera or of motion pictures, scholars, theoreticians, and critics have been intrigued by the subject of adaptations from one medium of expression to another. These mixed works invite investigations in several directions: they sharpen our perceptions of the formal values of individual works of art; they provide a field for studies of the relationships among the arts, and they offer systems which can be compared to the systems of other social structures. It is virtually impossible, moreover, to discuss an adaptation without taking into consideration the polysemous nature of its origin and the centrifugal character of its implications.

Few if any forms of art have depended as heavily as film upon the works of predecessors in different and earlier forms. From one point of view adaptations reveal to what extent *Ut Pictura Poesie*, just as from another point of view, they illustrate the differences in kind between language and visual images. Rightfully termed a pan art, film draws upon and transforms many models, suggesting that this ability to absorb and to adapt so readily may be one of the unique features of this twentieth-century art form. Yet many prescriptive and proscriptive purists object to the very concept of film adaptations, considering them to be mere copies or pallid derivations drawn from original works. Ignoring the practice of Shakespeare and other august artists sanctified by time, these aestheticians insist that the cinema refrain from borrowing from literature or the theater, and that it find its own form and mythos instead. Others, whose predilections are social and political, deplore the imitation of art rather than of life. It seems to me that such arguments evade the essential phenomenology of film, in which because of the particular nature of the medium, every film, whether it be an adaptation or an original, must employ its own means to find its own form and mythos. Moreover, art always grows out of art, and no facile polarization of art and life is possible, for art is not opposed to, but is a part of life.

In the following essay on the two versions of *Intruder in the Dust* I provide a detailed description of the various components of each work, based on an empirical investigation of their individual means and ends. Taken together, William Faulkner's novel and Clarence Brown's film version of that novel demonstrate that many factors—economic, historic, sociological, political, and psychological—must be considered in examining the relationship between the two works. As the pressures of these extrinsic forces are applied to specific works, they shape the unique aesthetic elements that are a characteristic of every art form. Accordingly, I have tried to examine the two *Intruders* in light of the extraordinarily different backgrounds from which each one emerged, and also to point out that, although aesthetically each version must be judged independently of the other, ultimately, in various complex ways, the novel and the film continue to interact with one another.

Before summarizing the content of this book, I would like to explain briefly its scope and its aims, and to tell the reader of what to expect and of what not to expect. The book is not a history of film or an analysis of film theory, any more than it is a history of the novel or novel theory. It is instead a particularized case history of the adaptation of a single novel into a motion picture. In recording the major steps in the process of this single adaptation I have tried to provide as complete an anatomy as possible, thereby including many disparate kinds of details ranging from the anecdotal and the pragmatic to the aesthetic.

My argument proceeds chronologically from an interpretation of the novel, including its critical reception and subsequent fate, to a discussion of the genesis and aftermath of the film, which reflects the response of the studio system to the political tensions and conflicts of the time. Next, I trace the revisions in Ben Maddow's screenplay from the treatment to the final version. Since early drafts of scenarios are rarely accessible to a critic, I have taken full advantage of the availability of this material to illustrate the process of adaptation from novel to screenplay. Finally, I deal with the film itself, interpreting and evaluating it, as well as pointing out that because of a shift in tone and in emphasis, the total meaning of the film differs somewhat from the meaning of the novel.

Several unusual aspects of this project remain to be discussed. First, it provides a professional portrait of Clarence Brown, who, although now retired after a career of more than three and one-half decades, is still one of Hollywood's most esteemed directors. Because he is a very private person, very little has been written about Clarence Brown. This book presents a view of him as seen through the eyes of several of his co-workers, and also a more subjective picture, drawn from his own words. In addition, since *Intruder* is generally conceded to be one of Brown's finest films, it offers a model for the directorial quality of his canon. Appearing one year after the publication of the novel, it was heralded as the best adaptation ever made of a Faulkner work.

Next, for readers particularly interested in William Faulkner, new insights are provided by Clarence Brown and by the cinematographer, Robert Surtees, into the complex personality of the man acknowledged to be the major American novelist of the twentieth century. Faulkner's probable contributions to the screenplay (for which he received no credit) are also cited and quoted.

Finally, this volume includes the complete scenario of the film version of *Intruder in the Dust*, as written by Ben Maddow, one of the most talented and eclectic writers in Hollywood. It is a model of its genre, and deserves to be read on its own as a major contribution to screen writing. Since no script can serve as an accurate record of a film, I have documented some of the changes from the script to the film, and in addition noted dialogue and action that was transferred from the novel to the script. A filmography of Clarence Brown's films and a primary bibliography and filmography of Ben Maddow's works are also provided.

In the preparation of this book, I have had the help and the cooperation of many people. I would like to express my gratitude to the following:

Clarence Brown for his interest and encouragement, and for extremely valuable insights and information; Ben Maddow for his kindness and patience in discussing the scripts and the film with me on several occasions; Dore Schary for a wealth of background information, given generously and in friendship; Robert Surtees for a remarkable memory of every aspect of the film from the purely technical to the personal. To these men, all of whom were directly involved in the making of the film, I am immensely grateful.

I would also like to thank Metro-Goldwyn-Mayer for granting me permission to publish the screenplay, and in particular Herbert S. Nusbaum who expedited the project, and whose legal expertise and knowledge of film history and technique were among my most valuable resources; Donald S. Klopfer and Gerald Summer of Random House for permission to publish the screenplay and quotations from the novel; William K. Everson for his helpful advice; John H. Dobson for the use of the Clarence Brown papers in Special Collections at the University of Tennessee Library; Douglas Lemza for providing a 16mm print of the film.

I also appreciate the encouragement of Neil D. Isaacs, whose book on *Walk in the Spring Rain* precedes mine, and Ski Hilenski, who compiled the Clarence Brown filmography with immense diligence and thoroughness.

In my discussion of Faulkner's novel, I have relied upon the works of many scholars and critics. I would like in particular to acknowledge the inestimable value of Joseph Blotner's biography of Faulkner. My discussion of the film is highly indebted to Beverle Houston, Marsha Kinder, and Lillian Wilds, whose perceptions of *Intruder*, as well as of many other films, have provided a basis for the interpretation in the last chapter of this book and for a continuing education in the art of the cinema. I am most grateful, too, to Blake Nevius without whose skillful and discerning reading I would be loath to consider a manuscript complete. Finally, I thank my husband, William Fadiman, who helps me in innumerable ways and who never fails to encourage me with wisdom and wit.

REGINA K. FADIMAN

Los Angeles, California
March, 1977

CONTENTS

ILLUSTRATIONS

PART ONE

Introduction

I
NOVEL INTO FILM

THE CREATION OF A NOVEL is a private act, performed by one individual who has only language by means of which to create and people his fictional world. Despite publishers, hawkers, and vendors of books, for the reader, too, a novel is a private experience. In contradistinction, the creation of a motion picture is a public act, a group endeavor which can involve as many as 128 crafts and numerous people from artists and technicians to administrators and executives. Film itself is only one of the means to the finished film, which relies not only upon language but upon the use of sophisticated electronic and photographic equipment to present images of real people among real objects in real places. For the viewer, moreover, whether in a motion picture theater or in front of a television screen, a movie is a social experience; the contexts both on and around the screen preclude the privacy of the written word.

When two works, such as William Faulkner's novel, *Intruder in the Dust*, and Clarence Brown's film adaptation of the novel belong to such different realms of experience, how do we discuss them? For a literary critic the novel forms a part of Faulkner's entire canon, and in particular of his fictional Yoknapatawpha world. A film critic, however, especially one who subscribes to the *auteur* theory, sees Brown's *Intruder* in relationship to the director's *oeuvre*, classifying it perhaps with his other films of small-town life or of childhood and adolescence. As for Faulkner's novels and Brown's films, only on this one occasion do the twain meet.

Yet, there is an undeniable relationship between an original work and its adaptation into a different medium of expression. Oceans of ink have already been employed to explore this relationship, and the debate still rages about fidelity to the original as against reshaping and change in the hands of adapters. Since this book deals with one novel and its film adaptation, I cannot avoid the stormy controversy, although I know well that these few drops of ink will scarcely turn the tide.[1]

First, let me state my creed. I do not believe that the concept of fidelity either to the letter or to the spirit of the original provides a valid criterion on which to base a value judgment, for the demotic use of this imprecise term in such a context is actually descriptive rather than evaluative. And although filmmakers, critics, and audiences persist in comparing a film to the novel or play on which it is based, such a comparison generally leads to crude oversimplifications of both works or to the use of one as the whipping boy for the other. Ultimately, each work must be judged on its own merits, and can best be compared to other works in the same medium or genre. For Faulkner's novels are verbal constructs, and Brown's films are assemblages of visual and auditory images.

There are fruitful ways, however, in which an original work and an adaptation can be discussed without violating the integrity of either work. For example, since no film adapted from a novel can or should transcribe everything in the original, the film can serve as an interpretation of the novel, selecting out components that reveal filmic and dramatic aspects of an author's style and structure. In responding to the exigencies of a different medium and audience and sometimes to a different period in time, a film can also discover themes latent in the novel. Or the filmmakers can ally themselves to the novel's tone, or can transpose it into another key. In all these ways, looking at an adaptation can sharpen our eyes to see more of the original.

On the other hand, if what has been selected out of the novel coheres into a new work of art, the resonance of a novel can enrich a film, resulting in a complex dialogue between the two. Although André Bazin says that the greatest adaptations are those that include and are more than the originals on which they are based, it is possible for each work to be aesthetically independent and to engage one another in the issues each raises.[2] One of the most interesting adaptations from the point of view of a debate between two works is Jean-Luc Godard's *Contempt*, adapted from Alberto Moravia's *Il Disprezzo* (translated into English as *A Ghost at Noon*). In the film Godard indirectly replies to and disagrees with the novel's patronizing and scornful attitude toward the film. In addition, Godard explained in an interview that he changed the character of the heroine to fit the actress who portrayed her: "If I had had another actress for Camille Javal, the film would have had a much stronger psychological side to it. . . . But with [Brigit] Bardot it was not possible. Her nature is different."[3] Godard thus responded to practical considerations which never beset the novelist, who is free to shape his characters at will. In so doing, the film director acknowledged the personality of the actor as it infuses and often transforms a work.

In contrast, Stanley Kubrick's adaptation of William Thackeray's *Barry Lyndon* distances and generalizes the characters who could be typified by any number of actors. The film closely approximates the nineteenth-century's fictional view of the eighteenth century, and in scope, style, tone, and mode is "faithful" to the genre. Both adaptations are excellent, although vastly different in their approaches and intents, for they satisfy what in my estimation is the primary criterion for judging a film adaptation: they transform the novels into rich, complex films in cinematic terms without simplifying or popularizing the issues of the originals. In the following discussion of the two *Intruders*, I shall try to keep in mind that criterion.

Intruder in the Dust in both its forms has had a strange history. When the novel appeared in 1948, during a period of mounting agitation for racial integration, it created a critical furor. Many reviewers who had been sincere admirers of William Faulkner were deeply troubled by its seeming "anti" or "go-slow" Civil Rights message, which these reviewers took to be outright political propaganda.[4] They severely criticized the contents of the long, tortuous speeches of the lawyer, Gavin Stevens, who was assumed to be the author's mouthpiece.[5] The leader of the attack on these grounds was Edmund Wilson, who, in his frequently quoted and reprinted *New Yorker* article, "William Faulkner's Reply to the Civil Rights Program," labeled the book a political tract.[6] In the North, Faulkner was called a gradualist; in the South, he was dubbed a "nigger-lover."

Yet, despite its mixed reviews the novel sold well, and its prepublication sale to Metro-Goldwyn-Mayer freed Faulkner from the desperate need for money that had plagued him for most of his life. In fact *Intruder* made it no longer necessary for him to spend time in Hollywood, which he disliked intensely, in order to supplement his income by writing scenarios for films.[7]

According to Joseph Blotner, on whose excellent biography of Faulkner I have depended for the facts relating to the publication of *Intruder* in 1948, it drew more attention to Faulkner than anything since the publication of the notorious *Sanctuary* seventeen years earlier.[8] This renewed interest reached its apogee in 1950 when Faulkner was awarded the 1949 Nobel Prize for literature.

5

Loew's Grand, Atlanta, Georgia.

6

The reception accorded the film was almost the reverse of that of the novel. After having been chosen by Metro-Goldwyn-Mayer director Clarence Brown and the head of production, Dore Schary, because of its so-called message (a liberal view for the Hollywood of 1948), the novel was turned into a film which many respected film reviewers extolled as the finest picture of the year. Still, at the box office the film fared poorly. It was one of the few films in Clarence Brown's long and distinguished career (fifty-one films in all) that scarcely earned its costs.

Why, then, although a near-critical failure which offended both liberals and conservatives alike, was the novel a monetary success? And why was the film, released only one year later, acclaimed by film critics and ignored by potential theater audiences? It would be an oversimplification to claim, as some critics do, that the film was better than the novel.[9] Actually, the answers to these questions must be drawn from an examination of the political temper of the period directly following World War II; from a consideration of sociological issues, such as the differences in tastes between film audiences and the reading public, as well as the differences in the quality of the reviewers for the two; and from an analysis of the disparate aesthetic requirements of the two media. In retrospect, the details of the genesis and subsequent histories of both versions of *Intruder* provide an illuminating study not only of changing tastes and attitudes but also of aesthetic criteria as they shift and often collapse under the weight of current political and sociological pressures.

It was nothing new, of course, for many reviewers to refuse to grant Faulkner his *donnée* and to deplore what they had frequently termed his tales of decadence, populated with degenerates, idiots, and soulless perverts. But in *Intruder*, as one reviewer observed, "the characters are decenter."[10] Although some found the style even more tortuous than in previous Faulkner works, this time the major target was ideological. In fact, Elizabeth Hardwick stated outright that the novel was, "in its odd way a 'novel of ideas.'"[11]

Philosophic concepts are always problematic in fiction. Some of our greatest classical works are marred by ideas that seem totally unacceptable to contemporary readers. And unless the topical issues of a particular time and place are expanded to include larger, more universal themes, a work which contains naïve, outmoded or offensive arguments may fail to survive the shifts in cultural values. Fortunately, in the nearly three decades since the novel's publication, scholarly critics have examined it closely and pointed out how the concepts expressed by Gavin Stevens function as part of the total novel; several have found viable explanations for his ideological role.

Cleanth Brooks points out that Stevens's speeches amount to about ten pages in all; he concludes that Stevens's "arguments do reflect a very real cultural situation, and the reader could learn from them a great deal about the problem of the South."[12] Olga Vickery describes *Intruder* as the initiation and coming-of-age of its sixteen-year-old protagonist, who, as part of his education, must learn to come to terms with the words and ideas of his uncle, the lawyer, Gavin Stevens. Vickery also notes that the loquacious Stevens is treated with "irony if not outright satire" and that the novel dramatizes the baffling discrepancy between rhetoric and behavior. Ultimately, deeds speak louder than words.[13] Andrew Lytle finds the novel more concerned with spiritual than political matters and John Lewis Longley, Jr., dubs Gavin Stevens a "quixotic, comic hero" who "jumps too hastily to conclusions and talks too much."[14]

When asked in an interview in Japan about Stevens's sentiments, Faulkner replied, "Well, now, you must remember that that was the character's opinion and it need not necessarily be mine. I'm writing about people, not trying to express my own opinion." He suggested, incidentally, that those Japanese interested in reading his works begin with *Intruder in the Dust* because it "deals with the problem which is important not only in my country, but, I think important to all people."[15]

In pointing out the relationship of the novel to the others in Faulkner's canon and in interpreting and explicating it more closely, literary critics over the years have found that it has indeed many redeeming features. The film, however, despite the superlative reviews when it appeared, has been practically ignored by subsequent serious film critics. This paradox is only one more in the long list of social and historic ironies that characterizes the relationship between the novel and the film. After the outburst of praise in both England and America, there has been a scarcely broken silence. A few references, however, have appeared.

Andrew Sarris classifies Clarence Brown under Subjects for Further Research, describing *Intruder* briefly as his American Gothic film.[16] Kevin Brownlow refers to it as "the finest picture ever made" on the subject of racial conflict in the South, and Charles Higham and Joel Greenberg find it "harsh and bitter . . . [but] perhaps too restrained, resulting in a rather mute and bland effect."[17] In a later book, Higham describes it as being "alive with Brown's sympathetic response to nature and to simple, uncultivated human beings." He adds that in "its sympathetic, uncondescending treatment of blacks it was well ahead of its time."[18]

Among the recent studies of the portrayal of blacks in film, *Intruder* always finds a place. Donald Bogle praises Brown for capturing "the character—savage and venemous—inherent in one typical small American town." He finds the film "tough-minded and complex" in showing that a black man on trial has "little chance for justice in our country . . . a statement on film twenty years before such statements were fashionable."[19] Daniel J. Leab discusses *Intruder* in a chapter entitled "Glimmers of Change." He is less impressed with its "platitudinous moments, most of them stemming from the sermonizing of the paternalistically tolerant lawyer" than with its "tough-minded sections" which do "not try to apologize for white actions and attitudes or to evade the issues."[20]

I have saved for the last the only long serious study of the film I have seen: E. Pauline Degenfelder's "The Film Adaptation of Faulkner's *Intruder in the Dust.*"[21] Although I disagree with some of her conclusions, I find her detailed examination of the film extremely useful in raising pertinent issues and in making analytical rather than impressionistic statements.

One critic of the film deserves special mention. He is, of course, William Faulkner. His response to a reporter included the following remarks:

> [QUESTION:] What do you think of the film?
> FAULKNER: It's good. I don't know much about movies . . . but I believe it's one of the best I've ever seen.
> [QUESTION:] Do you think it is true to your book?
> FAULKNER: I do. Of course you can't say the same thing with a picture as you can with a book any more than you can express with paint what you can with plaster. The mediums are different. Mr. Brown knows his medium and he's made a fine picture. I wish I had made it.[22]

Judging from these remarks, we can assume that Faulkner found form and content inseparable. His definition of fidelity, moreover, implies a reliance upon the single criterion offered in my opening remarks above. In fact, Faulkner's attitude seems to have been that he had made his point in the novel and that Brown should be free to express himself in the film.

Nor was Faulkner averse to a magazine serial sale in which chapter nine would be eliminated for popular consumption. In that chapter

Gavin Stevens delivers his long religio-political sermon, which, according to Faulkner, if deleted would leave the novel "a simple story of movement." He even offered to do the "paring and editing" himself. In fact, such editing might have resulted in a work closer to his original plans, for as he wrote his editor, the novel had "started out to be a simple quick 150 page whodunit but jumped the traces," and turned into "a pretty good study of a 16 year old boy who overnight became a man."[23]

A forty-one page abridgment of the novel did appear in 1948, but it was not the author's own paring.[24] Reading it is a useful exercise for anyone concerned with literary and film criticism. Far from being a simple story of movement, it is closer to a humorless parody of William Faulkner's style. The remaining traces of the novel's themes are negligible. Consequently, the abridgment leaves the reader wondering why the novel was written at all. Since film adaptations are also in one sense deletions, this abridgment can constructively be compared to the film, which, despite major changes and differences, emerges as being far truer to its source.

II
THE NOVEL

NINE YEARS AFTER *Intruder in the Dust* was published, Faulkner described its inception:

> It began with the notion— . . . a man in jail just about to be hung would have to be his own detective, he couldn't get anyone to help him. Then the next thought was, the man for that would be a Negro. Then the character of . . . Lucas Beauchamp came along. . . . he took charge of the story and the story was a good deal different from the idea . . . of the detective story that I had started with.[1]

In saying that Lucas Beauchamp "took charge of the story," Faulkner is more accurately describing the film.[2] For memorable as Lucas is in the novel, it is in his impact on Chick Mallison that the central meaning of the work lies. The characters and events have substance only as illuminated by the perception of the individual— in this instance, Chick. His consciousness *is* the center of the stage, whereas the episodes that comprise the narrative often occur either in the background or off stage. The significant action, therefore, is Chick's internal struggle to comprehend and to come to terms with his world. In this respect, *Intruder* is in the tradition of other Faulkner novels, such as *Light in August* and *Absalom, Absalom!*

It has been observed that Faulkner's "characteristic mode of structuring [is] through synthesis," that "reports, accounts, and conversations are the customary mode of telling us about action, which as a consequence is always filtered. Action itself is the most abstract element in Faulkner; the immediate and real thing is a musing upon or considering of such action. That is why every action is biased, seen through the eyes of a character with a prior attitude derived from his own personality."[3]

Intruder records the pattern and direction of Chick's growing perception. In the baroque and parenthetical style to which Edmund Wilson objected, and in the synthesis of the facts and legends, the parables and genealogies of his fictional Yoknapatawpha

County, Faulkner records the growth of a young Southern boy's mind, shaped by history and forever impressed by place.[4] Chick's mind is a storehouse of the facts, fables, and memories that through the years have endowed the history of Jefferson, Mississippi, with a mythic aura. Like those of any sixteen year old, Chick's impulses, feelings, attitudes, and responses have been shaped by his experiences and observations, but his consciousness differs in one major respect: it is an echo chamber continually reverberating with the words of his garrulous uncle, Gavin Stevens, who has carefully nurtured in his nephew a moral responsibility toward social justice. Stevens's grandiloquent speeches provide not only the external but also the internal dialectic that helps Chick to resolve successfully the crisis of achieving manhood in his community.[5] It is actually irrelevant whether Stevens voices Faulkner's personal opinions, for, as Cleanth Brooks has noted, his views reflect "a real cultural situation" which, in the context of the novel, Chick must understand before he can fulfill his destiny.[6] But Chick does not blindly accept his uncle's explanations and apologias. By the end of the novel, he has learned to evaluate Gavin Stevens's rhetoric by testing it against his own experience.

His uncle does, of course, help Chick to recognize ultimately that through social action he can, as Stevens says, fight against "'injustice and outrage and dishonor and shame'" (T 206).[7] When his uncle proclaims these truths Chick is "standing there almost naked . . . [before] his uncle's bright grave eyes." Stripped down to his basic "I-Am," he completes his passage into adulthood having experienced for himself the conflicts of the complex relationship between morality and society (T 207). But his response to his uncle's rhetoric contains an element of embarrassed self-deprecation and provides a clear indication that Chick's earlier magnified view of his uncle is now adjusted to a more realistic lens.

Central to the argument I wish to pursue are the suggestive remarks of Cleanth Brooks, who has defended and defined Gavin Stevens's use of the word *homogeneity* to mean "a community of values rooted in some kind of lived experience."[8] For it is around this concept of homogeneity, which assumes the existence of a true community, that every aspect of the novel revolves. Significantly, the filmmakers grasped the importance of the local Southern community as the setting for the novel. Although such practice was comparatively rare for Hollywood in the 1940s, the film was made almost entirely on location in Oxford, Mississippi. As a result, it captures the sense of community so vital to the meaning of both novel and film, and provides a valuable record of the homogeneity Gavin Stevens described.[9]

As a novel of initiation and education, *Intruder in the Dust* concerns the growth into maturity of a *Southern* boy. Charles Mallison, Jr.'s, test of manhood and his subsequent moral and ethical development must occur in the community in which he was born and in which his forebears had lived out their lives; the rites of passage must be performed on the land in which his people had set down their roots and from which for generations they had taken their sustenance. As the following passage illustrates, a relationship of long duration between a group of people and the land forms the consciousness of the group and of the individual within the group:

> And now he seemed to see his whole native land, his home—the dirt, the earth which had bred his bones and those of his fathers for six generations and was still shaping him into not just a man but a specific man, not with just a man's passions and aspirations and beliefs but the specific passions and hopes and convictions and ways of thinking and acting of a specific kind and even race: and even more: even among a kind and race specific and unique. (T 151)

For a Southern boy, moreover, it is necessary to come to terms with the past which, according to Gavin Stevens, is still very much present: "'It's all *now* you see. Yesterday won't be over until tomorrow and tomorrow began ten thousand years ago'" (T 194). That past includes the Civil War which for every Southern boy is crystallized into "'the instant when it's still not yet two o'clock on that July afternoon in 1863,'" when Pickett's brigades stood ready for "'Longstreet to give the word'"; every Southern boy of fourteen since that instant has thought, and still sometimes thinks: "'*This time. Maybe this time* . . . the golden dome of Washington itself to crown with desperate and unbelievable victory the desperate gamble . . .'" (T 194–95).

The novel's world revolves on a view of history observed from south of the Mason-Dixon line. The sharing of this view is a major factor in the Southern homogeneity that Stevens defends. It colors Chick Mallison's childhood picture of the North, one that he has found "no reason or means to alter and which he had no reason to believe in his old age would alter either" (T 152). He sometimes saw a "curving semicircular wall not high" from which "row on row of faces" looked down upon him, expressing an "almost helpless capacity and eagerness to believe anything about the South not even provided it be derogatory but merely bizarre enough and strange

William Faulkner, Clarence Brown, and "Will Legate."

enough" (T 152–53). To Chick it was "not north but North, outland and circumscribing and not even a geographical place but an emotional idea, a condition of which he had fed from his mother's milk to be ever and constant on the alert not at all to fear and not actually anymore to hate but just—a little wearily sometimes and sometimes even with tongue in cheek—to defy" (T 152).

Like many a novelist, Faulkner selects, heightens, and generalizes in order to create his fictional reality. But there is a basis in fact for the reality he creates. The distinguished Southern historian C. Vann Woodward has analyzed the powerful forces which contribute to what he has termed "the burden of Southern history" in his book of the same title. Woodward locates the distinctive character of the Southern heritage in its past, as it differs from the national experience; the past has, he asserts, formulated the Southern character. He points out that the American national character is founded on abundance and the American experience of success. But the South has known poverty and near-starvation (poverty has been a continuing part of Southern experience since the early years of the Civil War); it has also known failure, frustration, and defeat. The South until very recently was the only part of the nation to have lost a war. Woodward points out that in most of America opulence and success have combined to fuse into the "Legend of American Innocence," which results in a moral complacency that the South cannot share because it has lived with the guilt of slavery and known this social evil intimately. The experience of evil and of tragedy, therefore, are parts of the Southern heritage. Southerners are Americans, but they are not born free.[10]

If one is to achieve maturity in the South and become a responsible, moral human being, one must cope with the forces that have created the Southern character. Thus in order to fulfill his own potential for good, Chick Mallison must face up to and overcome the potential for evil still present in his Southern community. And he must work out these problems not by testing himself in the world at large but by remaining close to what Faulkner referred to as his "own little postage stamp of native soil."[11]

It is highly significant, I think, that in most major American novels of initiation and education, the young protagonist must leave his native place in order to confront a larger and less familiar world. But in the two Faulkner works that Olga Vickery calls novels of initiation and identity, *Go Down, Moses* and *Intruder in the Dust*, there are no departures and no farewell scenes. Both Isaac McCaslin and Chick

Mallison, moreover, learn to deal with the present only by traveling into the past, and since "'it's all *now*,'" neither of them ever leaves home (T 194). Instead, by remaining among his own people, each young man finds his identity.

I have dealt at some length with the themes of homogeneity and community because they are seminal ones for *Intruder in the Dust*. The form and logic of the narrative, the structural rhythm, and the point of view are all determined by this functional use of setting. And only in a community with the shared experience of Yoknapatawpha County could the characters perform the roles and functions assigned to them in the novel. The basic plot, which consists of solving the mystery of who killed Vinson Gowrie and of proving the innocence of the falsely accused Lucas Beauchamp and of saving him from being lynched, depends upon the "good guys" having the kind of knowledge which can only be obtained from life membership in a community in which people have lived together long enough to know each other's personal histories and habits, and can therefore predict their attitudes, responses, and behavior. In addition, the plausibility of the action from its inception to its resolution, as well as the motive for that action, is governed by the social, historic, and psychological setting of the novel.

It is significant that the novel opens and closes in the town square which is the center and symbol of the county's history as well as of its social institutions. The first two paragraphs firmly establish Chick hiding "under the shed in front of the closed blacksmith's shop across from the jail" while he watches the sheriff bring Lucas Beauchamp to jail for his alleged murder of a white man. In the first two paragraphs, before he remembers the meal he had eaten in Lucas's house four years before, Chick's mind rests briefly on the two men who have been and will continue to be his moral and ethical teachers: Lucas Beauchamp and Gavin Stevens. The former will contribute dramatically to Chick's understanding of the latter.

The rest of chapter one relates Chick's first encounter, which develops into an unforgettable confrontation, with Lucas Beauchamp. Many commentators on *Intruder* have described Chick's tumble into Lucas's creek as a kind of baptism. That term, of course, is being applied very loosely to convey the quality of an experience or ordeal that initiates, tests, or purifies. The language in which Faulkner communicates the peculiar characteristic of this initiation sounds the warning:

all of a sudden the known familiar sunny winter earth was upside down

Brown and company.

and flat on his face and still holding the gun he was rushing not away from the earth but away from the bright sky and he could remember still the thin bright tinkle of the breaking ice and how he didn't even feel the shock of the water but only of the air when he came up again. (T 5)

Ralph Ellison describes Chick's fall into the ice-coated creek on a Negro's farm as a metaphor, explaining that Chick "finds that he has plunged into the depth of a reality which constantly reveals itself as the reverse of what it had appeared before his plunge. Here the ice—white, brittle, and eggshell thin—symbolizes Chick's inherited views of the world, especially his Southern conception of Negroes."[12] From that day in "early winter four years ago" to the close of the fateful week of the novel's narrative present, Chick's painful education in reality continues (T 3).

He learns that what he had assumed to be the odor of a race is perhaps the odor "of a condition: an idea: a belief" (T 11), that what Negroes customarily eat may not necessarily have been chosen "because it was what they liked" (T 13), and that *"You dont have to not be a nigger in order to grieve"* (T 25). But above all, from his own shame at insulting Lucas's hospitality, a shame that has haunted him ever since, Chick learns that his "masculinity and his white blood" cannot be affirmed by demeaning the dignity of the Negro (T 26).

During the four years that are rapidly chronicled in chapter two, Chick tries to free himself of his debt to Lucas, and, more importantly, of his own guilt and shame. The chapter consists of what in film terms would be called a montage in which Chick is shown in his familiar milieu (in the square, working in his uncle's office to earn money for the gifts he sends Lucas, and at home, receiving from a white boy on a mule Lucas's reciprocal gift, the molasses). He seems unable to gain the upper hand with Lucas, to force him to *"be a nigger first, just for one second, one little infinitesimal second"* (T 22); he cannot return Lucas's gift of molasses because it "would only be the coins again for Lucas again to command somebody to pick up and return, not to mention the fact that he would have to ride a Shetland pony which he had outgrown and was ashamed of" (T 23).

But when Lucas, crossing the square, fails to speak to Chick on two separate occasions, Chick deludes himself into thinking he is at last free, free of the mistake and the guilt and the shame it engendered, free also of "the man, the Negro, the room, the moment, the day itself," all of which "had annealed vanished into the round hard symbol of the coin" which "swelled to its gigantic maximum" and seemed "to hang fixed at last forever in the black vault of his anguish like the last dead and waneless moon" and free of the reminder of the debasement "not merely of his manhood but his whole race too" (T 20–21).[13] The ironic refrain, "he was free," recurs over and over again as Chick tries but fails to buy the freedom of his conscience from the Negro, Lucas Beauchamp. Chick's frantic and futile endeavors are carried out in the customary manner and in the customary places of the members of his own kind and race. But it is not until he defies custom and digs up the grave of a white man to provide the evidence that will save the skin of a black man that Chick's conscience is at last free.

During the course of the novel, Chick returns to the town square nine times and to his own home six times.[14] Each time he goes to the square, he learns more about the society into which he as a man will be integrated and in which he will function in the future. Each time he returns home, he learns more about the three adults who compose his immediate family: his mother, his father and his uncle, all of whom have helped to shape his development. Each member finally acknowledges in one way or another that Chick has grown up.

As he moves from place to place among the familiar landmarks, Chick remembers his uncle's lessons in history. For example, when he goes with Stevens to Lucas's cell, the history of the county jail is provided, as well as the ironic fact that "it and one of the churches were the oldest buildings in the town, the courthouse and everything else on or in the square having been burned to rubble by Federal occupation forces after a battle in 1864" (T 50). The historic burning of the courthouse, the center of law and justice, anticipates and to some measure justifies the sentiments expressed in Stevens's strong statement that not one man in a thousand *"would hesitate to repulse with force . . . the outlander who came down here with force to intervene or punish him"* (T 215).

Appropriately, it is in the square that Chick experiences his deepest emotional crisis and loses the veil which he had not known was shielding his eyes. Looking pitilessly at the waiting crowd for the first time, he sees that they have already condemned Lucas Beauchamp, and that they are now waiting "not to see what they called justice done nor even retribution exacted but to see that Beat Four should not fail in its white man's high estate" (T 137). He sees

> the faces myriad yet curiously identical in their . . . complete relinquishment of individual identity into one WE . . . he now recognized the enormity of what he had blindly meddled with . . . he was responsible for having brought into the light and glare of day something shocking and

shameful out of the whole white foundation of the county which he himself must partake of too since he too was bred of it. (T 137–38)

Horror at the composite face of evil, and the realization that he is a part of it, fill Chick, for the last time, with a yearning to run away, thereby repudiating the human race. "But it was too late now, he couldn't even repudiate, relinquish, run," for he has incurred responsibility which he cannot evade. Facing the crowd and guarding Lucas Beauchamp (or so Chick thinks) sits Miss Habersham and his own mother, calmly mending his own sock (T 138).

Chick's bitterest disillusionment, however, occurs after the fratricide has been revealed, and after the mob, making no apologies or amends, has slunk away. Over and over again he repeats, "'They ran.'" He rejects Stevens's super-subtle and convoluted explanations of the crowd's retreat, culminating in the theory that they ran in horror and repudiation of Crawford Gowrie's fratricide, a denial of his "'citizenship in man.'" Accusing his uncle of defending or excusing the mob, Chick finally decides for himself that "'they were running'" not from Crawford, but "'from themselves . . . to hide their heads under the bedclothes from their own shame'" (T 202).

Later that same Monday, after he has at last slept, Chick returns with his uncle to the square. It is not empty at all now; the people make way for them "who could do it better." He thinks that now it is all right, *"Because they always have me and Aleck Sander and Miss Habersham, not to mention Uncle Gavin and a sworn badge-wearing sheriff"* (T 209). Suddenly, he realizes his

> fierce desire that they should be perfect because they were his and he was theirs, that furious intolerance of any one single jot or tittle less than absolute perfection—that furious almost instinctive leap and spring to defend them from anyone anywhere so that he might excoriate them himself without mercy since they were his own and he wanted no more save to stand with them unalterable and impregnable: one shame if shame must be, one expiation since expiation must surely be but above all one unalterable durable impregnable one: one people one heart one land. (T 209–10)

Thus among his own people in the square, with its courthouse, its church, its Confederate monument and its jail, Chick finds the self-knowledge and sense of true identity that makes it possible to forgive and to return in spirit to his own community.

The crisis in the community has its effect on Chick's personal relationships too. Each time he returns to his home, he discovers some astonishing new truth about either his parents or his uncle,

Faulkner astride his prize-winning Tennessee walking horse.

Gavin Stevens. From his mother, who Chick thinks will never forgive him "for being able to button his own buttons and wash behind his ears" (T 34), he learns that women cannot "really stand anything except tragedy and poverty and physical pain." When he had been "chasing over the country with the sheriff digging up murdered corpses out of a ditch: she had been a hundred times less noisy than his father and a thousand times more valuable" (T 208).

It was his mother who calmly accepted the fact of Chick's independent, brave action and who acknowledged his passage into adulthood by casually giving him coffee. It was his father who objected to the coffee and deprecated the achievement with "'Maybe I better go to work. Somebody'll have to earn a little bread around here while the rest of you are playing cops and robbers.'" (T 132). But Chick, who had always looked up to his uncle, and whose first impulse was to go to his uncle's office on that Saturday afternoon when he heard that Lucas had killed Vinson Gowrie, sees

> his father's noise and uproar flick and vanish away . . . not merely revealing but exposing the man who had begot him looking back at him from beyond the bridgeless abyss of that begetting not with just pride but with envy too; it was his uncle's abnegant and rhetorical self-lacerating which was the phony one and his father was gnawing the true bitter irremediable bone . . . being born too soon or late to have been himself sixteen and gallop a horse ten miles in the dark to save an old nigger's insolent and friendless neck. (T 133)

Just as Chick's recurrent visits to familiar places, such as the town square and his home, mark off stages of his growth, the two contrasting trips to the cemetery in the lawless wilderness of Beat Four provide him with new moral horizons. The first visit is in the terror of darkness which conceals the fearful and bloody deeds of Crawford Gowrie, as well as the vandalism, although well-motivated, of the three intruders. The second visit occurs in broad daylight in the presence of the representative of the law. This time, using the clues provided the night before by Aleck Sander's sharp ears and keen vision, the sheriff and the others discover the truth. Chick also learns that old Nub Gowrie had loved his son and was capable of deep grief. He thinks that one reason Lucas was not burned the night before was that Nub, usually quick on the draw, was more occupied with mourning than revenge.

Chick understands too why Crawford Gowrie had been able to keep his Luger pistol with one bullet in it in the county jail although "strangers would be asking for weeks yet what sort of jail and sheriff

Yoknapatawpha County had" (T 237). With that bullet, Crawford killed himself, saving his father the shame of a shocking, sensational trial in which he must attest to his own son's fratricide, and saving the community further disruption as well.

Chick Mallison's peregrinations among familiar places and people, and also to a wilderness beyond, function in the novel both thematically and structurally. On the theme level, they lead him into the discovery of a complex reality, which, in turn, forces him to explore deeper layers of his own psyche. Structurally, they form recurrent patterns which illuminate the moral topology of the novel. In addition, Faulkner has furnished the novel with an abundance of vivid detail which includes the history, gossip, and folklore of Yoknapatawpha County, as well as the genealogies of many of its inhabitants. Anecdotes from the past, many of them in the form of brief *exempla*, fill Chick's consciousness with fragments of the inherited wisdom on which he can draw to understand the motives and behavior of those around him.

Thus, like most of the inhabitants of Jefferson, Chick has heard the story of Lucas's excursion to Fraser's store, seven years before the events of the narrative present. At that time Lucas's cool insolence had outraged one of the white men from the crew of a nearby sawmill to the point where the proprietor's son had had to restrain "the foaming and cursing white man" from striking Lucas with a plow singletree (T 20).

Chick also knows why Lucas has waited to "tell him, a child about the pistol . . . remembering old Ephraim and his mother's ring that summer five years ago" (T 70). The Ephraim-story of the recovery of the ring has taught Chick a bit of folk wisdom:

> "Young folks and womens, they aint cluttered. They can listen. But a middle-year man like your paw and your uncle, they cant listen. They aint got time. They're too busy with facks. . . . If you ever needs to get anything done outside the common run, dont waste yo time on the men-folks; get the womens and children to working at it." (T 71–72)

Miss Habersham understands too why Lucas did not choose to confide in Stevens but in Chick instead. As she says, "'Lucas knew it would take a child—or an old woman like me: someone not concerned with probability, with evidence. Men like your uncle and Mr. Hampton have had to be men too long, busy too long'" (T 89–90).

Lucas Beauchamp and Eunice Habersham represent the elders of the tribe into which Chick is initiated and subsequently takes his place. Although one is black and the other white, they are continually linked in Chick's consciousness. He always thinks of them in terms of their advanced ages and of their resemblances to his own grandparents. On first seeing Lucas, Chick is immediately reminded of his grandfather. For example, Lucas wore a "broad pale felt hat such as his [Chick's] grandfather had used to wear" (T 6). A moment later, following Lucas to his cabin, Chick realizes that

> he could no more imagine himself contradicting the man striding on ahead of him than he could his grandfather, not from any fear of nor even the threat of reprisal but because like his grandfather the man striding ahead of him was simply incapable of conceiving himself by a child contradicted and defied. (T 8)

Other references to the similarities between Lucas and Chick's grandfather appear sporadically throughout the novel.

As for Miss Habersham, the moment Chick notices her, sitting primly in his uncle's office, he observes "one of the round faintly dusty-looking black hats set squarely on the top of her head such as his grandmother had used to wear" (T 75). Later, too, Chick thinks about "the hat which on anyone else wouldn't even have looked like a hat but on her as on his grandmother looked exactly right" (T 130).

Chick is aware too of "a fragment of the country's chronicle" which includes Lucas's and Miss Habersham's progenitors (T 7). Lucas was the "son of one of the old Carothers McCaslin's, Edmonds' great grandfather's, slaves who had been not just old Carothers' slave but his son too" (T 7). Miss Habersham's "name was now the oldest which remained in the county. There had been three once: Doctor Habersham and a tavern keeper named Holston and a Huguenot younger son named Grenier . . . but all gone now, vanished except the one" (T 75–76).

The two old people are frequently associated and are described in comparable terms. Their clothes and jewelry are somewhat archaic: Lucas's gold watch and toothpick; Miss Habersham's watch "suspended by a gold brooch," which she wore just as Chick's grandmother had and which "since his grandmother's death no other woman . . . wore or even owned" (T 75). In addition, Lucas chooses the same hard chair in Stevens's office "which nobody else but Miss Habersham had ever chosen" (T 241). Both are independent, erect, and solitary; Lucas is friendless and kinless, Miss Habersham is forlorn (T 187).

These surrogate grandparents, each in his and her own way, exemplify the highest values of an honorable tradition and teach Chick moral truths about courage, dignity, and justice. They show the Southern boy that he is not free and that he cannot escape his responsibilities. Lucas Beauchamp, moreover, forces Chick to establish his own, independent selfhood. It is in facing Lucas Beauchamp through the prison bars that Chick realizes that he alone of all the white people Lucas would have a chance to speak to "would hear the mute unhoping urgency of the eyes" (T 69). Thus for the first time in the novel, at the moment of his supreme test, Chick thinks of himself not just as "he" but as "Charles Mallison junior" (T 68). It is Charles Mallison, Jr., who moves from assuming, along with the rest of the white population, that Lucas is guilty to proving his innocence. With Miss Habersham to encourage him and Aleck Sander to join in, he performs the heroic task that saves Lucas's life. Comic though the trio of saviors may be, they still exemplify how the virtues of a homogeneous society can be passed on from one generation to the next and to both Negroes and white people alike.

In Faulkner's fictional Jefferson of nearly thirty years ago racial prejudices and conflicts provided the testing-ground for Chick Mallison's moral growth. They still exist in the real world today, and they continue to provide the testing-ground for the moral growth of the whole nation. Ultimately, in its concentration on individual conscience, the novel presents a world in which the moral confusions of the social process must be evaluated in terms of spiritual and ethical goods, and looks forward to the day when "'Mass becomes man again conceptible of pity and justice and conscience even if only in the recollection of his long painful aspiration toward them, toward that something anyway of one serene universal light'" (T 201).

III
THE BACKGROUND
OF THE FILM

ALTHOUGH *Intruder in the Dust* was not the only film released in 1949 which dealt with the Negro problem, it had unique characteristics.[1] The novel from which it was adapted was written by a Southern author of great eminence, and it was made almost entirely in his hometown of Oxford, Mississippi. It was directed by a man whose father and grandfather were Southerners, and who himself had spent his boyhood and youth in Knoxville, Tennessee. As a director, moreover, Clarence Brown commanded among his professional peers great respect and prestige. In addition, the film starred two Southerners: Claude Jarman, Jr., who played the role of Charles Mallison, Jr., and Elizabeth Patterson, who played Miss Eunice Habersham. It also provided one of Hollywood's first atypical roles for a black man, played by the Negro actor, Juano Hernandez. The genesis of the film, as well as its aftermath, illuminates aspects of Hollywood's hyphenated product rarely brought to light, and reveals how this art-industry tried sincerely to serve the Muses and at the same time to satisfy the marketplace.

During the era of the major studios, approxomately 80 percent of Hollywood films were adaptations of plays, classical novels, or current best sellers. The reasons for this phenomenon were more often economic than aesthetic.[2] A combination of factors determined the selection of film fare, some of which explain the choice of Faulkner's controversial novel. The author's prestige and the many years since any of his works had been adapted to the screen (*Sanctuary* and "Turn About" in 1932) were undeniable extrinsic considerations.[3] What were the intrinsic values of this novel for the screen?

Primarily, Hollywood searched for works with absorbing plots, interesting characters, and fresh settings or familiar settings used in fresh, new ways. Faulkner's so-called detective story, therefore, had immediate attraction because the mystery-detective tale had become a film staple, with a built-in guarantee of box-office appeal. In the days of the B movie such thrillers were legion. Today, television is glutted with an apparently infinite number of variations of the same standard fare.[4] Interesting characters *Intruder* also provided, although the assortment may have lacked the conventional stereotypes that were so frequently employed. Its youthful protagonist, however, was well suited to attract the potentially large audience for films about children, of which *Intruder* was only one of many. Clarence Brown had made the immensely successful film starring Claude Jarman, Jr., *The Yearling* (1946), as well as *National Velvet* with Elizabeth Taylor and Mickey Rooney (1945). Metro had turned out a number of Andy Hardy stories from 1938 to 1947, several with Mickey Rooney and Judy Garland; the latter also appeared in the all-time favorite, *The Wizard of Oz* (1939).

Unique and most memorable of the novel's cast of characters is the old Negro, Lucas Beauchamp, on whom so much of *Intruder*'s meaning rests. In the use of this character the film departed from the usual detective story and also from the previous subjects for films featuring children.

The setting of the small Southern town was fairly fresh. Many films, of course, had been set in the antebellum South, but few had exploited that region in the contemporary period with its atmosphere of violence that Faulkner evoked. The novel, therefore, offered its adaptors many of the basic ingredients required for a film.[5] It provided something old and something new: a murder mystery, the solution of which results in the achievement of maturity in its adolescent hero, as he as well as the reader is forced to examine the causes and results of racial bigotry and injustice.

How did this film come to be made at Metro-Goldwyn-Mayer during the presidency of Louis B. Mayer, a man rarely moved to espouse liberal causes? Clarence Brown and Dore Schary have contributed the background information that helps to answer the question, and even though both men were discussing a film made more than twenty-five years ago, their recollections were almost identical.[6]

Clarence Brown instigated the project. His interest in making a film version of *Intruder in the Dust* emanated from a shocking event he had witnessed as a young man in Atlanta in the summer of 1916. Brown was sitting in the balcony of the Bijou Theater when a violent race riot broke out, which resulted in several lynchings. The young man rushed out of the theater and witnessed one lynching. From that day to the present, he has never forgotten it. He said that the riot began because of an alleged rape. As the Negroes came into town with their market baskets to shop on Saturday, they were grabbed up almost before they could leave the streetcar. As Brown remembers it, fifteen Negroes were slaughtered in one night; one hundred and fifty in a fortnight. In addition, there was one rape per night. Although Brown's memory of the date and the figures may not be precise after more than fifty years, the horror in his voice as he told the story was in no way diminished. The trauma of that experience lasted a lifetime.

Thirty years later, in 1948, after reading the galleys of Faulkner's *Intruder in the Dust* Brown rushed to the office of Louis Mayer and tried to convince him to buy the property at once. Mayer opposed the project at first, but Brown, a close friend of Mayer and also a top director at MGM, was in a position to be insistent.

He had an ally in Dore Schary, who had just become the vice-president of Metro in charge of production. Schary had been given the authority to buy any story costing under $75,000 and to produce the films based on these stories without interference from Mayer. Schary remembers having read the galleys of *Intruder* straight through as soon as they were submitted to him. He was immediately enthusiastic about obtaining the novel for Metro because he liked the story and thought that Faulkner's name would lend an aura to the film and evoke respect.[7]

Schary confirmed Brown's statement that Mayer was at first reluctant. With a smile, Schary said that Mayer knew his new production head's reputation for "message pictures," but that Mayer thought he could handle him. As it turned out, it was Schary who handled Mayer. Schary realized that Mayer was not very sophisticated about stories (his favorites were about motherhood), so in Scheherazade-style he told it to Mayer, who never read the novel, but finally agreed to let Schary and Brown make the film, mainly because of his respect for Brown. Schary added that Mayer was not really a bigot, but that he never understood the point of the story. With amusement, Schary explained that "Brown made it Kosher."

Both Brown and Schary felt a deep commitment to the film. Brown described it as a true labor of love and added, "this picture was for *me*." He said it was the easiest film he ever made. "You work much harder to make a flop," he observed. Although Schary worked closely with Brown and screenwriter Ben Maddow on the script, and later with Brown on the cutting, he insisted that the major credit for the film belongs to Clarence Brown, who began the project, sincerely believed in it, and handled it with great integrity. He also said that Ben Maddow wrote a superb screenplay.

When the script was completed, Brown, determined to film it on location, went to Oxford, Mississippi, to seek the cooperation of the leading citizens there. At first, he found the mayor, the city council and the Chamber of Commerce hostile to the project, but by combining persuasion with threats he finally won their agreement. When asked what sort of arguments he used, Brown said he told them that he knew his business (a truer statement was never made), and that if they did not cooperate with his work in Oxford he would make the picture in Hollywood and do whatever he pleased with it. He noted wryly that the town "came around" to his point of view. In fact, Brown was so convincing that R.X. Williams, the mayor of Oxford, agreed to act in the film. He played the role of Mr. Lilley, a representative townsman who speaks to Gavin Stevens and Chick Mallison on their way to visit Lucas Beauchamp in his jail cell. Lilley's name, of course, carries an ironic connotation in the novel that the mayor may have failed to see, but that gains a sharper edge in the film for the initiates who know the actor's official position.

There were actually no altercations between the director and the natives of Oxford during the shooting of the film, although 90 percent of the crowd scenes were made up of townspeople and students of the University of Mississippi. The *Oxford Eagle* was filled with reports of the film's progress, with human interest stories about the "sixty" Hollywood people who had been brought to Oxford, and with editorials urging the inhabitants to cooperate with the project. One editorial (10 March 1949) stresses the economic advantages that the film would have for the town of Oxford, guaranteeing that the film would not be a "quickie" but "the best film possible." Allaying the concerns of those who feared that the worst side of the community would be portrayed and that Oxford would "be held up to shame and ridicule," the editors assert that "searching diligently to determine what we have to be ashamed of, we have failed to find anything at all."

The *Eagle* followed every development in the progress of the film. It announced, for example, that "Edmund and Ephraim Lowe, identical twin sons of Mr. and Mrs. Ed Lowe, were cast in the roles of the 'Gowrie Twins' by Mr. Brown upon sight." The University of Mississippi provided a list of the local people in the film. Mrs. James W. Silver, wife of the chairman of the History Department, was in a crowd scene.[8] Her husband was reported to have spent much time on the set, taking photographs. Professor Harry M. Campbell, an associate professor of English at the time, who has since written a good deal on Faulkner, also appeared in a scene in front of the Lafayette County Jail.[9]

Brown was invited to address many local citizens' groups, and was interviewed by numerous Southern newspaper reporters. In the *Memphis Commercial Appeal* (19 March 1949) he said: "As a Southerner, I believe this motion picture can be a great accomplishment toward nationwide better understanding of the true relationship between the races in the South and of the gradualism which is solving this very old problem. Mr. Faulkner's book is the first thing ever written upon that theme." He quoted chapter seven in particular as "the most eloquent statement as to the true situation in the South." Brown obviously was not using the term "gradualism" in a pejorative sense.

The filming of a novel by William Faulkner in his hometown in the Deep South was national news. The *New York Herald-Tribune* (15 May 1949) printed the schedule:

> In January, M.G.M. dispatched a photographer to Oxford to shoot hundreds of stills of location settings with Faulkner's assistance. From these, Brown and the writer, Ben Maddow, were able to visualize what they had to work with.
>
> . . . .
>
> In February, Brown visited Oxford, spoke to civic groups, etc. Shooting began on March 10 with a company of 54—14 actors and 40 technicians.
>
> . . . .
>
> Brown adhered mostly to type casting. The village barber, Brooks Patton, plays a barber in the picture. The Marshal, Garland Kimmins, portrays the role of a marshal, and even the Mayor is seen in a prominent role.

Three themes run through the numerous interviews that Brown held with the press: (1) the value of using real locations for achieving authenticity; (2) the benefits to people outside of Hollywood of a true view of the professionalism and hard work of filmmakers; (3) the splendid cooperation of the Oxfordians. Thus the director was completely successful in persuading the community that the project would do much for Oxford, so that the attitude of the townspeople evolved from resentment to approval. "Faulkner was the first major event in Oxford," said Brown, "and the filming and World Première [11 October 1949] of *Intruder in the Dust* was the second." Numerous photographs in the Clarence Brown Collection at the University of Tennessee Library show the filmmakers hard at work amid a crowd of fascinated local bystanders.

The *Oxford Eagle* (6 October 1949) published a special edition of the newspaper to commemorate the world premiere of *Intruder in the Dust*. It quoted Clarence Brown as saying that the location work in Oxford was "inspiring." An article in the same edition by Barrett C. Kiesling says that Brown shot for only three days in Culver City before leaving for the Deep South, and that he would not have used studio sets at all had he known what he would be able to get with the cooperation of the mayor and the people of Oxford. He photographed there for six weeks, using the exterior and interior of the ninety-year old Lafayette County Jail, the famous square, the buildings (many of which were rebuilt after having been burned by Union troops in 1864), an abandoned church and graveyard deep in the wilderness of the Holly Springs National Forest, and St. Peter's Episcopal Church, which has a cross on top of its spire. Kiesling claims that over five hundred Oxford citizens appeared in the film. The great innovation, according to the article, was the use of indoor sets on location. In the past, it was customary for film companies to shoot only exteriors on location, thereby risking expensive delays because of uncertain weather. There may have been more local pride than accuracy, however, in these remarks, for, according to the director's shooting script, a number of shots, both interior and process, were taken at the studio in Culver City.[10]

The eleventh of October was proclaimed "William Faulkner Day" throughout Mississippi by Governor Fielding Wright. Mayor Williams (the Mr. Lilley of the film), who owned the Lyric Theater, completely remodeled it and put in a new screen to do full justice to the photography. The local citizens turned out en masse for the world premiere. Only Oxford's single world-famous resident was reluctant to attend; he was finally persuaded by his indomitable great-aunt.

The festivities began several days before the major event. Clarence Brown, his wife, Marian, and two of the leading actors in the film, Elizabeth Patterson and Porter Hall, returned to Oxford for the occasion. The other principals could not attend because of other film commitments. Brown was presented with a key to the city, and received the title of honorary citizen of Oxford. Representatives of a dozen Southern newspapers, *Life* magazine and Movietone News covered the celebration. Most astonishing of all, William Faulkner actually granted an interview to the press and willingly answered questions. He thought the film was one of the finest he had ever seen, and did not object to the changes that had been made: "There

31

had to be some changes in transferring the story from one medium into an entirely different one," he said, "and I think it has been well handled." When asked what he liked best he answered, "Well, I liked the way Mr. Brown used bird calls and saddle squeaks and footsteps in place of a lot of loud music telling you what emotion you should be experiencing."[11] He also praised Juano Hernandez's performance.

The people of Oxford were very proud of the film and of their participation in it. Clarence Brown confided with amusement that at the premiere none of the local actors who had been given lines to speak in the crowd scenes realized that their own voices were not used, but that voices of professional actors were later dubbed in. In fact, all of the film had to be dubbed to eliminate the ordinary noises of the streets of Oxford.

Clarence Brown was particularly proud of the dubbing. He had had twenty-five actors standing by in Hollywood, whose voices were to be looped for those of the townspeople. He picked the voice that best fit the face on the screen. He was also pleased with the score, which used only indigenous music, such as the tunes blaring forth from the loudspeakers in the mob scene and the church hymns at the beginning of the film. He said that no separate score was written for the film; background mood music was never used.[12] Robert Surtees, who photographed the scenes shot in Oxford, said that the professionalism of the dubbing was one of the most outstanding aspects of the film and that *Intruder* had been nominated for a sound award, a particularly remarkable feat on Brown's part since he had come from the era of the silents. Most silent directors, Surtees added, thought of sound as the enemy.[13]

Surtees, one of the most gifted and admired cinematographers in Hollywood, said that he learned much from working with Brown. He spoke of Brown as a great technician, whose previous engineering training was very useful. Two or three weeks before the shooting began, the directors and cameraman began to discuss what Surtees called "the emotions" of the scenes, planning far in advance the light-dark contrasts and the low-key lighting, which blurs contrasts in some of the shots.

In photographing the action, three or four cameras were used for the large crowd scenes, including a hand-held Ciné Kodak, which Surtees had used from time to time since 1927. He also explained that day-for-night shots were sometimes used because it was impossible to keep the light sky out of a large panoramic shot.

Although the director's script allocates some of the graveyard scenes to the second unit, no other cameraman was employed, according to Surtees, and the first unit did second unit work to save overhead costs. Harry Stradling, Sr., however, photographed the few interior scenes shot in Hollywood before the company went to Oxford.

It was Brown's custom to rehearse with the actors for an hour or two before shooting. He rehearsed as long as possible without breaking the Actor's Guild regulation in which actors must have twelve hours off after each working day. According to Surtees, Brown was not a temperamental man, but he was a perfectionist. Still, he did not take advantage of his powerful position in the studio to shoot an excessive number of takes, for which Surtees particularly admired him. Like a businessman, Brown was always conscious of costs and tried to work at normal speed.

One sequence that Surtees particularly remembers is the day-for-night scene of Crawford Gowrie carrying a body over the front of his mule, which was photographed from a long distance to achieve ambiguity. Many trees interfered with the shot, so that Surtees requested time to have them trimmed. To his surprise, Brown allowed two days for the green-man to remove dead branches. Then the leaves and the trunks of the trees in the foreground had to be painted black. For the desired effect, the film was underexposed. When the sequence was finished, Clarence Brown cheered; he knew even before seeing the daily "rushes" that it would be a pictorial achievement of high artistic merit.[14] Surtees also remembered that the graveyard scenes presented difficulties. Parts of this long sequence were shot on two separate nights. On the second night, the light was different, so that the grave had to be moved to a new position in order to achieve shots that would match those of the previous night.

The solution to one technical problem illustrates the director's resourcefulness, as well as his engineering training. Porter Hall, who played the role of Nub Gowrie, had to sink slowly into quicksand. The technicians at Metro had spent weeks constructing an apparatus to simulate quicksand. Unfortunately, it did not work, but Brown remembered a picture he had made years before for Universal in which he had used oatmeal to create a similar effect. He purchased one and one-half tons of oatmeal and covered it with a little sand to convey the desired illusion. Surtees also remembered the sequence but thought that chicken feed had been used. He said that it fermented and developed such a bad odor that the town

Robert Surtees checking camera for quicksand scene.

authorities ordered the filmmakers to dispose of it.

Although the natives liked and respected Clarence Brown, and politely followed his directions for the scenes in which they appeared, they nevertheless regarded the intruders with a mild degree of skepticism, from which an occasional awkwardness arose.[15] Knowing well the Deep South of 1949, Brown had warned Juano Hernandez, the Puerto Rican Negro who played Lucas Beauchamp, that he might be subjected to insults. At first Brown and Hernandez stayed at the best hotel in town, accommodations which both men agreed were far from deluxe. Then, according to Brown, Hernandez managed to meet the richest Negro in town and to promote an invitation to stay at his home for the duration of his Oxford stay.[16] Robert Surtees remarked that the local people could not believe that Hernandez, a black man, was earning fifteen hundred dollars a week, and thought he must be part white.

Hernandez, in fact, was able to help his director solve a very irritating problem. At first, the Negro stand-ins would work for a couple of hours and then disappear. It seemed that they thought Hollywood was an evil place and that all people from Hollywood must be the sons of Satan. Hernandez preached a sermon at the Negro church and convinced them that such fears were totally unfounded. Phil Mullen in the *Oxford Eagle* (6 Oct. 1949) took full advantage of this development:

> Through the close association with the MGM company for two months, Oxford learned how false is most of the glamourized and scandalized publicity about Hollywood people.
> Just as did Hernandez, and the other visitors, learn how false is most of the Northern publicity about Southern racial conditions.
> Even though he is recognized as one of the outstanding dramatic artists of the day, Hernandez quickly agreed that he would follow the natural pattern of social segregation in his stay in Oxford.
>
> . . . .
>
> Just as he worked closely with director Brown and the white actors of the company, and all enjoyed a mutual respect and affection, so he discovered that in Oxford Negroes and white men work closely together in all fields of endeavor and enjoy the same mutual respect and affection.

In an interview in *Ebony*, Juano Hernandez praised Clarence Brown, William Faulkner, and Ben Maddow. He said that they

> were wonderful, fighting for the dignity of Lucas Beauchamp in every scene. But as for Oxford . . . I went down there with an idea of what I'd find and I didn't get to change my mind. But nothing goes on in Oxford that doesn't go on in New York City. I didn't have to play at being Lucas

Beauchamp. I've been him too many times. When I tried to buy a home in Hempstead, Long Island, I was mobbed and so was my family.

Brown found Elzie Emanuel, the young Negro Hollywood actor who played Aleck Sander, less cooperative, perhaps because his was a more stereotyped role. *Ebony* reported that Emanuel "figures in what is perhaps the unhappiest moment of the film, a scene in which he bugs his eyes and trembles in the best Stepin Fetchit manner when he goes to the cemetery to dig up the murdered man's grave. Although he fought strenuously against the characterization, he was finally forced to do the stereotype."[17]

According to Brown, by disputing his direction of the grave-pit scene, Emanuel provided the only sour note in the filming. Brown settled the altercation by secretly placing a loudspeaker that made a variety of moaning and groaning sounds inside the coffin so that the young actor was genuinely frightened. Surtees, too, remembered that Brown played several practical jokes on Elzie Emanuel, including the use of a white sheet floating down from a tree and a loudspeaker emitting eerie sounds, in order to frighten him and make him respond properly.[18]

During the filming, Clarence Brown and William Faulkner became good friends who respected each other. The two men had in common their Southern backgrounds as well as their experiences in piloting their own planes. "Faulkner," said Brown, was an "elusive little devil." Frequently, looking into a store window, he would see the author's reflection peering over his shoulder, but when he turned around Faulkner would be gone. He was always wandering about and then suddenly disappearing.

While the film was being made, Faulkner was busy constructing a boat and had to get permission from the construction boss to leave the job.[19] But on Sunday, his day off, he habitually cooked breakfast for Brown and some members of the cast at Rowan Oak, his antebellum plantation.[20] As for the boat, "it never got off the dock," said Brown, but Faulkner did invite him and the cast to come aboard. On one such occasion, when Lila Bliss, who played Mrs. Mallison, started to tell an off-color story, Faulkner left the boat.

Robert Surtees, too, spoke of the author with great admiration, saying, "Faulkner entranced me; I really wanted him for a friend, and went out of my way to make him one." Surtees was full of anecdotes about Faulkner, with whom he had hoped to make a series of documentaries on the South. He described him as the most reticent man he had ever met, adding that he never wanted to intrude. Surtees also mentioned Faulkner's disappearing act, even when walking and talking with him and Brown. Faulkner's explanation was that when the conversation was finished and when there was nothing more to say, he left. Shooting parts of the film two or three miles from Faulkner's home, Surtees noticed big holes and ruts in Faulkner's driveway, which Faulkner explained were kept there to discourage people from visiting him. Surtees remembers, though, that Faulkner was sufficiently interested in the filming of *Intruder* to drop in occasionally to see the "rushes," sitting inconspicuously in the back of the room and making no comments. One of the author's chief delights in the film was the casting of his Tennessee walking horse in the role of Chick Mallison's horse, Highboy.

Surtees also said that Faulkner's sense of humor was very close to that of Will Rogers, and he attributes to Faulkner a comment that might easily have been made by Rogers: "The trouble with church," he said, "is that they have it on the wrong day and I can never make it." Surtees added that, metaphorically speaking, William Faulkner and Will Rogers "contributed more" to his life than any men he had ever met. Surtees found Clarence Brown to be a very warm-hearted, though solitary, man. When the Oxford shooting was completed, Brown thanked Surtees with tears in his eyes and told him that he was "the nicest guy" he had ever worked with.

The filmmakers returned to Hollywood, and Brown at once set to work dubbing and editing the film. As is customary, the completed director's cut was shown to Dore Schary, who had the right to re-edit it as he saw fit. Schary, however, suggested very few changes, deferring in most cases to Clarence Brown. The only changes Schary made involved the pace of the film. By eliminating some of the establishing dolly shots at the beginning, he improved the timing and thus energized the film.[21] Otherwise, the finished film followed the director's cut.

At the preview Louis Mayer became very upset and demanded changes, complaining that "the picture was about a colored man who had no respect for white people, that the man [didn't] remove his hat in the presence of white people or say 'no, sir,' or 'yes, sir,' and that he [was] just too independent."[22]

Schary chuckled as he remembered telling Mayer, "that's what the book is about—an independent black man who feels himself equal to the white man. One of the fine points of the book and the film is that the lawyer, Gavin Stevens, is sensitive enough to take the black man's money at the end." Mayer kept repeating that he ought to have some respect because "after all, he is a colored man," but Schary insisted that the film be released as it was, with no changes. Finally, Mayer countered with his strongest argument: "It won't make any money." But standing firm, Schary replied, "we made it because we wanted to make a distinguished picture that was really about something."

The film was completed within about fourteen months from the purchase date of the book, as part of a new speed-up policy that Schary had initiated. It was one of forty pictures that he supervised during his first year at the studio; he remembers that the writing and filming of *Intruder* went particularly smoothly. As it turned out, Mayer was right about one thing. Although it cost comparatively little, the film did not make money.[23]

Schary said that although the Metro publicity departments in both Los Angeles and New York thought it was a "marvelous picture" and did their best to sell it, they could get few bookings in the South. Even in the North, despite the publicity of the press preview in Inglewood, California, the Oxford premiere, and the big New York opening, white audiences avoided it. Schary suspects that in 1949 they too thought that the Negro in the film was too independent. Nevertheless, Schary added, "for Clarence Brown, it was a real cause."

The Memphis Board of Censors approved the picture, but its chairman, Lloyd T. Binford, in some respects agreed with Louis B. Mayer in his view of the film. "No Southern Negro would act the way the one in the picture does," he said. "For that matter, I don't think any one would act that way." Still, the censor board voted unanimously to permit showing the film in Memphis because "there's no social equality in it at all."[24]

Once on its way, the film inspired encomia on the part of the majority of critics. Brown's personal tally shows that 98 percent of the reviews were highly favorable. The influential Louella O. Parsons rhapsodized in the *Los Angeles Examiner* (12 November 1949), pronouncing *Intruder* "dynamic, exciting, . . . superior to the original story [which I seriously doubt she ever read] . . . one of the few real classics in Hollywood." In a more sober tone, Ralph Ellison judged it "the only film [dealing with Negroes] that could be shown in Harlem without arousing unintentional laughter [because] . . . Negroes can make complete identification with their screen image. Interestingly, the factors that make this identification possible lie in its depiction not of racial, but of human qualities."[25] Harrison Carroll predicted wrongly that "when Academy Award time rolls around . . . *Intruder in the Dust* will stand as a giant among contenders" (*Los Angeles Evening Herald and Express*, 12 November 1949); he called the film the peak of Brown's long career and found Surtees's camera work distinguished. The headline of the *Hollywood Reporter* (11 October 1949) stated that "Brown Vitalizes Faulkner Novel" and went on to claim that the director had imbued the work "with a reality that it never possessed on paper" and had "multiplied a thousand fold" its dramatic impact. Bosley Crowther in the *New York Times* (23 November 1949) proclaimed that "it is probably this year's pre-eminent picture and one of the great cinema dramas of our times."

There were, of course, some reservations. Dick Williams, in the *Mirror* (Los Angeles, 12 November 1949), said that the film touched too lightly on a controversial subject. Ezra Goodman, in the *Daily News* (New York, 12 November 1949), found that it failed "to come forth with a coherent viewpoint." He suggested that making the film in Oxford was a disadvantage: "It is not easy to get perspective on a lynch story when shooting in the heart of the deep South with the cooperation of its citizens." The *New Yorker*'s John McCarten was predictably pejorative. In a bored tone he granted that "the film has its moments of suspense" and that regarded as elementary melodrama "it is fairly satisfactory." He found "the piece as a whole . . . nowhere near as interesting as the Faulkner novel from which it was adapted." He added, moreover, that "in its mores of the Southern peasantry, it frequently borders on the ludicrous, attempting to invest with dramatic dignity characters who seem as superficial as comic-strip types."[26] Emily Wister, however, writing in a Southern newspaper (*Charlotte News*, 23 January 1950), found that "the South, particularly Mississippi, comes in for some hearty slaps in this picture and the sad thing about it is most of the charges are true. . . . It's a good story, honestly told and fearlessly portrayed."

By and large the Negro press praised the film. Gertrude Gipsom wrote in the *California Eagle* (17 November 1949) that it was one of the "best presented of the so-called 'racial' pictures," but that "these films always successfully bring out the point 'that Negroes have a place and should remain there.'" Robert Ellis, in the same journal, found it "a dynamic movie, one of the most sincere ever to be made in Hollywood." Nevertheless, he objected to the scenes showing the Negroes hiding rather than helping to free Lucas Beauchamp. The *Richmond Afro-American* (11 February 1950), called it a "clinical study

Brown and Faulkner.

of portions of the South still festering with the poison of prejudice and . . . as adult an opus as Hollywood has delivered during this era of preoccupation with minority" [*sic*]. Walter White, secretary of the National Association for the Advancement of Colored People, in the *New York Tribune* (13 November 1949), announced that *Intruder* made him feel "exultant." He was glad that the film did not follow the novel too closely and "excised Faulkner's special pleading and racial quirks without alteration of the basic story he told so well." He added that it took "no stand whatever on the issue of states' rights versus Federal action on the issue of lynching." The film, White said, indicated that Hollywood was maturing.

In the motion picture profession, *Intruder* was unquestionably a *succès d'estime*. Clarence Brown received and preserved in his scrapbook about fifty congratulatory and complimentary letters. Among those who wrote him were many of the best-known men in the film industry, such as Jerry Wald, John Huston, Melvin Frank, Fred Zinneman, Joseph Cotten, and Dudley Nichols. Dore Schary sent Brown an interoffice communication (13 June 1949): "Dear Clarence: For the record—and from my heart—I believe *Intruder in the Dust* is a truly magnificent and important picture, and I'm very happy for you for having delivered such an impressive film and such a telling blow to bigotry and hatred." Although they were close friends, there was no letter from Louis B. Mayer to Clarence Brown.

On 29 November 1949, a few weeks after the premiere in Oxford, Schary wrote to Brown again:

> I know how depressed you are about the lack of business, but don't let that destroy the fact that you've made a great document, one of which you must constantly be proud and one of which I will always be proud. While we are in a profit business, we occasionally must be prepared for a commercial loss as long as we know we have gained dignity and stature.
>
> If we had to do it all over again, tomorrow, I'd be in back of you once again, knowing how much art and conviction you would have to contribute. My congratulations and my confidence.

When the English reviews came out, Schary again wrote to Brown (15 March 1950): "Congratulations on the English notices . . . they must bring you enormous satisfaction. Again my congratulations and my conviction that *Intruder* will be a picture that will have a long life and will in time grow in importance."

One letter from Oxford, Mississippi, pays testimony to Clarence Brown, not as a film director, but as a human being. It was written by Alberta Dishmon, the Negro schoolteacher who was cast in the role of Parlee, Aleck Sander's mother and the Mallison's maid. She had no previous acting experience and was filled with trepidation about appearing in the film. After he had returned to Hollywood, she wrote Brown that she would never cease being grateful to him for having given her the courage to do it. Knowing and working with him, she added, had been inspirational.

Despite the lobby cards and posters that exploited the film in letters of fire as sensational and daring, Bradford F. Swann in the *Providence Sunday Journal* (30 April 1950), noted: "It is, I suppose, one of the sad aspects of the movie business that, having been arrogantly ignored when the Academy Awards were being distributed, *Intruder in the Dust* was faintheartedly relegated to the lower half of a dual bill with a big technicolor western."

For Brown, his film version of *Intruder* is still a source of great pride. It earned him the British Academy Award for the Best Director of 1949. He is pleased that it was labeled "uncompromising."

In 1971 Clarence Brown read in the newspaper that a film class at the College of the Desert, near his home, was planning to show *Intruder in the Dust*. He and his wife went unrecognized into the auditorium. The professor in charge announced that he had never seen the film, and told the members of the class that they would have to judge it for themselves. The Browns, fearing that this young audience might spurn the film, were tempted to leave. But they mustered up the courage to stay. To their astonishment, the film evoked overwhelming approval. As Brown was leaving, he introduced himself to the professor, who persuaded him to stay to talk with the class. The informal question-and-answer period lasted for more than an hour. At one point Brown polled the twenty black students present and found that all of them were, in his words, "mad about it." In turn, they asked him about Juano Hernandez and he was delighted to have the opportunity to tell them in particular about his intelligence and great dignity.[27]

Intruder in the Dust is still shown from time to time on television, at film festivals and at museums in retrospective series.[28] It has been shown at two Clarence Brown Film Festivals, one at the University of Tennessee in May, 1973, and another at the College of the Desert in 1971. The 16-millimeter rights to the film are owned by Films Incorporated, who report that it continues to be rented, particularly by colleges and universities. The distributors feature the film on a program they have assembled for classes in social studies, and for a new series named "The American Challenge Film Program," where its theme is described as "caste and class in the South," and where it is classified with such films as *Citizen Kane*, *The Grapes of Wrath*, and *Wilson*.[29] A recent reference terms it Clarence Brown's "most acclaimed film."[30] By now, as Dore Schary predicted, *Intruder* has become a Hollywood classic.

IV

THE SCRIPTS

ANY DISCUSSION of a film adaptation should begin with the script, for the writing of a script is the first stage in the making of a film. Furthermore, the script records the changes in narrative structure from novel to film, and can be useful as a verbal sketch of the film, providing that the director has in general followed its outline. In some instances, like a study for a painting or a work of sculpture, a film script can have artistic merit on its own. Ben Maddow's version of *Intruder in the Dust* is a fine example of its genre. Although Maddow would probably deny the validity of the genre as such, having stated publicly that he thinks of a scenario only as a means to an end, his skillful interpretation of the novel, his ability to match Faulkner's dialogue, and his ingenuity in dramatizing Faulkner's off-stage episodes provide a model of the screenwriter's art. This screenplay deserves careful consideration before moving on to a discussion of the film.[1]

The script published in this volume, approved for production by Clarence Brown on 8 December 1948, was Ben Maddow's final version, completed in little more than two months. Not only was it written with dispatch, but it was written entirely by Maddow, an unusual procedure in the Hollywood of the forties and fifties.[2] By and large, with the exception of a few minor changes of dialogue and modifications of settings, the script serves as an accurate blueprint for the narrative progression of the film.[3]

The earliest versions of any script are rarely available; fortunately, the treatment Maddow submitted and the early drafts of the screenplay are extant. Because a comparison of these documents with the final screenplay provides useful insights into the process of adaptation, I shall devote the following pages to a description of the variations found in two preliminary drafts. I would like to suggest that the reader read the published script at this time in order to follow the ensuing description of the revisions from earlier to later versions. Since the approved script is included in this volume, I shall deal with it, as well as with the director's shooting script, more briefly.[4] But first, a few definitions are in order, and also an explanation of the general procedures of the Hollywood troika system of the period of *Intruder*, in which an approved script was the result of the composite efforts of the writer, the director, and the producer.

The writing of a treatment is often the first step in the preparation of a script. Its purpose is to explain the characters and their motives in depth to the director and the producer, as well as to suggest the development of a story line. A treatment is never intended for the screen. Although treatments vary in quality and technique, the form has its own set of conventions. A third-person narrator, generally in the present tense, describes the characters and most of the action. Dialogue is used sparingly, usually only for key scenes and for dramatic encounters. In fact, except for occasional references to camera action or film editing (typed in capital letters), treatments resemble short stories in their alternation between dialogue and the long descriptive passages which set the scene and explain the mental processes of the characters. Unlike short stories, however, treatments are oriented toward an audience of viewers rather than of readers, and emphasize the visual and auditory imagery that the audience will see and hear.

After the treatment has been analyzed at one or more story conferences, the writer begins to compose the first pages of the screenplay, incorporating into it the suggestions of the director and the producer. The writer, in general, does not complete a first draft before submitting it, but prepares instead a few scenes at a time for story conferences with his director. He then revises his earlier pages according to the decisions reached at these conferences, and also composes first drafts of the next group of scenes for the next story conference. What emerges is truly a process script, containing scenes written and revised on many different dates. The rejected pages show the number of times individual scenes were altered, and record everything from significant structural changes to seemingly trivial variations of a word or two.

As the old scenes are being approved and the new ones are being revised, a final version is emerging. When this version, parts of which are again altered, receives the director's "okay," it is considered complete, and the writer's job is done. This version is called the approved screenplay and is the one usually published for students of the film. It is, however, a composite of revisions, executed on different dates, and sometimes even written by different authors. Thus it is usually impossible to identify ideas, scenes, or passages contributed at story conferences by the director and the producer.

First, the treatment. Ben Maddow's treatment for *Intruder in the Dust* is a document of considerable literary skill and cinematic imagination. It is divided into seventeen sequences, each of which has been given a title that refers to the central idea of the sequence.[5] Taken together, the titles provide a convenient outline of the narrative structure of the treatment and, astonishingly at such an early stage of composition, of the final film as well.[6] Following Faulkner's method, Maddow has employed many interior monologues, indicated by underlinings in the typed treatment. Of course, these interior monologues were not intended for the screen in that form and some of the ideas they express have been put into dialogue in the earliest pages of the screenplay.

As a document, the treatment is interesting on several counts. It records the process of simplifying and selecting from a much longer and more complex novel those elements which the screenwriter considers dramatic and visual, while at the same time trying to preserve as much as possible of the central meaning of the original.[7] It also illustrates the process of dramatizing actions which may be of vital importance, but which, for a variety of reasons, may be only indirectly reported in the novel. A good example of such a scene in *Intruder* is the capture of Crawford Gowrie, to be discussed in more detail presently. In fact, this treatment is an ingenious record of deletions, additions, and transferences; it illustrates as well the writer's insights into character and theme, and his suggestions for cinematic imagery. Sequentially it follows the novel more closely than the approved script or the film. A more detailed description would be useful, I think, in tracing the process by which this particular novel was transformed into a motion picture.

In the act of simplifying the novel's complex murder plot, Maddow has reduced the number of corpses to one. He explained that it would have been ludicrous, and perhaps even confusing, to have filmed first a strange body in the grave and then an empty grave.[8] He solved the problem by eliminating entirely the character of Jake Montgomery, whose body in the novel is found in Vinson Gowrie's grave. In addition, the treatment eliminates the roles of Chick's mother and father, although they do ultimately appear in one sequence of the film, and Chick's mother is also shown again in the montage in which Chick selects a dress for Molly Beauchamp. The exchange of gifts between Chick and Lucas has also been deleted, as well as any mention of Lucas's white blood. Needless to add, most of the long historical and political passages of the novel do not occur in the treatment.

Although Maddow has eliminated some minor characters, he has invented a climactic scene that dramatizes the capture of Crawford Gowrie and increases the roles of both Lucas Beauchamp and Nub Gowrie. Both men wait alone together in Lucas's cabin for the murderer to fall into their trap. Despite their differences in color, the two former antagonists discover that since they are both widowers they can understand each other's grief and can therefore communicate in human terms. Gowrie shows his courage and rectitude in his insistence on alone facing and apprehending the murderer, who is, of course, his own son, Crawford. Lucas picks up the rifle with which Crawford had killed his own brother, and pitches it into the quicksand. With this gesture, Lucas betrays his first sign of strong emotion; his face shows "depth of anger and impatience and a desire to be done with this thing that had nearly meant his death, upside down, disfigured and disemboweled by fire."[9]

The screenwriter, moreover, has introduced and fleshed out the character who lurks behind the evil action but never actually appears in the novel—Crawford Gowrie, the murderer himself. By introducing Crawford early in the treatment, and by individualizing him as the leader of the potential lynch mob, Maddow heightens the threat to Lucas, as well as the dramatic suspense. From time to time, the action returns to the square in order to maintain the sense of imminent danger. In fact, the center section of the treatment develops two parallel actions which intensify the tension and conflict; the frantic activities of those who are working to clear Lucas are intermittently intercut with scenes of the increasingly restive mob. The novel, too, frequently reminds the reader of the danger to Lucas, either by describing actual scenes in the square or by recording Chick's mental anguish and fear of a lynching, which in his mind he sees as clearly as Macbeth's dagger.

In the treatment Maddow has suggested numerous cinematic equivalents for Faulkner's prose, using images and techniques that instantly convey an idea which in the novel is developed more leisurely and on occasion more subtly. Many of these early suggestions, however, do not, and perhaps cannot appear on the screen.

For example, the treatment opens with an instant statement of the major menace: the word "Burn." As the camera pulls away, the letters B-U-R-N are seen to be part of the name of the owner of the barbershop. This image runs consistently throughout. At the end of the flashback of Chick's visit to Lucas's cabin, Chick is seen flinging away the coins he had tried to give Lucas "into the broken ice where he had fallen [that] morning." Aleck Sander has resumed the rabbit hunt, and impatiently shouts to Chick, "Fire! Fire! Whyn't you fire?"[10] The ripples of the creek then dissolve into the image of the square as the sheriff's car approaches, bringing Lucas to the jail from which at any moment he can be dragged out and burned alive.

Moreover, from the first view of Crawford Gowrie, striking a match, to the last sequence of the treatment in which he sets fire to the steps of Lucas's cabin, he is always associated with fire. It is Lucas who puts out the flames, choking them with heaping spadefuls of earth, a highly symbolic scene that was never transferred to the screen. Although the capture of Crawford is not tied in the film to arson of any sort, Crawford is still nearly always identified with the flame of a match.

In the film but not in the novel the sheriff's car which brings Lucas to jail has a flat tire. One critic noted that this detail suggests "the collapse of justice."[11] This action with its concomitant dialogue was invented for the treatment and carried over to the screenplay and the film. The dialogue in two terse sentences clearly lays out the two sides of the conflict, as well as hinting at sabotage or vandalism: "'Somebody try to slow you down, Sheriff?' . . . 'Maybe. Somebody that don't know me, anyhow.'"

Often the treatment invents visual details which provide an ironic comment on lawyer Stevens. For example in his office hangs a framed print of Pontius Pilate washing his hands of the truth. Later, musing about his white world, Chick thinks of his uncle Gavin, "taking up his big volume of Cervantes and then putting it down again in his restlessness, irritation, and worry."[12] In addition, Maddow uses a good deal of Faulkner's imagery, such as the black and white hands gripping the jail bars (T 69) and "Miss Habersham in motionless silhouette on the sky above" (T 103). Maddow adds that she stands by the grave "like some sort of spinster angel with a wreath and a light." He also develops the "carnival" atmosphere (T 135), the "holiday" (T 136), "almost gala" (T 137) of the mob scene in the square.

There is a consistency in Maddow's movement from image to symbol or metaphor that gives the treatment an unusually literary quality. Having used an image of a fish hook at the beginning to evoke Chick's memory of falling into the creek, the scenarist picks it up again near the end of another of Chick's interior monologues in which he thinks, "And now they are fishing for Crawford, and Lucas is the bait."

Maddow has also suggested the use of expressionism in photographing the faces of the crowd: "The faces watching him [Lucas] are quite ordinary, simple people, but they seem to him, *and now to the camera* [the camera is often personified in the treatment; references to it are always underlined] a series of grotesque, death-pale heads, an ice-cold eye behind a steel-rimmed lens, or an ear with tufts growing out of it or a hooked nose like a hawk or an owl, or a mouth still surrounded by the white-face of lather forgotten in the excitement and drying out in the noon heat of the square." In the sequence entitled "The Holiday," however, the treatment points out that the people gathered to see the lynching "are in no way extraordinary," and in the highly inventive sequence, "Deadlock," which describes the confrontation between Crawford Gowrie and Miss Habersham, Maddow repeats it again: "Fat or thin, tall or short, men, women, and children, they are no different in appearance than the audience that will see them on the screen."

In addition, Maddow has invented a dramatic scene to objectify the initiation theme of the novel, one in which Chick bravely admits to Nub Gowrie that he has violated a Gowrie grave. The treatment also illustrates Lucas's role in Chick's development by showing Chick's imitation of Lucas's gesture (wiping off his hat), and it dramatizes Miss Habersham's contribution to Chick's education by shifting to her the recognition of his well-earned adult status, symbolized by her encouraging him to drink a cup of coffee.

In general, Maddow's original concept employed a wider range of cinematic techniques than was used in the final screen version. He thought in terms of tricky dissolves, such as one in which the flame of a match dissolves into a shot of Lucas Beauchamp, and another in which Nub Gowrie awkwardly and tenderly wipes the sand from his dead son's face, wiping out the whole screen-image as well.

Although significant changes were made as the screenplay took shape, the basic narrative structure remained the same. Maddow's major additions and deletions were carried over from treatment to film: Crawford Gowrie as menace, first to Lucas and then to Miss Habersham, continued to lurk outside the jail; Nub Gowrie himself apprehended his son; and neither Jake Montgomery nor his corpse appeared in the film.

On 5 November Ben Maddow submitted the first seven pages of

his first version of the screenplay. From that date to 29 November he continued to deliver in chronological order additional batches of pages as he wrote them. Taken together, these pages represent the first complete scenario, probably written over a period of about four weeks. During the same period Maddow was revising pages of his earliest draft in accordance with decisions reached at a series of story conferences held with Clarence Brown and, on occasion, with Brown and Dore Schary. As a result of these revisions an intermediate script was created, one that stands between the treatment described above and the final script "okayed" by Clarence Brown. This intermediate script can be appropriately termed the process script, for it illustrates clearly the script "in process" as well as the process of collaboration between screenwriter, director, and producer.

This process script is in screenplay form consisting of dialogue, descriptions of settings, and instructions for character-placement, camera shots (such as dissolves and fades), and editing. It begins with a series of shots of the Jefferson town square, then moves to the barbershop where the preliminary exposition occurs concerning the "nigger" who shot a white man in the back. Next, the church steeple is described: "Instead of a cross, the spire is crested by the curve of a great wooden hand, forefinger pointing to heaven."[13] Bells have been ringing, but now they stop. A siren is heard. Cross cuts follow between the barbershop and the church in which the voices of the Sunday worshippers, singing hymns, are mingled with the shriek of the siren. There is no sign of Chick Mallison. As the sheriff's car approaches the jail, the camera looks closely at a pair of "handcuffed dark gnarled hands."

After Lucas's hat has tumbled off and been retrieved, and after he has been escorted by the sheriff to the steps of the jail, he looks at the men in the square, seeing them subjectively as threatening monsters. Then he spots one friend, who is trying to remain anonymous in the crowd. It is Chick Mallison. A voice-over provides the words that Chick thinks but does not say: "I shouldn't have come. . . ." Following Lucas's instructions to tell his uncle that Lucas wants to see him, Chick runs home.

Next, a new scene has been added, part of which comes from the novel. It shows Chick at Sunday dinner with his parents and his uncle and communicates clearly that Chick's parents still treat him like a child. Resentfully, he tears off the napkin that his mother has tucked like a bib under his chin. Gavin tries to explain that Chick despises

Claude Jarman, Jr., and William Faulkner.

being babied in this way and that after all Chick is sixteen years old.

After showing his confusion about what attitude to take toward Lucas Beauchamp, Chick leaves the table in anger. Obviously disturbed, he rushes to his room. Gavin Stevens follows Chick and asks about his special concern for Lucas. As the camera passes Chick's hunting rifle, in a wooden rack hanging on the wall, the scene dissolves into a shot of Chick and Aleck Sander hunting rabbits near the creek on Lucas's farm. The flashback begins with a voice-over, but soon becomes a series of dramatic scenes. Occasionally during the flashback Chick adds additional reflective remarks in a voice-over. The flashback in this version and all subsequent ones is thus placed after Lucas's request for a lawyer, and narrated by Chick in his bedroom to Gavin Stevens. Here, the subsequent exchange of gifts between Chick and Lucas, in which Chick tries but fails to repay his debt, is covered by rather awkward dialogue between Chick and his uncle. The approved script introduces instead a rapid montage of shifting images which conveys the visual information, accompanied by Chick's voice-over.

Thus the internal action of the treatment has been externalized, achieving the double advantage of informing both Gavin and the audience of Chick's special interest in Lucas. In the novel it is taken for granted that Gavin already knows. Although the fishhook symbol of the treatment has been eliminated, the image of the rifle in Chick's bedroom not only introduces the tale of the rabbit hunt but also foreshadows the future direction of the plot.

In general, the differences between the treatment and the process script fall into two categories: (1) changes that result from using more of the novel's episodes and background ideas, and (2) changes that result from the screenwriter's (or the director's or producer's) newly invented plot action. For example, Lucas Beauchamp's white grandfather is not mentioned in the treatment but is referred to in the process script when Chick tells his uncle about his misadventure in the creek. In addition, the encounter and subsequent dialogue with Mr. Lilley on the way to Lucas's cell has been transferred from the novel to the screenplay in a shortened but otherwise verbatim version (T 47–49).

Frequently in the novel during the fearsome night at the cemetery and later at home and at the sheriff's, Chick's troubled thoughts return to the menacing mob in the square. As a counterpart to Chick's anxiety, the process script, like the treatment, cuts back to the square six times during the race against time to find the evidence that will clear Lucas Beauchamp. Each cut to the town square in-creases the suspense, showing the crowd's mounting impatience as various members taunt Crawford Gowrie until he is finally forced to take some sort of action. Parallel scenes of the two excursions to the graveyard are intercut with shots showing the increasing pressure on Crawford, who finally threatens to set fire to the jail, now guarded only by the reluctant Mr. Tubbs and the imperturbable Miss Habersham. In this respect, the process script is closer to the novel than to the film.

In shaping the material, a major revision was engineered so that in the final version of the script (and in the film as well) all the shots of the restless mob after Lucas's imprisonment have been strung to-gether and withheld until Vinson Gowrie's body has been found. A certain amount of cumulative suspense has thus been sacrificed to achieve the shock and horror of the dissolve from Nub Gowrie's silent grief as he gently wipes sand from his dead son's face to the raucous, bloodthirsty mob in the square. This long, sustained se-quence depicting the thrill-seekers who fill the square and who goad Crawford Gowrie into threatening Miss Habersham is one of the great strengths of the film and one of the most memorable se-quences to be found in any motion picture. Faulkner's verbal de-scriptions of the carnival mood, which could at any moment explode into brutality and violence, have found here stunning cinematic equivalents.

The process script also objectifies Chick's thoughts about the silent, fearful Negroes inside the dark cabins he passes on the way to the Caledonia Chapel. A series of wordless scenes convey the terror of the Negroes, watching behind closed doors. In the film, their faces are illuminated by the lights of Miss Habersham's car, but neither Chick nor Miss Habersham can see them. Instead, they communicate to the audience the mute dread that afflicts the Negro community.

Perhaps the major difference between the treatment and all of the later versions occurs in the sequence of the capture of the murderer. Instead of using Lucas Beauchamp as bait, the sheriff himself waits in the cabin for the murderer to appear. He is joined by Nub Gowrie, whom he has summoned to be a witness to the event. Consequently, Sheriff Hampton's role is greatly enhanced. Although the filmmak-ers had first sought to enlarge Lucas's role, they modified their original intention and substituted Sheriff Hampton for Lucas in this sequence. I assume that this revision was based on the improbability

53

of a scene in which in the Mississippi of 1949 a Southern redneck (Nub Gowrie) would sit down with and talk quietly as an equal to a black man. Such a scene, moreover, might have invited jeers and hisses from some members of an audience in the Deep South.[14]

In the novel, of course, the sheriff, accompanied by Lucas, apprehends the criminal, so that the use of the sheriff in the film follows its source. But Nub Gowrie's role is greatly enlarged in the film, for he becomes the actual agent of his son's capture and alone faces Crawford's raised rifle. In addition, Maddow has composed a scene in which old Nub Gowrie and Sheriff Hampton take the handcuffed Crawford through the mob collected in the square and into the jail. The sheriff tells the crowd that Crawford is the man who murdered his own brother, and old Nub confirms it. At that point, the crowd silently breaks ranks and its members shuffle away. In a film, such a scene is almost obligatory; this one emphasizes ironic justice, for it has been Crawford Gowrie to whom the mob previously looked to provide its ghoulish entertainment. The novel, of course, does not relate Crawford's trip to the jail, because its narrative point of view never strays outside of Chick Mallison's consciousness, and Chick at that moment is at home in bed. The novel, however, reports at second hand that Crawford Gowrie was allowed to commit suicide in jail (T 237), a detail that was not carried over to the screen.

One point that Maddow stresses in even the earliest version of the script is Lucas Beauchamp's moral superiority to the people who are willing to convict him on purely circumstantial evidence. When Lucas is finally persuaded to tell what he knows of the murder, the scene dissolves from an image of the light hanging from the ceiling of his cell to the lights of the truck which the lumber-thief is driving. In a flashback narrated by Lucas, we are shown the reenactment of the murder, as well as Lucas in the role of witness to the theft. But neither Lucas nor the screen audience ever sees who fired the shot. Lucas therefore states emphatically that even though he may suspect the murderer's identity, he will not name a man whom he did not actually see fire the gun. After Vinson Gowrie has been shot and has fallen to the ground, Lucas's hand touches the pocket that holds his own gun. Using the gun image for the transition, the process script then returns to the narrative present in the cell. Matching his previous action, Lucas now touches his empty pocket, the one in which the "Colt fawty-one" was formerly kept. This device, however, is not used in the film.

A late and significant alteration appears in the process script following the flashback montage of the exchange of gifts between Chick and Lucas. In the novel when Lucas passes Chick without speaking, Chick thinks that he is at last freed of his shame and guilt. But when he later learns that Lucas's wife has died, he realizes that Lucas had failed to see him because he was grieving for her. He thinks, "with a kind of amazement: *He was grieving. You don't have to not be a Nigger in order to grieve* . . ." (T 25). In the script he says to his uncle, "'I reckon you can be sad or proud, or even lonely, inside a black skin too.'" As a result of this new knowledge, Chick goes to see Lucas, not at his house but on neutral ground at Fraser's store, where Lucas customarily goes on Saturday afternoons. In a voice-over, Chick introduces the scene which is then dramatized on the screen. The Gowrie boys are present, Fraser's son, and the ubiquitous Lucas. Lucas's cool indifference to the white working men, his nonchalant self-assurance so infuriates Vinson Gowrie that he lunges at Lucas with a pole, shouting, "'you goddam biggity burr-headed Nigger!'" (corrected to "'you lousy biggity burr-headed ——!'"). Speechless, Chick watches. Then in a voice-over he explains, "'I didn't go after him. I couldn't. I don't know why. Maybe because Vinson Gowrie was white, and I was white and Lucas Beauchamp was not. And right in these woods—on a Saturday afternoon—just yesterday—he killed Vinson Gowrie. Shot him in the back.'" As the scene returns to Chick and his uncle in the bedroom, Chick is still caught up in his memory of the episode at Fraser's store. "'And yet,'" he says, "'he thinks I'm his friend.'" At that moment he informs Stevens that Lucas wants a lawyer.

In the novel Chick is not present but learns through hearsay of this confrontation at Fraser's store (seven years before the murder) between Lucas and "three youngish white men from the crew of a nearby sawmill," who are not named (T 18–20). He remembers having heard it when he thinks about Lucas's arrogant independence, his refusal to be obsequious to white men or to behave in other respects like a black man.

By adding this scene to the film and by making Chick its silent witness, the filmmakers have gained two strong advantages. First, in placing the clash between the white man and the Negro nearer to the date of the murder, and in specifying that the man who tried to attack Lucas was none other than Vinson Gowrie, the film strengthens the circumstantial evidence against Lucas by giving him a motive for the murder. Second, by placing Chick in the scene and by stressing that he had lacked the courage to stand up for Lucas, who in fact had actually done nothing to inspire such wrath, the adaptors have given Chick an additional motive for wanting to expunge his shame by helping Lucas during his present and far greater crisis.

The introduction of this scene, moreover, into the process script and, later, into the film provides a parallel with a scene to follow in which Chick behaves in a different fashion; the scene in which Chick Mallison manfully steps forward and admits to Nub Gowrie that it was he who dug up a Gowrie grave. This scene, demonstrating Chick's courage at this tense moment, was also created by Ben Maddow for the film. The film's two parallel tests of Chick's moral courage therefore serve to illuminate a major theme of the novel, for Chick's contrasting responses illustrate dramatically that he has advanced rapidly on the road to manhood.

Changes of a different order can also be observed in the revisions of the process script. In the rewriting of some scenes, for example, passages of dialogue have been shortened. Others are longer and more explicit, particularly those passages which refer to the dangers and terrors of entering Beat Four and of risking the ire of the brawling Gowries. Such additions increase the sense of peril to Lucas that pervades the whole film, as well as to Chick in profaning a Gowrie grave. It is astonishing, incidentally, to observe how much of Faulkner's dialogue appears in all versions of the script and finally in the film.[15] Many of Lucas's speeches, as well as those of the sheriff, Nub Gowrie, and the members of the crowd are taken from the novel. My annotations of the screenplay provide the textual references to these lines, so that the reader can compare the two versions and can note Faulkner's gift for re-creating the spoken vernacular.

Other alterations from process to approved script add or emphasize more pointedly details from the novel such as Chick's flash of memory of how Lucas came to own his own land, which he had inherited because he was the first cousin of the white man who owned it. In the voice-over of the flashback to Lucas's cabin, Chick refers to the familiar Negro smell and names the Negro food which was to have been Lucas's dinner but which he gave instead to his guest, Chick.

Such lines may have been added to give more information about Lucas and also to convey the kind of knowledge and attitudes that Chick held from having been raised in a community in which the Negroes and whites lived in close propinquity. The new passages also anticipate the added dialogue in which Miss Habersham explains to Stevens why he did not believe Lucas, and why Lucas in turn did not trust Stevens with "the fact that he was innocent":

MISS HABERSHAM: You're a white man. Worse than that: you're a grown white man.
STEVENS: I'm sorry about that.
MISS HABERSHAM: So there's a wall grown up between you. Lucas can't see through it, and neither can you.
STEVENS: I'm sorry about that, too.

From process to approved script, the changes are few; the additions seem to have been made in the interest of clarity in character motivation. For example, the approved script lengthens Mr. Mallison's instructions to Chick about staying home and adds his smug comment that "'It's happened before and it's bound to happen again. There's nothing for any of us to get excited about.'" It also provides dialogue to get Mr. Mallison out of the way by having him say he is going to Memphis, and later, adds a line referring to Mr. Mallison's having departed. This new dialogue functions to strengthen and make more plausible the relationship between Chick and his uncle.

New dialogue also explains more than Faulkner does. After Chick tells Gavin about having tried to pay for Lucas's hospitality, he now adds: "'I was so angry. I was so awfully ashamed. He knew what I didn't know—what I didn't have sense enough to understand. And he knew all the time, and I didn't—that I was his guest.'"

When Chick first meets Crawford Gowrie, Crawford now explains, as much for the audience as for Chick, "'He [Lucas] killed my kid brother.'" In the cemetery, when the three conspirators see the distant figures of the man on the mule, Chick emphasizes the danger by saying, "'But suppose he saw us. Suppose he comes back and catches us.'" To Lucas's reluctant discussion of the murder at the beginning, "'There was two folks, partners in a sawmill'" the approved script adds, "'There was two *white* folks'" (my italics). And Gavin's too explicit reply, "'You told him his partner was robbing him'" has been changed to "'You told him somebody was robbing him.'"

In addition, the approved script removes the following speech which conveys to Aleck Chick's reluctance to carry out Lucas's instructions and Chick's desire to escape:

CHICK: Well, I'm not going to any graveyard or dig anybody up, not in the middle of Beat Four, up in those piney hills where the Gowries live—!
ALECK: Well, I never tole you to.
CHICK: I'm going the other way.

On the other hand, the approved script adds a scene to account for Miss Habersham at the end of the crisis. While Stevens is responding to Chick's outrage about the mob's running away, he looks down from his office balcony and sees her driving off in her car below. She shouts farewell and adds, "'I've got to get home to my chickens. But if you ever get into trouble again, let me know.'" Stevens then comments to Chick, "'You see, *we* were in trouble, not Lucas Beauchamp.'"

One cut in dialogue provokes speculation. The reference in the process script to the smell of Lucas's and Molly's quilt has been removed. Formerly Chick had said, "'I knew the smell of this quilt: all my life I guess. But I never noticed it before.'" This line may have been deleted because it could have been misunderstood and therefore been offensive to both Negroes and white liberals. If used, the concept would have had to be more fully developed, as in the novel, linking the odor to poverty instead of to race. Rather than making the dialogue tediously didactic, the filmmakers dropped the concept.

At Schary's insistence, however, Maddow wrote into the last scene two message lines. He himself objected to these lines, and many critics share his distaste.[16] Like the novel, the last line of dialogue in Maddow's treatment is Lucas's humorous "'my receipt.'"

The process script adds new dialogue between Chick and Stevens, spoken as they look from the balcony down on the crowd through which Lucas walks. Chick insists that they "'don't see him . . . don't even know he's there.'" Stevens replies, "'They do. The same as I do. As long as he lives. Proud, stubborn,—insufferable: but there he goes: the keeper of my conscience.'"

The approved script is even more explicit. To Stevens's dialogue is added the following: "'They do, the same as I do. *They always will'*" (my italics). At the end of the last line quoted above, the two words, "'our conscience,'" are added, along with directions that they be delivered into the camera "as if to the invisible audience." The film transfers these two words to Chick, ending with the words "'our conscience, Uncle John.'"[17]

Finally, the approved script eliminates various unnecessary establishing shots that slacken the pace, and also compresses informational shots into a tighter, more economic drama. It excises the sequence in which the sheriff returns to the square for the Negro prisoners who are to dig up the grave on Monday morning, and instead dissolves directly from the scene in the sheriff's kitchen to a shot of his car speedily conveying prisoners through the countryside to the cemetery. In addition, Chick's greetings to his family at Sunday dinner are now conveyed by his off-stage voice, which accompanies a close-up of each person he speaks to, thereby introducing the members of the family to the audience at the same time. An exterior shot of Lucas's cabin to show that evening is approaching has been eliminated, the time-change is demonstrated instead by the lighting of a lamp inside the cabin.

The next version, which is the director's shooting script, provides valuable information on the actual process of photographing this film. It is broken up into shots to be taken by the second unit, day-for-night shots, and process shots.[18] Most of the alterations in the shooting script, written in or crossed out by hand, involve minor changes of dialogue and deletions of descriptions of setting, action, or camera position. In other words, the script's stage directions for various reasons were not always followed. In fact, Maddow did not intend that his suggestions for the camera and for cutting be accurately transcribed into film. He customarily wrote them into a script as a way of persuading the director to imagine the film in advance. Having written for documentaries and worked with a movieola, he found that written references to cutting were useful in marking changes of perception.[19]

The shooting script, while somewhat closer to the film, is still not an accurate transcription because once a shot or a sequence is recorded on film there is no practical reason for the director to indicate the changes on his script. Instead, improvisations on the set are recorded on film and later described in the continuity script. For example, the next to last sequence of the film contains several lines of dialogue found only in the film and the continuity script. In the scene in which Lucas comes to Stevens's office to pay his fee, just before the last verbal exchange between Stevens and Lucas, Stevens asks, "'Just one thing more—why didn't you tell me the truth? That night in the jail?'" Lucas replies with another question: "'Would you have believed me?'"

The reiteration of Stevens's obtuseness may have been introduced here because of certain very late and very interesting changes in the shooting script. They can be found on the script's two pink sheets, numbered forty-one and forty-two and dated "3/19/49," and on its five blue sheets, numbered sixty-five through sixty-nine, and dated "3/21/49." These pages, in fact, may contain some dialogue written by William Faulkner and woven into Maddow's version of those scenes. In addition to the different color and later dates of these pages, they have been typed on a typewriter different from the one used for the rest of the screenplay.[20]

In discussing the filming of *Intruder* in Oxford, Joseph Blotner says that "Faulkner agreed to read the script . . . and help with any revisions Brown wanted. The Studio would have its contract writers working on this property, but it might be a better script if the author worked on it, too, even if much of what he wrote were not used. The result was that Faulkner would eventually read the 113–page scenario, approving most of the scenes, changing a few others slightly, and revising the last scene considerably in an effort to make it less sentimental."[21]

Actually, there is no indication in the shooting script or in the film of Faulkner's effort in behalf of the last scene, and, as I have recorded, from version to version it grew not less but more sentimental.[22]

But there is an indication that Faulkner may have added some dialogue elsewhere to more clearly delineate the character of Gavin Stevens. The following lines have been substituted (on the pink pages) for the previous ones in the sequence outside the jail after Chick's and Gavin's first visit to Lucas in his cell, and before Chick's return to see him alone:

> CHICK: You are going to help him, aren't you?
> STEVENS: Of course I am ... whether he wants me to
>   or not. Ask for a change of venue ...
>   plead him guilty...
> CHICK: Then maybe he'll tell you what really
>   happened.
> STEVENS: I know what happened. He killed Vinson
>   Gowrie... no matter what provacation [*sic*]
>   ... and he probably had plenty ...
>   nevertheless he killed a man.
> CHICK: But there was something -- something he
>   started -- wanted to tell you.
> STEVENS: I know the answer to that too. He was
>   getting ready to tell me the lie he knew
>   I couldn't believe, <yet which> and being
>   his lawyer, I'd have to pretend I did. No,
>   I know what happened and I know the only
>   cure for it. Come on, let'us [*sic*] go
>   home.[23]

The preceding dialogue confirms the truth of Lucas's later comment to Chick: "'A man like your uncle, he ain't got time. He's too full of notions.'" It contains some of the ideas of the novel found on pages sixty-four and sixty-five, and in the more complicated use of the "'yet which'" (altered, not in Faulkner's handwriting, to "'and'") suggests Faulkner's prose.

The five pages dated 21 March occur in the sequence in the sheriff's kitchen, and replace five previous pages. Several modifications can be seen, most of which, like the preceding revision, concern the character of Gavin Stevens. For example, when Stevens suggests that the sheriff should be the one to get Nub Gowrie's permission to open the grave, the sheriff replies, "'But you're a lawyer, you're the talker.'" In addition, Stevens quotes Aleck's grandfather here and echoes Lucas's earlier comment:

> "Oh, yes, I've heard that before too. I heard Aleck's grandfather tell Chick and Aleck that once. If you want to get anything done, don't bother the men folks with it, they're too cluttered up with facts. Get the women and children to working at it. Is that what you mean?"

Certain key lines formerly spoken by Miss Habersham have been lengthened and given to Gavin Stevens:

> "It's more than that; there's a wall grown up between us. Lucas can't see thru it and I won't. Or maybe that's wrong; we're the ones who can't see thru it because we're the ones who are blind. . . ."

These pages emphasize Stevens's change from the stubborn certainty that Lucas was guilty to a baffled regret that he, Stevens, could have been so wrong. Their thrust seems to be to discredit Stevens as spokesman for the South. Could Faulkner have written in these changes in light of the reviews of the novel which assumed that Stevens spoke for him? At any rate, I am familiar with some of Faulkner's typing habits, and the irregularities in the typing of these pages may well indicate that they were typed by him. They do not follow the strict conventions of studio practices; nor do the new scenes provide as full directions for actors and camera as the pages written by Ben Maddow.[24]

So much for the scripts, which represent, after all, only one of the many, complex components of a motion picture. Nonetheless, they do reveal how the choices, decisions, and selections from the multiple possibilities inherent in the source shaped the final artifact. They also illustrate the contribution, so often neglected, of the screenwriter, without whom there would have been no film. In the case of *Intruder*, Ben Maddow's excellent scenario provides the foundation for nearly every foot of the film.

V

THE FILM

In his *Theory of the Film*, Bela Balázs contends that the subject of an original work and an adaptation can be the same, but that the contents of the two are different. "It is this *different* content that is adequately expressed in the changed form resulting from the adaptation." The true artist uses the existing work of art as "raw material . . . as if it were raw reality," which he regards from the "specific angle of his own art form."[1] The film version of *Intruder in the Dust* is an excellent example of Balázs's theory, for while both the novel and the film deal with the near-lynching of a Negro, innocent of the crime of which he is accused, and with the determination of a young boy and his two accomplices to prove the Negro's innocence, the emphasis and the emotional tones are so different that the content is transformed.

Instead of Faulkner's dense rhetorical blocks, his convoluted and half-hidden plot and his picture of a world presented through the intensely subjective eyes of Chick Mallison, we have Clarence Brown's mode of handling the dramatic and pictorial components that comprise the complex surface of the film, and Brown's treatment of the cinematic images that create "the sensuous layer of film meaning."[2] For it is in the convergence of the plot and the style, as well as in what André Bazin terms the "plastics of the image," that meaning is found.[3]

The changes from novel to script discussed previously (such as the elimination of Jake Montgomery's corpse, the use of Crawford Gowrie as a major character, and the dramatization of his arrest) contribute to the changed content, but less obvious factors, which I shall discuss presently, are equally important in altering the tenor of the film.

Because the novel is set in the mind of Chick Mallison and because every action in the novel gains in validity and meaning through Chick's responses, the primary source of interest lies in Chick's development of an independent moral and social conscience. In addition, as I have noted above, the structure of the novel emphasizes the effect of the community, of its history, and of its shared experience upon the psyche of its young hero. As members of that community, Lucas Beauchamp, Miss Habersham, Chick's parents, and his deeply admired uncle all contribute to his growth.

Like other novels of initiation and education, Faulkner's *Intruder* emphasizes the need for perception and the power of perception in apprehending the truth from the welter of circumstances and appearances. Mature awareness demands close observation, insights, and intuition. Mystery-detective stories also stress the theme of perception, so that in combining the initiation and the detective novel, Faulkner's *Intruder* fully exploits this underlying premise. Nor does Brown's film depart from the norm. The shift from novel to film, however, lies more in what is perceived and in how it is perceived at the mythic level of human experience. Thus a theme latent in the novel becomes of primary importance to the film.

The most memorable images in the film are those of the morbidly fascinated faces of the crowd and of the commanding figure of Lucas Beauchamp, with his watchful, wary eyes. Whenever he appears, Lucas dominates the scene; when he is absent, his emblematic power remains in the mind's eye. His larger-than-life stature achieves heroic and mythic proportions, which are reinforced by the choreography of the crowd scenes, moving back and forth across Courthouse Square. Like a Greek chorus, the townspeople register the tensions that strain their society and that threaten to erupt in an orgy of evil. The near-collision of these two opposing forces suggests the ritual of the sacrifice or the casting-out of the scapegoat, a figure prevalent in myth and in fiction whom Northrop Frye has called the *pharmacos*. The *pharmacos* is a victim onto whom society attempts to transfer its guilt even though he is innocent of the crime attributed to him and guilty only in being a member of a society or "living in a world where such injustices are an inescapable part of existence."[4] In its most ironic form, the myth of the scapegoat transfers the evil to the whole society; it is this viciousness in society that the film forces us to recognize.

In theorizing about the unique qualities of film as an art form, Parker Tyler finds that "the true field of the movies is not *art* but *myth*." He defines myth as "specifically a free, unharnessed fiction, a basic prototypic pattern capable of many variations and distortions, many betrayals and disguises, even though it remains *imaginative*

FAULKNER'S *Intruder in the Dust*

truth."[5] Perhaps, then, it is the nature of the medium itself to mythologize its subject. Still, the raw material of the novel provides several possible myths; it contains rituals of both sacrifice and initiation, as well as Cain and Abel archetypes. Why, then, does the film emphasize so strongly the myth of the scapegoat, forcing the characters in the film and the audience in the theater to look so closely at this brutal rite?

If it is from the "plastics of the image" that a film molds its content, the images of Juano Hernandez are the most powerful in the film. His physiognomy and his performance provide the most significant clues to its meaning. In fact, Faulkner said that Juano Hernandez "in this role creates the third great Negro character in fiction—Uncle Tom, Emperor Jones and now Lucas Beauchamp."[6] So compelling is Hernandez's characterization of Lucas Beauchamp that it heavily outweighs the inadequate and inexpressive performance of Claude Jarman, Jr., as Chick Mallison, thereby shifting the emphasis from the latter to the former. Furthermore, David Brian's lackluster performance in the role of John Gavin Stevens provides neither an equivalent for Faulkner's prose nor a counterbalance to the compelling visuals of the mob scenes. Shorn of most of the rhetoric assigned to the character in the novel and unable to command the intensity of audience-response awarded to the mob scenes of the film, Brian's low-key performance contributes to the altered meaning of the film. In addition, without the complexity and the irony with which the novel develops the Chick-Stevens relationship, the interest shifts from Chick's rites of passage to the ironic reversal of the scapegoat myth.

The change in narrative structure from novel to film reinforces the scapegoat theme. The reader first meets Lucas as the proprietor of his own land, standing firmly in his gum boots, an axe on his shoulder, and regarding with neither pity, commiseration, or even surprise Chick Mallison, the intruder on his property (T 6).[7] But in the film our first image of Lucas shows him already a prisoner, in a close shot of his handcuffed black wrists resting on the back of the seat of Sheriff Hampton's car. As the sequence progresses, the camera dramatizes the conflict by showing the dignified, composed Negro facing the large group of white men gathered in the square.

Even before Lucas appears, the film establishes the background for this conflict between the society of Jefferson and its chosen victim. Initially, we see a cross, visible over the opening titles. Immediately, the camera pans down to show the church steeple, the tower, the church, and the group waiting to enter. At the same time, the church bell tolls. The next shot establishes the bell in close-up, followed by a long shot of Courthouse Square. Thus in three shots the director has presented images that convey the paradoxical poles of the film. The cross is an instant sign for traditional Christianity, sacrifice, and martyrdom, but it is also a symbol of crucifixion and, in its most demonic sense, of white supremacy and the Ku Klux Klan as well. As the bell tolls, we see in the background the courthouse, a diminished image of legal justice, and we hear the ringing that reminds us of for whom the bell tolls. As it explores the environment of Courthouse Square, the camera notes that the group waiting to enter the church is only a small part of a larger scene.

Next, the scene dissolves to the interior of the barber shop from which in depth focus the square outside can be seen. Dialogue between the barbers and their customers provides the preliminary exposition, explaining that one of the Gowrie boys has been shot in the back by a "nigger," and that all the "darkies" have disappeared. Immediately, Brown cuts to the square, this time to seven old men loitering at the base of the Civil War monument, erected in 1907, a date which links the past and the present, for it is midway between the end of the Civil War and the date of the film. A hymn being sung inside the church can be heard:

> The morning light is breaking
> The darkness disappears
> The sons of earth are waking
> To penitential tears.

A cut to the interior of the church establishes in a long shot the whole congregation, singing, but we also hear, off stage, the shriek of a siren. In a series of rapid cuts, all three groups, those in church, those around the monument, and those in the barbershop react to the siren. The members of the last group hurry into the square to enjoy the excitement. The sheriff's mud-spattered car with one flat tire moves into the scene as a rapidly increasing crowd runs after it. A cut to the interior of the car shows a medium close-up of a pair of handcuffed black hands. Finally, moving very slowly, Lucas Beauchamp follows the sheriff and the deputy out of the car. Hitting the top of the car door, Lucas's old-fashioned beaver hat tumbles off and the sheriff picks it up for him. The camera rapidly tracks back and forth among the curious spectators. Quick cuts focus on their fascinated expressions. Lucas, however, appears indifferent to their taunts as he walks between the rows of men to the door of the jail. At the door, he turns and looks calmly from side to side. The camera speeds through the crowd, recording what Lucas sees. Suddenly, it stops at the figure of a boy with lowered eyes. It is Chick Mallison, whom the theater audience immediately perceives to be totally different from the others in the crowd. Spotting Chick, Lucas coolly instructs him to tell his lawyer-uncle to come to the jail. A bystander snorts "'Lawyer! He ain't even gonna need an undertaker.'" Ignoring this prediction, Lucas turns his back on the tense, expectant faces of the crowd and enters the jail, as Chick starts for home.

In this first sequence, ironic contrasts are everywhere: in the mingling of the siren's shrieks with the hymn of the Sunday worshippers; in the symbolic words of the hymn ("The darkness disappears") and the reality of the missing "darkies"; in the mass of white faces and the single black one; in the imposing new courthouse (the original one was burned by Union troops) and the much older jail (which was left standing), and in the eager faces of the men whom the sheriff calls "boys" and the troubled young face of Chick Mallison. As it tracks back and forth, the camera forces us to look at the faces of the townsmen, helping us to see how these individual members of what Faulkner calls a homogeneous community can be fused into a monstrous, implacable mob. The film thus exposes not only the members of the community, but also both the negative and positive aspects of its tradition.

The recurrent motif of the film is the image of the eye, which signifies its theme of perception. Appropriately, the key image is the enormous close-up of the all-seeing eye of Lucas Beauchamp, peering through the iron, crisscross bars of his prison cell. The shot follows Chick Mallison's protest that he cannot carry out Lucas's instructions to dig up the body because it is already too late. As in the novel, Lucas replies "'I'll try to wait,'" but to the multiple ironies of that line, the film adds the close-up of the eye (T 73).[8] By means of a dissolve, this image lingers on the screen and blends into the next image of Chick running from the jail and unexpectedly encountering Crawford Gowrie. The eye-image and the dissolve thus work together to convey the impression that Lucas foresees and oversees all.

Not only does the film contain innumerable shots of characters observing, watching, looking, peering, and staring, but its dialogue, editing, and camera techniques reinforce these images. In addition, alternate modes of perception are counterpointed so that what is at first invisible, or at least obscured, is ultimately revealed to contain further truths. This concentration on pairs of eyes staring intently, often in silence and with either fascination or fear, helps to create the film's atmosphere of uneasiness and foreboding. Even conventional point-of-view and reaction shots take on a deeper, more penetrating meaning as we see the characters in the context of this conflict engaged in the act of seeing and perceiving. In addition, slight but consistent modifications from novel to film are consonant with the film's emphasis on the eye.

In the novel, for example, Chick and his uncle, on their way to Lucas's cell, pass the bullpen where "in tiered bunks against the farther wall lay five Negroes, motionless, their eyes closed . . . immobile orderly and composed . . . as if they had been embalmed" (T 56). But in the film, the eyes of the Negro prisoners are open, eloquently communicating their mute fear. On another occasion in the text, Chick senses during his midnight ride to the cemetery the invisible presence of the "black men and women and children breathing and waiting inside their barred and shuttered houses," whereas in the film these images appear on the screen (T 96). The camera takes us beyond what Chick can see as the lights from Miss Habersham's car flash across and illuminate the interiors of the cabins along the way. We see the silent, fearful Negroes, waiting. A mother covers three children; two men and a woman sit at a table, ignoring the barely touched food. From another cabin, a man cautiously opens the front door and peers through the crack as Chick gallops by on Highboy. So powerful and so moving are these views of the potential victims of a mass hysteria that no dialogue is necessary.

In addition, it is the power of the image that, despite the warning of his mother, draws Aleck Sander out of their cabin on the Mallison's property. In the novel Aleck Sander responds to Chick's familiar whistle (T 85); the film shows him peering at Chick (who is saddling Highboy), through the bars of the venetian blinds at the window. Then almost as if hypnotized, Aleck moves toward what he sees. And although he mutters, "'Gonna do no good—be burned just the same,'" he finds himself part of a dangerous mission.

Although limitations of space prevent detailed descriptions of every scene organized around the seeing (or unseeing) eye, several patterns should be noted. There are, for example, a series of staring-down confrontations. Two such confrontations occur between Chick and Lucas in Lucas's cabin, directly after Chick's mishap in the creek. In the first, Lucas orders the unwilling Chick to "strip-off" so that his wet clothes can be dried; in the second, Lucas

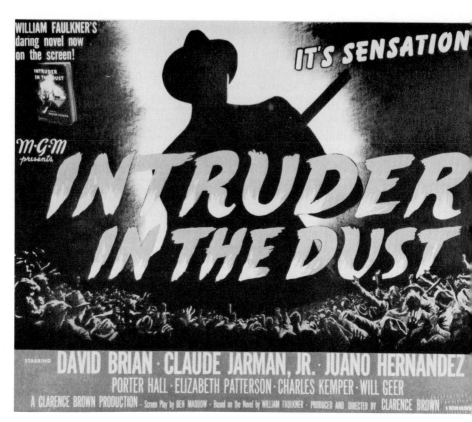

Advertising poster for the film.

refuses to take the coins with which Chick tries to pay for his **meal**. In both confrontations, by his formidable strength of will, Lucas masters Chick, who, under Lucas's determined stare, lowers his eyes.

In a scene invented for the film, however, Chick faces up to Nub Gowrie and admits that it was he who proved that Vinson's grave was empty. Manfully, Chick meets Nub Gowrie's eye.

There is also the confrontation between Crawford Gowrie and Miss Habersham, who is blocking the entrance to the jail in order to prevent the commission of an unconscionable crime. Crawford eyes her warily and then threatens to ignite the gas that he has spilled at her feet. With unruffled composure, she refuses to move. A close shot shows her threading a needle and ordering Crawford to get out of her light, a line which has both a literal and a metaphoric meaning. He backs away as she angrily addresses the mob, commanding the men to go home. The wall of watchful faces breaks up as the men reassemble in smaller groups, aware that Crawford has backed down.

In the next to last sequence, after Lucas has paid Stevens's two-dollar charge for the broken pipe, there is a final exchange of penetrating glances between the two men. Stevens asks Lucas why he did not tell him the truth that night in the jail. Lucas looks directly at the lawyer and asks "'Would you have believed me?'" This time, it is Stevens, not Chick, who lowers his eyes.

In contrast, Lucas will not even bother to look at the men loafing around Fraser's store, who eye him with overt hostility. Close-ups show both Crawford and Vinson Gowrie glaring at Lucas with contempt. Lucas's impassive demeanor and his total silence further incite Vinson's rage. When Vinson tries to assault Lucas, Chick, tensely watchful, steps forward but finds his knife frozen in his hand. Although Fraser's son averts the attack and prevents further violence, it is Lucas's slow, deliberate, and dignified movement that controls the pace of the scene.

In fact, with his mesmeric gaze and his authoritative manner, Lucas controls the pace of every scene in which he appears. In the long jail sequence in which Stevens tries to pry information out of him, Lucas's slow responses increase Stevens's vexation. But Lucas can and does act more rapidly. When Chick returns to the cell door alone, Lucas directs him with brisk authority.

In two of the film's major sequences the theme of perception is expressed in the symbolic treatment of the source of light. The staging of the previously mentioned scene in Lucas's cell, and of the midnight cemetery sequence, establishes significant parallels between Lucas and Miss Habersham in their relationship to the light, parallels which are further emphasized by the camera and the cutting.

When Stevens enters Lucas's cell, he finds the old man asleep on the cot, with his face covered by a newspaper to screen it from the glaring light of the single bulb hanging from the ceiling above. Stevens removes the paper, exposing Lucas to the light. From that moment on, Lucas on center stage is illuminated by the light. His enormous eyes follow Stevens as he paces back and forth, improvising his totally erroneous version of the crime. The interplay of light and shadow on the faces of the two men takes on a symbolic significance in which Lucas is identified with light and Stevens with shadow. Stevens's nervous pacing frequently carries him out of the light, and occasionally casts a shadow over parts of Lucas's face. When the lawyer passes in front of Lucas, he obscures him entirely, and throws his own distorted shadow-image on the wall of the cell. Standing in the doorway, Chick, as always, closely observes the scene.[9] Separate close shots dramatize the reactions of each character; with his penetrating and skeptical eye, Lucas follows Stevens's steps, all the while exposing the foolishness of his words. For Stevens's rhetoric obscures the truth just as his pacing image frequently dims the light. Lucas's poise, moreover, provides an ironic contrast to Stevens's ill-concealed frustration.

When Stevens drops and breaks his pipe, Lucas, fully aware of his lawyer's limitations, seizes the moment to signal to Chick by requesting a can of tobacco. The broken pipe, incidentally, replaces the broken fountain pen, discussed after the fact in the novel. Clarence Brown explained that the substitution was made because a pipe in an actor's hand is a more useful prop. As an instrument for writing legal briefs, the broken pen perhaps signifies the inadequacy of reason alone, whereas the loss of the pipe suggests, in true Ahab-fashion, the end of Stevens's self-assured and smug serenity. The substitution of pipe for pen also functions pragmatically to provoke Lucas's request for tobacco. Chick perceives the dire plea behind Lucas's calm manner, for in contrast to his uncle's blindness, Chick is the one who sees.

The graveyard sequence is introduced by the only extreme long shot in the film. It shows Chick, Miss Habersham, and Aleck Sander searching among the gravestones for Vinson Gowrie's newly dug grave. Once found, the terrified gravediggers communicate as much by glances as by words. Miss Habersham's flashlight and a full moon illuminate the scene. Crickets, bird-calls, and the harsh scraping of the shovel are the only sounds. When a covey of birds suddenly flies off, the flapping wings sound like a clap of thunder. Miss Habersham starts and looks nervously after them. Clouds drift over the moon, shadowing her face, as the scene darkens.

The tension in this long sequence is increased by the careful manipulation of camera distances and angles, and by the frequent reaction shots which punctuate it. In addition, a parallel between Miss Habersham and Lucas is established in the composition of several shots which resemble those of the previously discussed sequence in Lucas's cell. In the latter, Lucas sits under the light with Stevens and Chick in the foreground on either side of him. In the former, Miss Habersham stands above the grave holding the flashlight, while Aleck and Chick on either side in the foreground shovel dirt from the grave. In each sequence respectively, Lucas and Miss Habersham are identified with the source of light. Here, the filmmakers have found visual means to equate these two elders of the community in their superior moral vision, just as in the novel Chick associates them with his own grandparents, thereby granting them respect and authority.

In a second pair of parallel shots, the camera forces us to see Chick, under Lucas's tutelage, growing in stature. The climax of the graveyard sequence is, of course, the discovery of the empty coffin. It is shown, not in a close-up, but in a close shot which includes the image of Chick's legs, somewhat magnified in size by the camera's proximity. As the camera pans up to show Chick's reaction to the astonishing sight, we are reminded of Chick's first view of Lucas Beauchamp in the first flashback. Chick has fallen into the creek and is climbing up its steep bank when he sees two huge boots. Following Chick's view, the camera slowly pans up to reveal a statuesque figure of heroic proportions looking directly down at Chick. Shot from below, Lucas towers over Chick, but in the cemetery it is Chick, looking down into the coffin, whose size the camera angle has increased.

After each member of the trio has reacted to the shot of the empty coffin, the sequence closes with the only complete fade-out in the film. Having begun with the film's only extreme long shot, the graveyard sequence has thus been bracketed to emphasize a different order of experience in time and space, one in which its participants have had to explore a wilderness beyond temporal law. They have had to follow their own consciences and instincts to discover an order of truth that lies beyond circumstantial evidence and provides irrefutable proof.

As the film presses on to its final plot revelations, new relationships emerge to increase our perception. In the second cemetery sequence, one-armed Nub Gowrie commands all attention as he maneuvers his gun and questions the evidence of the preceding night. Once the grave is proven to be empty, the search for the body is on. A frantic chase ensues in which the camera speedily tracks along with the scrambling men and dogs; black prisoners and white men are united in the search for truth. The pace accelerates as Nub discovers the corpse, buried in quicksand, while the others use every means possible to rescue him from sinking. The corpse is then retrieved from the water and the thin layer of sand covering it, while the howling dogs intuitively express the father's grief. Nub's eyes are filled with tears as he wipes the sand from the face of his dead son and then covers it with his hat. The others watch in total silence as the scene ends.

The silence is followed by a shocking crash of music and a dissolve to a close shot of a loudspeaker blaring out the tune of "Running Wild."[10] We are now in the carnival atmosphere of the square. Men are arriving in busloads and other men, women, and children, already gathered, are eagerly waiting for their bestial entertainment to begin. A depth-focus tracking shot reveals that the assemblage has grown to a massive size. Pans pick up individual images of men playing cards, a woman applying lipstick, a girl with a yo-yo, and another with an ice cream cone. Ironically, it is a woman with an infant in her arms who challenges Crawford Gowrie to begin the barbaric fun. Carrying a can overflowing with gasoline he begins the walk past the fascinated watchers; among them is one whose mouth slavers in anticipation. All eyes follow Crawford as he confronts Miss Habersham at the jail door.

After Crawford fails to depose Miss Habersham, the camera tracks in past the groups of waiting men and then pans up to show the barred window of the cell, where Gavin Stevens is again trying to pry information out of Lucas Beauchamp. This time, Gavin wants the murderer's name. Lucas insists that he did not see the person who fired the shot. He explains, moreover, in his own words: "'I ain't seen no rifle. I don't wanter send no man to jail I ain't seen pussonally.'" A close-up of Lucas leads into the flashback in which he explains exactly what he has seen.

At this point in the film there can be no doubt that the whole matter of perception has been broadened to include the perceptions of moral truths. And throughout the film, the dialogue has reinforced the theme. For example, in the new previously mentioned pages of the shooting script in the sequence in the sheriff's kitchen, pondering over why he had failed to believe Lucas, Stevens says, "'It's more than that. There's a wall grown up between us. Lucas can't see through it and I won't. Well, maybe that's wrong. We're the ones who can't see through it, because we're the ones who are blind.'" Immediately, a shot of a closed door appears on the screen, serving as a metaphor for the wall through which Stevens cannot see.

Allusions in the script to seeing, of one sort or another, are far too numerous to list. One more example must suffice. After the flashback showing the murder, Lucas is baffled by why the killer chose Vinson for his victim when he could so easily have chosen him. Stevens, whose perception is improving, explains: "'Because the killer watched you every inch of the way. . . . here was his chance, to murder the man from whom he stole the money and to see you lynched for that very same murder. . . . The scheme should have worked—by every reason of geography and psychology and the past two hundred years of this country's history.'" Incorporating in his own person the evil side of his society's tradition, the murderer has perceived a way to turn these prejudices to his own advantage. He has, he thinks, found a scapegoat to pay the price for his own vicious deed. But Crawford has misjudged the man he had hoped to make his second victim.

The last sequence in Lucas's cell ends with Lucas still watching and waiting. To protect him, the sheriff closes and locks the door; the camera then pans down to show a close shot of the keys in his hand; the keys dissolve into a medium close shot of Crawford Gowrie standing in the center of a group of his companions. Without dialogue, the images foreshadow the resolution.

The sheriff now lays the trap for the real killer. He gives Stevens the task of preparing the bait by announcing to the crowd that Lucas is undeniably innocent. A desperate and angry murderer, the sheriff knows, will become vindictive and try to kill the man who has thwarted his plan. Now Hampton goes to Lucas's cabin to set up his smoke signal. While he kneels to prepare the fire, the startling image of two legs appears behind him. It is Nub Gowrie, whom the sheriff has summoned to be a witness to the scene. Both men wait for the murderer to appear. Nub Gowrie sits in the rocker next to the

Clarence Brown receiving the key to the City of Oxford, presented by Mayor R.X. Williams and an award from the State of Tennessee, presented by Governor Gordon Browning (holding document), on the occasion of the world premiere.

large wedding picture of Lucas and Molly. As a long-time widower, he identifies with the more recently widowed Lucas and talks of his own life and of how hard it has been to raise five boys alone. As he counts out his sons on the fingers of his hand, a shot rings through the window, shattering the glass, and a voice shouts, "'Come on out here, you runnin' black nigger.'" Knowing the truth which he has earlier suspected, Nub insists on bringing in his own son alone. With a calm command and a level glance, he forces Crawford Gowrie to turn over the gun, the same one that had killed his own brother.

In the preceding cabin scene, Nub Gowrie is paralleled to Lucas Beauchamp in several ways. We see his legs first, just as we have earlier seen Lucas's boots before viewing the whole man. The dialogue also reinforces the experience they have in common: the widower's condition of loneliness. Moreover, as Nub's eyes widen and as he admits he knows who carries a 30–30 rifle, it is clear that he is now fully aware of who killed his son. Other matters also become clear, for just as Lucas Beauchamp will not name a man whom he has not seen commit the crime, Nub Gowrie has hesitated to lead a lynch mob against a man who may not have been guilty of the crime.

Returning to the square in the dark of night, the sheriff's car now holds a different prisoner, one whose handcuffed wrists are white. The mob chases the car, crowding around it as Nub exits, followed by his son, Crawford. With the sheriff, they walk to the jail door and stand for a moment to address the crowd. Several shots show Crawford's tight-lipped face. Masterfully composed, the last shot of the three men is eloquent. Crawford stands in the middle with his back to the crowd, an abject image of disgrace. The sheriff, at his right, is half-turned toward the crowd, while Nub, on the left directly faces his fellow townsmen and quietly confirms their suspicions.

For a moment, the members of the crowd remain immobile in horrified silence, while the camera pans over their faces exposing their guilty, silent shame. All at once they break ranks and shuffle away. Chick and Stevens watch the sea of cars from the balcony above. From their superior position the people and the cars look small as, with some justification, the man and the boy look down on the crowd. Suddenly they spy Miss Habersham. Intent on getting on with the business of feeding her chickens, she braves the traffic jam and shouts from below to offer her assistance should Chick and Stevens get in trouble again. Continuing in her role of nourisher of the flock (which includes the boy, Chick, and Gavin Stevens, as well as her farmyard chickens), Miss Habersham demonstrates that she is the kind of woman who is not cluttered and gets things done. Grasping truth intuitively, Miss Habersham represents the humanitarian side of the communal tradition. She ignores Stevens's easy assumption that Lucas killed Vinson Gowrie and suggests that "'Maybe he didn't.'" To all objections to digging up the grave, she replies, "'But somebody's got to do it.'" And she herself helps Chick to get it done.

The final two scenes show at last a normal Saturday afternoon in the sunny town square of Jefferson, Mississippi. A wagon filled with Negroes makes its way through the crowd, in which blacks and whites mingle normally and a phonograph plays in progression "Tiger Rag," "Raucous Ruckus," and "Hand Me Down My Walking Cane." After Lucas has paid his two dollars and received his receipt, Chick and his uncle again look down from their exalted positions, watching Lucas make his way through the crowd below. Because of his height and his archaic garb, Lucas stands out among the people milling around. As he proceeds on his independent and impervious path, Chick insists that "'They don't see him,'" that "'They don't even know he's there.'" The image confirms Chick's view, for like Ralph Ellison's Invisible Man Lucas seems to evoke no recognition at all from the townspeople who have so grievously wronged him. Gavin Stevens's retort, however, contradicts the image: "'They see him. . . . they do. . . . they always will, as long as he lives.'" Stevens proceeds to explain that Lucas is the keeper of his conscience, and Chick graciously includes his own, in the line, "'Our conscience, Uncle John.'" A crescendo of romantic background music prepares the viewers for the final fade-out.

These last two speeches, followed by the lush music, are so explicitly moralistic that they have rightfully been accused of sentimentality.[11] There is ambiguity, however, in the contrast between the image and the word that creates a certain ironic deflation of Stevens's optimistic assurances. For a truer statement of what the people perceive, we must recall their shocked and silent withdrawal from the vision of the fratricide. In that scene there is no discrepancy between the image and the word, for Stevens correctly assesses the reason for their repulsion and dismay. They *are* indeed running away from themselves.

As viewers, though, the film will not permit us to run from ourselves, but constantly implicates us in its tests of our own perceptions. In the foregoing series of shots from Lucas's face, to the jail keys to Crawford Gowrie, the continuity increases our awareness.

The film also employs a technique, advanced for its day, of deliberately courting audience recognition of the true criminal. It provides three opportunities for the more attentive to identify the true murderer. I do not refer here to Crawford Gowrie's presence in the square, for his brother's death justifies in the eyes of the mob his anger and his desire for revenge. But the distant view of the man on the mule whom the trio of saviors watch so anxiously, and the rapid image in the second flashback of the man driving the truck, as well as the offstage voice heard by the sheriff and Nub Gowrie inside Lucas's cabin, all tease and test our own powers of perception.[12]

In addition, carefully spaced close-ups emphasize significant details, magnifying images that become symbols of truth and forcing us to grasp the unseen from the seen: the tolling bell on the church spire, followed much later by its demonic counterpart, the loudspeaker entertaining the mob in the town square; Lucas Beauchamp's handcuffed black wrists; the gleaming coin rolling on the floor of Lucas's cabin, the symbol of Chick's guilt of which we are reminded in the close-up of the moon at the cemetery; the Negro food Chick eats in the cabin, knowledge of which is part of his background; Lucas's enormous eye behind jail bars; Chick's ear on the other side, listening; the two pairs of hands, one black and one white, grasping the bars, both implicated in the search for truth; the shot of Highboy's head, his agitation showing his premonition of danger; the empty grave, and later, the bullet that provides the proof of Lucas's innocence; the mule's hoofprints which Chick discovers; Nub Gowrie's tear-filled eyes; the can being filled with gasoline; the barred window of Lucas's cell; the keys to the jail; and the numerous images of the faces of the townspeople, watching, waiting, and reacting.

Natural sounds of footsteps on hard, wooden floors, of rusty hinges on heavy doors, of horses' hooves, of phonograph records and of voices singing hymns—all these serve to make us aware of the lack of the customary background music and even of the moments of silence. Silence, like the invisible, has a meaning, too.

Perhaps it was Brown's soundtrack with its lack of background music and its use of natural sounds that inspired so many reviewers to praise the film for its realism. Or perhaps its having been shot on location in Oxford prompted its first commentators to praise its "genuine realism, its documentary quality [that] puts the stamp of super-reality on every scene," and its achievement in reaching one of the "all-time highs in motion picture realism."[13] Such phrases as "stark realism" and "raw realism" recur frequently in the panegyrics to the film, but what the term "realism" means here is not quite clear. I suspect that it is being used loosely as a synonym for excellence.

The description of the film thus far, however, clearly reveals that its theatrical and pictorial elements have been far too artfully shaped and composed to be classified with direct forms of realism, such as *cinéma vérité* or docudrama. Instead, the settings have been meticulously selected, and the action has been framed, often creating stylized tableaux, in order to create the illusion of reality. Reality and realism should not be confused, for the conventions of the latter express only one view of the former.

The dynamic rhythms of the camera energize the film, providing configurations of imagery that heighten its significance, and the editing cannily manipulates the emotional responses of the audience. Together, the montage and the fluid camera create the atmosphere, mood, and tone of the film. But nothing is haphazard or accidental; all is carefully crafted. And even the soundtrack, although employing natural sounds, is not in its effect naturalistic, for in working contrary to film convention, it creates an eerie, ominous atmosphere.[14] In all, *Intruder* can be described as a well-made film that employs a high degree of artifice artfully to convey its meaning.

Nor is *Intruder*'s cinematic use of the objective world of Oxford any more literal than Faulkner's creation of the fictional Jefferson. Each exterior setting in the film is deliberately chosen for its emotional and dramatic possibilities, and each interior is carefully furnished to depict the tastes and traditions of its occupants.[15] Furthermore, these settings frequently serve to reinforce the ironic level of the film, and to emphasize the contrasts between the positive and negative sides of the tradition; for the ability of the camera to present multiple images simultaneously enhances the power of film to exploit the paradoxical aspects of existence.

For example, in a small town most of the residents know each other, so that it seems quite natural for Chick and his uncle to chat with Mr. Lilley on their walk to the jail. Entrusted with Mr. Lilley's message that he will join the prospective lynchers as soon as he can, Chick and Stevens proceed toward the square and are nearly run over by a car full of wildly cheering and screaming men. At the same time, a view of the Confederate monument in the background reminds us that the tradition includes the attitudes of men like Mr. Lilley and his friends, "'which proves again how no man can cause more grief than that one clinging blindly to the vices of his ancestors'" (T 49).

Probably no setting in the film conveys the contradictory aspects of the tradition more vividly than the jail with its chipped, scarred walls and its heavy, iron double-doors, which serve both to protect and to imprison Lucas. As Stevens and Chick walk up the stairs with Mr. Tubbs, the jailer, we see the texture of the wall in sharp focus and the strong diagonal line of the stair railing, bifurcating the screen. The bannister seems to illustrate obliquely the divisive social impulses, as well as the conflict in the mind of the jailer, whose sneering contempt for "niggers" does not prevent him from trying to safeguard his Negro prisoners. The scene shows us, on the one hand, that the tradition includes a respect for the law and a strong sense of duty, later expressed in Miss Habersham's pithy statement: "'Someone's got to do it.'" On the other hand, there are false attitudes that prevent seeing truth: the threat of lynching, objectified in the constant association of Crawford Gowrie with the flame of a match, and Mr. Mallison's smug, conventional comments that "'It's happened before and it's bound to happen again. Nothing for us to get excited about.'" It is with these conflicting attitudes that Chick must grapple.

Sunday dinner at the Mallisons' is set in a typical middle-class Southern home, with its gleaming silver on the buffet and its centerpiece of garden flowers. Parlee and Aleck Sander wait on table in the traditional roles of servants of white people.

But in Lucas's cabin we see him as master of his own hearth, where the fire is warm in contrast to the barren, winter landscape outside. His gold toothpick glitters as he stands, legs spread apart, in front of the fire or rocking back and forth on his heels contentedly watching Chick eat the side meat and greens that were to have been his own dinner. On the mantel above the fire is a glass filled with long rolls of paper which Lucas uses to light his pipe. It is exactly like the one on Gavin Stevens's desk. Above the mantel hangs a picture portraying a Western scene of covered wagons and a dark-faced man on a white horse. Most conspicuous of all is the large wedding portrait of Lucas and Molly on the table beside Molly's rocking chair. The pride and contentment this elderly couple feel in their home is evidenced in its cleanliness and order, in Lucas's stance and in Molly's proprietary rocking. Without a line of dialogue, she conveys strength and dignity. Although more humble than Lucas, she is serene. Until Chick, in trying to establish his white supremacy, desecrates their hospitality, the scene glows with warmth and humanity.

In addition to the rich detail of the settings, Brown's placement of the actors helps to convey meaning. Several shots of the film are framed so as to demonstrate the process of Chick's increasing awareness. When his uncle is in command, Chick, like an apprentice hero, often stands on the thresholds of doorways. He walks behind his uncle, imitating his stride. Placed either between or behind Stevens and Sheriff Hampton, his shorter stature is conspicuous.

In other positions, his moral growth is symbolized. When he urges the complacent Stevens to hurry to the jail before a lynching can occur, Chick is standing on the stairway looking down on his uncle in the hallway below. At the foot of the stairs, Stevens says, "'Lucas should have thought of that before he shot a white man in the back.'" Here the visuals bear out that the usual relationship between Chick and Stevens is reversed. Later, when his uncle refuses to help him obtain the telling bullet, Chick firmly closes the door between them, and leans against it in discouragement. Then he suddenly makes up his mind and moves rapidly to get his horse. Although he still speaks of escape, he is quick to fall in with Miss Habersham's plans. When they start on their quest, Chick is in the lead.

Brown's favorite transitional device is the dissolve; it also functions for him flexibly in several other ways. It compresses time and space, driving the action forward so that the tension rarely sags, and it provides the shock effect of the shift from the close shot of Nub Gowrie's silent grief to the blast of the loudspeaker in the square. In contrast, the long, tracking shots of the crowd vary the pace and have a distinguishing rhythm of their own, just as the single complete fade-out after the shot of the empty grave enhances its emotional content.

There is also a correlation between the effect of the dissolves and the general coloration of the film. Using black-and-white film on the subject of Negro-white relations, a more conventional director probably would have chosen to stress the contrasts. But Brown worked against the obvious by blending the black and white into variegated grays. He shows the cars covered with dust. He dresses most of his actors in clothes which photograph in the range of gray. Several of his landscapes and skies look bleak and gray.[16] This lack of strong contrasts between the white and black tones is reinforced by lap dissolves, which fuse the images and break down sharp color distinctions. And as the diction of this paragraph implies, the color tones of the film can be used to describe the blending of white and black people in the community of Jefferson as well. For just as on the plot level we see the melding of races in the square after the truth has been discovered at the end of the film, the gradations and shadings of color throughout the film represent an artistic choice that illustrates visually the novel's theme of community and homogeneity.

In his old-time white waistcoat and formal black coat, Lucas is set apart from the crowd. Defying the community's determination to make him act like a "nigger," he arrogantly demonstrates his pride and independence. His appearance and manner mark him out for what he is: the grandson of one of Jefferson's early white settlers.[17] In his refusal to fit into the stereotype of the Negro, he achieves a Promethean grandeur, and he also forces Chick Mallison to see beyond the limitations of his inherited prejudices. For stereotypes, without doubt, limit perception.

Lucas's determined denial of the role of scapegoat transfers the guilt to society where it ultimately belongs. Because he is neither lynched nor driven out of the community, the mythic structure of the ritual sacrifice is modulated. Ultimately, more emphatically in the film than in the novel, Lucas is revealed to be morally superior to any man in his milieu, and Crawford Gowrie is fleshed-out to incorporate society's most vicious and barbarous tendencies. In the darkest moment of the film, when Crawford Gowrie is taken to the jail, the camera forces us to see the white faces of the mob. They do not gloat over the triumph of justice. Instead, the camera exposes and condemns their complicity in the perpetuation of injustice. Faced with the realization that the murderer is one of them, they run from the horror of their own potential for violence and evil.

In both the novel and the film the fratricide carries a resonance beyond its explicit plot function. It reaches back into history to our fratricidal Civil War, and it implies that we are still denying brotherhood. In its largest sense it suggests that racial bigotry is a form of fratricide. Finally, we are forced to recognize that Jefferson, Mississippi, is only one small community in a larger society that includes, as Faulkner might have put it, all mankind.

NOTES TO PART ONE

1. In addition to the writings of Serge Eisenstein, Erwin Panofsky, Rudolph Arnheim, Siegfried Kracauer and André Bazin, all of which are well known to and frequently cited by critics and students of film, I have found the following works useful in dealing with adaptations: George Bluestone, *Novels into Film* (Berkeley and Los Angeles: Univ. of California Press, 1966); Susan Sontag, *Against Interpretation and Other Essays* (New York: Farrar, 1966); Raymond Durgnat, *Films and Feelings* (Cambridge, Mass.: M.I.T. Press, 1967); W.R. Robinson, ed., *Man and the Movies* (Baton Rouge: Louisiana State Univ. Press, 1967); Robert Richardson, *Literature and Film* (Bloomington: Indiana Univ. Press, 1969); Neil D. Isaacs, *Fiction Into Film: A Walk in the Spring Rain* (Knoxville: Univ. of Tennessee Press, 1970); T.J. Ross, ed., *Film and the Liberal Arts* (New York: Holt, 1970); Marsha Kinder and Beverle Houston, *Close-up: A Critical Perspective on Film* (New York: Harcourt, 1972); Gerald Mast and Marshall Cohen, *Film Theory and Criticism: Introductory Readings* (New York: Oxford Univ. Press, 1974); and a new journal devoted to the relationship between film and literature, *Literature/Film Quarterly*, ed. Thomas L. Erskine (Salisbury State College). Ronald Gottesman and Harry M. Geduld have listed numerous books and articles on adaptations in their *Guidebook to Film* (New York: Holt, 1972), pp. 30–35. And another book on this subject that is to be published in 1977 is Bruce Kawin, *Faulkner and Film* (New York: Unger, in press).

2. *What is Cinema?* Vol. 1, trans. Hugh Gray (Berkeley: Univ. of California Press, 1967), p. 143.

3. Toby Mussman, ed., *Jean-Luc Godard* (New York, 1968), p. 146. Quoted in Alfred Guzzetti, "The Role of Theory in Films and Novels," *NLH*, 3 (1972), 555.

4. Malcolm Cowley typifies this plight. After praising various prose passages, Cowley found that Faulkner used the story as a text for a series of sermons delivered by Gavin Stevens; Cowley adds that "the tragedy of intelligent Southerners like Faulkner is that their two fundamental beliefs, in human equality and in Southern independence are now in violent conflict" ("William Faulkner's Nation," *The New Republic*, 18 Oct. 1948, pp. 21–22). For a summary and sampling of contemporary reviews of the novel, see Joseph Blotner, *Faulkner: A Biography*, II (New York: Random, 1974), pp. 1262–63, 167; and John Basset, ed., *William Faulkner: The Critical Heritage* (London: Routledge and Kegan Paul, 1975), pp. 30–31, 343–49. Basset notes that *Intruder* "received almost no negative comments in Britain" (p. 347).

5. On several occasions Faulkner denied that Stevens was his mouthpiece. See Malcolm Cowley, ed., *The Faulkner-Cowley File: Letters and Memories, 1944–1962* (New York: Viking, 1966), pp. 17–18, 110–11; and James B. Meriwether and Michael Millgate, ed., *Lion in the Garden: Interviews with William Faulkner, 1926–1962* (New York: Random, 1968), pp. 160–61, 166.

6. Robert Penn Warren, ed., *Faulkner: A Collection of Critical Essays* (Englewood Cliffs: Prentice-Hall, 1966), p. 219, rpt. Edmund Wilson, *Classics and Commercials*

(New York, 1950). Wilson said that the novel had suspense and excitement, and that Lucas Beauchamp and his milieu live, but he deplored Faulkner's prose style and thought that the novel contained a "kind of counterblast to the anti-lynching bill and to the civil rights plank in the Democratic platform." Gavin Stevens's "long disquisitions" Wilson found so "'editorial' in character that it is difficult to regard them merely as a part of the presentation . . . of the uncle's personality."

7. Michael Millgate, *The Achievement of William Faulkner* (London: Constable, 1966), pp. 42–43.

8. Blotner, pp. 1244–58. *Intruder* sold over 15,000 copies in trade edition (p. 1264).

9. Reviewers of the film too numerous to cite stated that it was superior to the novel. Several reviewers of the novel claimed that it suffered from the Hollywood influence. Paolo Milano in "Faulkner in Crisis," *The Nation*, 30 Oct. 1948, pp. 496–97, called the novel a Gothic thriller with "touches of a movie scenario . . . in its race-against-time pattern." Maxwell Geismar in "Ex-Aristocrats Emotional Education," *Sat R* (25 Sept. 1948), p. 8, claimed that "even Jefferson, Miss., . . . has come under the influence of Hollywood." A recent literary critic finds the film an improvement on the novel, although "faithful to the book almost to the point of literary enslavement in the early sections." He adds that the last section of the film "is a good lesson in adaptation; it is the strongest possible argument for leaving the literary text on the printed page" (Joseph W. Reed, Jr., *Faulkner's Narrative* [New Haven: Yale Univ. Press, 1973], pp. 208–209). In general, Reed classifies the novel as one of Faulkner's failures, taking the argument full circle back to Wilson by saying "Edmund Wilson was right. *Intruder* . . . is an unsuccessful pamphlet" (p. 202). But as James B. Meriwether has noted, Reed's "chapters on the novels are rendered virtually useless by ignorance of previous criticism and scholarship, by factual errors, and by narrow critical sympathies. Throughout, the book gives the impression of belonging to an earlier age of Faulkner criticism" (James Woodress, ed., *American Literary Scholarship* [Durham, N.C.: Duke Univ. Press, 1975], p. 138).

10. Orville Prescott, "Outstanding Novels," *YR*, 38 (1949), 381–82. Prescott adds that Faulkner "has never mastered the rudiments of his craft. His novels are disorderly, inchoate, undisciplined, diffuse, torrential and opaque." He finds *Intruder*, however, easier to read than previous novels. Prescott recommends as "much more impressive, perhaps the best American novel of the year" James Gould Cozzens's *Guard of Honor*, a value judgment which puts Prescott's criticism in perspective.

11. "Faulkner and the South Today," in *A Collection of Critical Essays*, p. 227, rpt. from *PR*, 15 (1948), 1130–35. Hardwick found the situation brilliant (although she misread it and thought that Lucas pretended to be a murderer), and the theme one of the "South's appalled recognition of its sins." She adds that Faulkner's "states' rights pamphlet . . . falsifies and degrades his fine comprehension of the moral dilemma of the decent guilt-ridden Southerner" (pp. 228–29).

12. *William Faulkner: The Yoknapatawpha Country* (New Haven: Yale Univ. Press, 1963), p. 422.

13. The quotation is from "Gavin Stevens: From Rhetoric to Dialectic," *Faulkner Studies*, 2 (Spring 1953), 2. The paraphrase is of part of the argument in chap. 8 ("Initiation and Identity") of *The Novels of William Faulkner* (Baton Rouge: Louisiana State Univ. Press, 1964), pp. 124–45.

14. "Regeneration for the Man," *A Collection of Critical Essays*, pp. 231–37, rpt. from *SR*, 57 (Winter 1949), 120–27. Lytle points out Chick Mallison's effort to preserve his spiritual integrity, and shows that the symbolism suggests baptism and regeneration. The Longley quotation is from *The Tragic Mask: A Study of Faulkner's Heroes* (Chapel Hill: Univ. of North Carolina Press, 1957), pp. 36–37. Michael Millgate also comments on the comic aspects of the novel (*The Achievement of William Faulkner*, p. 218). Millgate, incidentally, says that the technique of the first view of Lucas Beauchamp in the novel "perhaps suggests an influence from the cinema," but Millgate's suggestion is not in any way pejorative (p. 219). Eudora Welty found

Intruder "marvelously funny" and noted that the "political views delivered outright as a speech, are made, rightly enough, another such shading of the story" ("In Yoknapatawpha," *HudR*, 1 (1949), 597, 598.

15. Meriwether and Millgate, *Lion in the Garden*, pp. 160–61, 166.

16. *The American Cinema: Directors and Directions, 1929–1968* (New York: Dutton, 1968), p. 228.

17. *The Parade's Gone By* (New York: Knopf, 1968), p. 138. Brownlow lists Clarence Brown as one of the "handful of directors who ever influenced the photography of their pictures" (p. 212). The quotation is from Charles Higham and Joel Greenberg, *Hollywood in the Forties* (London: Zwemmer, 1968), p. 79. For a brief discussion of Brown's style, see William K. Everson, "Clarence Brown: A Survey of His Work," *Films in Review* (Dec. 1973), pp. 577–89.

18. *The Art of the American Film, 1900–1971* (Garden City, N.Y.: Doubleday, 1973), pp. 113–14. A reference to the film occurs in Martin Quigley, Jr., and Richard Gestner, *Films in America, 1929–1969* (New York: Golden Press, 1970), p. 182: "Humanity at its worst—lynch law and mob rule—was shown without flinching . . . [in] what is probably one of the most horrible, as well as the most gripping sequences that has ever been recorded in an 'entertainment' motion picture."

19. *Toms, Coons, Mulattoes, Mammies and Bucks: An Interpretive History of Blacks in American Films* (1973; rpt. New York: Bantam, 1975), pp. 217–20.

20. *From Sambo to Superspade: The Black Experience in Motion Pictures* (Boston: Houghton, Mifflin, 1975), pp. 157–60.

21. *Literature/Film Quarterly*, 1 (Spring-April 1973), 138–49. I have recently discovered an interesting, early, long study of the film: Dorothy B. Jones, "William Faulkner: Novel into Film," *FQ* (formerly *Quarterly of Film, Radio and Television*), 18 (Fall 1953), 51–71.

22. Edwin Howard, *Memphis Press-Scimitar*, 12 Oct. 1949.

23. Blotner, p. 1252.

24. *Omnibus*, 2 (Dec. 1948), 88–129. The author of the abridgment is not given.

CHAPTER 2

1. William Faulkner, *Faulkner in the University: Class Conferences at the University of Virginia, 1957–1958*, ed. Frederick L. Gwynn and Joseph L. Blotner (1959; rpt. New York: Vintage Books, 1965), pp. 141–42.

2. This point will be developed in the chapter devoted to the film.

3. R.G. Collins, "Triptychs, Sequels, and Serials: Varieties of Structure in Faulkner," paper presented at MLA annual meeting, Dec. 28, 1975, pp. 8, 12.

4. See n. 6, chap. 1. Warren Beck defends Faulkner's prose style, noting that he "is trying to render the transcendent life of the mind, the crowded composite of associative and analytical consciousness which expands the vibrant moment into the reaches of all time, simultaneously observing, remembering, interpreting, and modifying the object of its awareness. To this end the sentence as a rhetorical unit (however strained) is made to hold diverse yet related elements . . . which is perhaps the nearest that language can come to the instantaneous complexities of consciousness itself" ("William Faulkner's Style," in *William Faulkner: Three Decades of Criticism*, ed. Frederick J. Hoffman and Olga W. Vickery [New York: Harcourt, 1960], p. 153, rpt. from *American Prefaces* (Spring 1941), pp. 195–211.

5. Robert H. Elias in "Gavin Stevens: Intruder?" (*Faulkner Studies*, 3, No. 1 [Spring 1954], 1–4) finds that the role of Stevens's words and the attitudes they convey "appear dramatically within the context of Chick's problems" (p. 1). His voice serves as both conscience and consciousness and is systematically and effectively embodied in the novel. Olga W. Vickery says that "Gavin Stevens' circumlocutions suffer in comparison with Chick's actions. . . . Faulkner . . . is attempting to bridge the gap between words and deeds by sustaining the parallel between them" (*The Novels of William Faulkner*, p. 144).

6. Brooks, p. 421.

7. Pagination refers to the Random House 1948 edition of *Intruder in the Dust*. The Modern Library College Edition (New York: Random, n.d.) has identical pagination. References to the novel will be cited as follows: (T #). I have taken the liberty of occasionally regularizing Faulkner's punctuation in quotations from the novel in order to clarify my use of the quotation.

8. Brooks, p. 421.

9. John Dobson, librarian of Special Collections at the University of Tennessee Library, told me that several scholars interested in the Oxford of the forties have come to examine the still photographs in the Clarence Brown Collection, which provide a better record for the purposes of these scholars than a visit to present-day Oxford.

10. (Baton Rouge: Louisiana State Univ. Press, 1960), rev. ed. 1968, pp. 19–22.

11. Meriwether and Millgate, *Lion in the Garden*, p. 255.

12. "The Shadow and the Act," *The Reporter*, 6 Dec. 1949, p. 17.

13. The shot of the moon in the cemetery sequence of the film is reminiscent of this passage.

14. In the last chapter there is a time dislocation that indicates that Chick has driven Lucas to get the flowers for Miss Habersham, and then returned to his uncle's office, just off the square. If this trip is considered, Chick goes to the square ten times and to his home seven times.

CHAPTER 3

1. *Intruder*, together with *Pinky*, *Home of the Brave*, and *Lost Boundaries* (three films dealing with other aspects of the Negro problem) were often referred to as a cycle of movies on that subject. All four films were released in 1949.

2. William Fadiman, *Hollywood Now* (New York: Liveright, 1972), p. 107.

3. Personal interview with Dore Schary, Sept. 22, 1974.

4. Faulkner said that "there was a tremendous flux of detective stories going about at that time and [his] children were always buying them and bringing them home" (*Faulkner in the University*, p. 141). William Van O'Connor suggests that Faulkner's work in Hollywood on *The Big Sleep* helped to turn him toward or strengthen his interest in the detective story. Faulkner worked on the script of Raymond Chandler's novel in 1944. See *The Tangled Fire of William Faulkner* (Minneapolis: Univ. of Minnesota Press, 1954), p. 136n.

5. Paolo Milano called the plot of the novel hackneyed and the setting conventional. He added that these choices were deliberate on Faulkner's part to leave the author free for his essential concern: the depths of conflict within each character (p. 496).

6. Personal interview with Clarence Brown, Feb. 24, 1972.

7. The details of the sale of the film rights to Metro are recorded in Blotner, pp. 1253–54, 1257. It is still customary for agents and book publishers to submit galleys to all potential buyers at the same time. The practice is called multiple submissions.

8. In an author's note in James W. Silver, *Mississippi: The Closed Society* (New York: Harcourt, 1963), new enlarged edition 1966, Professor Silver emphasizes Faulkner's sincere interest in and desire to help to ameliorate the racial strife in Mississippi.

9. See Harry Modean Campbell and Ruel E. Foster, *William Faulkner: A Critical Appraisal* (Norman: Univ. of Oklahoma Press, 1951). Professor Campbell's numerous articles and reviews are listed in John Bassett, *William Faulkner: An Annotated Checklist of Criticism* (New York: David Lewis, 1972).

10. These shots are listed in the explanatory matter preceding the script. In an interview with Philip K. Scheuer (*Los Angeles Times*, 30 Oct. 1949), Brown said that the interior shots of the action in both Lucas's cabin and Chick's bedroom were shot in the studio in Hollywood.

11. Howard, 10 Oct. 1949.

12. There is background music at the close of the film.
13. Personal interview with Robert Surtees, Aug. 6, 1975.
14. Rushes (or dailies, as they are sometimes called) are often shown as soon as they are developed so that the director can evaluate his material as soon as possible.
15. Surtees attributed Brown's popularity in Oxford partially to his being a teetotaler.
16. Hernandez's host was G.W. Bankhead, an undertaker.
17. Aug. 1949, p. 28.
18. Robert Ellis in the *California Eagle* (17 Nov. 1949) found it "cruel of producer Brown to jockey the young Negro player, Elzie Emanuel, into a Willie-Best-Eye-rolling comedy part." Ben Maddow remembers being shocked when he saw the scene. He attributes the direction of Emanuel to a convention inherited from the silent and early sound films (Degenfelder, p. 145).
19. Joseph Blotner discusses the construction of the boat fully (pp. 1254–56, 1258–59, 1288–89, *et passim*).
20. Blotner (p. 1254) describes Faulkner's farewell party for the cast, to which Juano Hernandez could not be invited because of the problem of having to invite the whole Bankhead family also.
21. Schary said that Brown was one of the first directors to use dolly shots. His use of them began in silent films.
22. Schary's words are quoted here and in the next paragraph.
23. Schary said that the film cost about $1,200,000 or $1,300,000; Brown said that it was made for under $500,000.
24. Howard, 10 Oct. 1949.
25. Ellison, p. 19.
26. Pt. 4, 26 Nov. 1949, pp. 84–85.
27. Hernandez died in 1970. *Intruder* was his first film.
28. It was shown at the Los Angeles County Museum and at Filmex in 1975.
29. The headquarters of Films, Inc. are at 1144 Wilmette Avenue, Wilmette, Illinois 60091.
30. Harry Haun, *Los Angeles Times*, 14 Oct. 1973. Harry Haun has been the movie editor and critic of the Nashville *Tennessean* since 1963. No full-length study of Clarence Brown's canon has been made to date. One is at present being written by Ski Hilenski, who prepared the Brown filmography for this volume.

CHAPTER 4

1. In "Screen Writers' Symposium," *Film Comment*, 6 (Winter 1970–71), 95, Maddow said that "there is no such animal as a screenwriter," that people who write screenplays "are monsters because it is the grotesque fact that they have responsibility but no power." He listed *Intruder*, however, as one of the films he had written for which he wanted to be mentioned. In 1973 Maddow spoke to a class I was teaching at UCLA on the novel and film versions of *Intruder*. He stated that he saw no permanent value in screenplays.
2. Faulkner probably unofficially added a few lines; these additions will be discussed near the end of this chapter.
3. The dialogue changes are noted in the script published in this volume. As a director, Brown was known for his integrity toward a script, seldom departing from the agreed-upon version. He did not follow the instructions for camera positions and editing in the script or the settings as described and improvised by Maddow, who did not go to Oxford and therefore could not include precise detail. A more accurate description of a film can be found in the continuity script, which is prepared after the film has been edited. It records the "number, kind, and duration of shots, the kind of

86

transitions, the exact dialogue and sound effects" (Harry M. Geduld and Ronald Gottesman, *An Illustrated Glossary of Film Terms* [New York: Holt, 1973], p. 137). It also lists the cast of characters, cites locations, and lists names of compositions used in the score. It serves the technical purpose of functioning as a record of the film. Four pages of *Intruder's* continuity script can be found in Appendix B.

4. The shooting script, sometimes called the director's script, is a copy of the screenplay that the director uses during the daily filming. It includes technical information, such as the director's plans for the composition of shots. Directors vary considerably in the amount of information they record on their shooting scripts.

5. A list of these titles has been included in Appendix A.

6. Maddow discussed the story-line thoroughly with Brown before beginning the treatment. Personal interview with Ben Maddow, Jan. 13, 1975.

7. In his comments to my class (1973) Ben Maddow said that plays were usually pared down to essentials and were therefore harder than novels to adapt into films because the adaptor must invent new action. Maddow, incidentally, holds the view that an adaptation of a serious novel or play should try to be faithful to the spirit of the original.

8. Maddow lecture, 1973. A student found the film flawed because it did not establish the suspicion that Lucas may have been guilty of the murder. Maddow replied that neither the novel nor the film intended to raise that suspicion, and that the meaning of both works was predicated on the audience's realization of Lucas's innocence from the beginning.

9. The quotation is from the treatment.

10. Maddow has substituted "fire" for the novel's "shoot him" (T 17).

11. Degenfelder, p. 143.

12. Faulkner has been quoted as saying that Cervantes is one of his favorite authors, but neither Cervantes nor *Don Quixote* is mentioned in *Intruder* (*Faulkner in the University*, pp. 50, 145, 150).

13. The wooden hand on the church spire is not used in the film. Ben Maddow explained that his descriptions of settings and buildings were intended to be followed literally in the design of the film. When he wrote the script he had no idea that the film would be made in Oxford because location pictures were seldom made at that time. Although Maddow never visited Oxford, he had traveled extensively in the South. He had also studied hundreds of photographs made by the Farm Security Administration under Roy Streicher. The list of Maddow's publications in his Bibliography shows that photography has been one of his continued interests.

14. Maddow concurred with my explanation of the improbability of such a scene in 1949.

15. In his discussion of Faulkner's style, Warren Beck says that "there exists in almost all of Faulkner's work a realistic colloquialism, expressing lively dialogue that any playwright might envy" ("William Faulkner's Style," p. 148).

16. Maddow lecture, 1973.

17. The film uses the name John Stevens instead of Gavin Stevens.

18. Robert Surtees said that these shooting plans may not always have been carried out. As noted in the previous chapter, Surtees explained that no second unit was taken to Oxford. He also explained that a special process camera for process shots is always taken on location and used for protection, in case additional shots are needed in editing. His was a Bell and Howell camera, a particularly steady one, because no movement can be allowed when shooting a process background. In addition, a particular kind of film and scale are necessary. He customarily took extra location shots after the actors had completed their scenes. The procedure is now different, he added (Surtees interview, Aug. 6, 1975).

19. Maddow interview, Jan. 13, 1975.

20. In addition, the line "She's the only lady anywhere that ever held a jail with a twenty-gauge spool of thread" occurs only in the film and the continuity script.

21. Blotner, p. 1278.
22. Blotner's note (p. 169) credits Professor Patrick Samway, J.J., for his analysis of Faulkner's work on the scenario of *Intruder*. Professor Samway may have had access, which I lack, to manuscript evidence of suggested revisions never added to Brown's shooting script, and, if filmed, later cut out of the film. Faulkner probably did contribute the dialogue in the next-to-last sequence above. Perhaps, though, Professor Samway is referring to these lines and considering both the office and the balcony dialogue as a single, final scene.
23. The ellipses occur in the screenplay. The symbol < > indicates deleted words.
24. Ben Maddow thinks it very likely that Faulkner made these changes and added the dialogue in the next-to-last sequence. He said that Clarence Brown never wrote anything himself in the screenplays he directed (interview, Jan. 13, 1975).

CHAPTER 5

1. "Art Form and Material," rpt. in Mast and Cohen, *Film Theory and Criticism*, pp. 270, 272.
2. Durgnat, p. 198.
3. Bazin, p. 24.
4. *Anatomy of Criticism* (Princeton: Princeton Univ. Press, 1957), p. 41.
5. "Preface" to *Magic and Myth of the Movies*, rpt. in Mast and Cohen, *Film Theory and Criticism*, p. 584.
6. "Phil" Mullen, *Oxford Eagle*, 6 Oct. 1949.
7. Richard Pindell makes the extremely interesting and valid point in "The Ritual of Survival: Landscape in Conrad and Faulkner" (Ph.D. diss., Yale Univ. 1971, pp. 142–43), that Lucas Beauchamp is a proprietary figure, a figure recurrent in Faulkner's fiction.
8. Brooks (pp. 284–85) discusses the several meanings and ironies in Lucas's "'I'll try to wait.'"
9. Degenfelder says that "the adolescent rite of passage underlies both novel and film, but receives greater emphasis in the film." She adds that Chick is frequently photographed on thresholds and in doorways, citing as an example, his remaining in the doorway to Lucas's cell in this scene as well as in several others. I agree that Chick's positions in doorways is symbolic of his "subservient or marginal position, signifying his "'threshold' situation,'" but I do not think that the emphasis in the film is on his rite of passage. The dominant figure in the scene with Lucas, Stevens, and Chick in Lucas's cell is unquestionably Lucas. He controls the scene, so that the major thrust of its meaning shifts from the adolescent Chick to the potential scapegoat, Lucas (pp. 139, 140).
10. Ben Maddow approved the revision from the original intercutting of the scenes in the square with those of the cemetery to the shock and surprise of the sudden shift to the square. The long sequence in the square, Maddow said, was much more powerful and original than the intercutting would have been.
11. Degenfelder, p. 147, n. 9. Maddow also explained to my class that Dore Schary insisted on this explicit, moralistic ending. Maddow dislikes it, as do many students to whom I have shown the film. The novel reads as follows: "Lucas Beauchamp once the slave of any white man within range of whose notice he happened to come, now tyrant over the whole county's conscience" (T 199).
12. Faulkner also buries clues, but readers can turn back the pages and put the evidence together. In the film the viewer must watch very closely.
13. *Showman's Trade Review*, 15 Oct. 1949; *Look*, 25 Oct. 1949, p. 140. *Look* actually said, "a long sequence showing the silent terror of the Negro citizens as the town's lynch spirit mounts is one of the all-time highs in motion picture realism." The billboards and theater posters advertising the film quoted out of context, "one of the

all-time highs in motion picture realism." Apparently, realism was considered a selling point.

14. Durgnat makes this point in his discussion of realism and expressionism (pp. 89 ff.).

15. See Durgnat, p. 102, on the symbolism of architecture.

16. This blending is far more apparent on the 35mm. print than on any 16mm. version I have seen. Sidney Solow, president of Consolidated Laboratories (which develops and processes Hollywood films), explained that reducing the size of film tends to emphasize color contrasts. I assume that the 35mm. print kept by MGM which I saw may be termed the authentic version, representing the filmmaker's intention. It is a print of the first quality. Films vary, however, in several respects from print to print, so that the grey tones which I found characteristic of the Metro print may be less obvious even on other 35mm. prints. Because of their technical inferiority, Brown dislikes his films to be shown in 16mm. prints (Everson, p. 579).

17. Because Lucas's father was the offspring of Carrothers McCaslin's incestuous relationship, Lucas is both the grandson and the great-grandson of old Carrothers.

PART TWO

Intruder in the Dust

SCREENPLAY BY BEN MADDOW

THE NOTATION
IN THE SCREENPLAY

KNOWING FULL WELL that no screenplay can serve as a transcription of a film, I have nevertheless emended Ben Maddow's screenplay to show significant changes from script to film. The following symbols have been used: deleted dialogue and shots are indicated by < > brackets; new dialogue, shots and set-descriptions are enclosed in [ ] brackets; dialogue closely resembling the dialogue of the novel is followed by a reference to the page of the text in parentheses; longer series of shots, action, and dialogue are indicated by an asterisk and explained at the bottom of the page.

In general, I have ignored minor changes such as single-word differences. In addition, I have not attempted to record every changed shot, for to have done so would have confused the reader unnecessarily and also would have interfered with the coherence and integrity of the script as Maddow composed it. The order of the action, therefore, is sometimes slightly rearranged or timed differently in the film. For the most radical change in action from screenplay to film, I have referred the reader to the pages taken from the continuity script, which have been reproduced and are included in Appendix B.

Limitations of space have prevented a full description of the sets in the film, but I have noted changes of certain visual details. New details of set-decoration that have been described in chapter five have not been cited again in the screenplay. The dates, which because of typing conventions sometimes appear at the top of the page and otherwise on the left side, indicate the dates of Maddow's submission of scenes. In printing the screenplay I have followed as nearly as possible the format of the original one.

Clarence Brown's shooting script is marked to show process, studio, day-for-night, and second unit shots as follows:

Process [a shot coordinated with another image created by rear projection, making the resulting picture look like a single shot]: p. 9, #23; p. 47, #164; p. 56, #196, #197; p. 70, #266.

Studio [a shot made in the studio instead of on location]: p. 13, #52; p. 20, #78; p. 45, #161; p. 47, #166.

Day-for-night [a shot filmed in daylight but made to look as if it had been shot at night by the use of camera filters]: p. 55, #195; pp. 57–60, #207–22.

Second unit [a shot made by a second crew, composed of an assistant director and an assistant cameraman, who photograph locations and scenery, as well as sequences that involve spectacular action]: p. 56, #198–202; p. 60, #224; p. 62, #231, 233, 235, 237; p. 63, #239, 240; p. 70, #265; p. 102, #406; p. 105, #421.

The scenes in Lucas Beauchamp's cabin were shot in Hollywood before the company went to Oxford. In an interview with Harry Haun in the *Los Angeles Times* (14 Dec. 1973), Brown said that the sequence in Chick Mallison's bedroom was also shot at the studio. Next to shot fifty-eight on page fifteen of the shooting script, the word "Oxford" has been written, implying that the previous shots of the action in Chick's bedroom were not made in Oxford. In addition, the words "Oxford interior" appear next to the dialogue on the staircase (p. 30, #121), which follows the bedroom sequence.

The illustrations appearing here with the screenplay are still photographs rather than reproductions of individual frames of the film. Some of the "stills" were made concurrently with the actual shooting of sequences but were photographed from a slightly different angle. Others were photographed independently and were used to publicize the film. Because a single frame cannot epitomize the dramatic essence of a scene, these photographs were selected to illustrate characteristic moments that contain the emotion and meaning of several sequential frames. Thus the illustrations depict the setting and the properties used in the film, which sometime differ from the precise description of the setting and "props" found in the screenplay. The illustrations, however, accurately follow the sequence of the action of both the film and the screenplay.

THE ANNOTATED
SCREENPLAY

INTRUDER IN THE DUST

FADE IN:

LONG SHOT - EXT. DAY

From a high angle, down toward the Courthouse Square of
the town. It is the county seat, a town of perhaps
thirty-five hundred in northeast Mississippi, the center
of life for all the rolling bottom land and back roads
and gullies and hills sprouting paintless cabins and
second-growth long-needle pine.

In the center of the Square, in the dry sunlight of a
Sunday morning in May, there is a Confederate monument of
weather-stained marble. On the far side is the courthouse
with its classic Georgian columns, and on a corner just
opposite, on a street giving entrance to the Square, is a
brick mansion with a front yard, steps, a porch and barred
windows: the County Jail.

On the west side of the Square are the revolving stripes
of a barber shop, its entrance graced with the two chairs
of a bootblack stand. On the south side, closer in the
f.g., are the open doors of a large church.

These three, the church, the barber shop and the jail, are
the only places open on Sunday morning. And the church
bells are ringing out for the morning service.

Scene 1.

2   MED. LONG SHOT - TOWARD THE OPEN DOORS OF THE CHURCH

the steps and lawn dotted with thirty or forty people,
talking quietly and enjoying the air before the bell in
the tower ceases and they must go in. In the f.g. are
the low concrete wall, the green plot and the bronze
pedestal of the monument, old men and restless dogs
waiting there in the sunlight, and beyond them, the glaze
of asphalt from the open Square. SOUND of church bells
continues.

3   MED. LONG SHOT - EXT. DAY

Again toward the Square, including as much of it as
possible: Courthouse and jail, sun-baked asphalt, a few
dusty cars and trucks parked between white lines. As the

3-48 bells continue the CAMERA PULLS SLOWLY BACK INTO the
doorway of a barber shop.

In the f.g., in silhouette, black against the sunlight,
is a shoe-shine stand just inside the entrance; and a
man's feet in dusty shoes planted firmly on the foot rest.

                    Man's Voice
          Say - am I going to get my shoes shined?
                         Barber's Voice (from inside)
          Not today, Mister.
The feet swing down. The man, a truck driver, BLOCKS OUT
MOST OF THE SQUARE, as he faces toward the barber shop.
                    Truck Driver
     Where's the boy? [Where's the shine boy?]

97

Scene 1.

FULL SHOT - INT. DAY

Into the crowded barber shop as he enters, CAMERA
FOLLOWING BEHIND him.

> Truck Driver
>
> Where they all at? Seems to me I ain't
> seen one darky on the road since
> yesterday.

> Barber
>
> Ain't you heard?

> Truck Driver
>
> No. (he's on his way to a door at the back
>   of the barber shop, opens it; it's
>   marked "Bath", and now he pauses)
> Heard what?

> A Customer
>
> One of the Gowrie boys --

> Another Customer
>
> --been shot dead.

CAMERA HAS MOVED IN MED. CLOSE TOWARD the truck driver's
face.

> Truck Driver
>
> A Gowrie? Shoot a Gowrie? Now who'd do
> a fool thing like that?

MED. SHOT

TOWARD a barber and the customers, leaning forward,
stopping their conversation to hear the answer and see

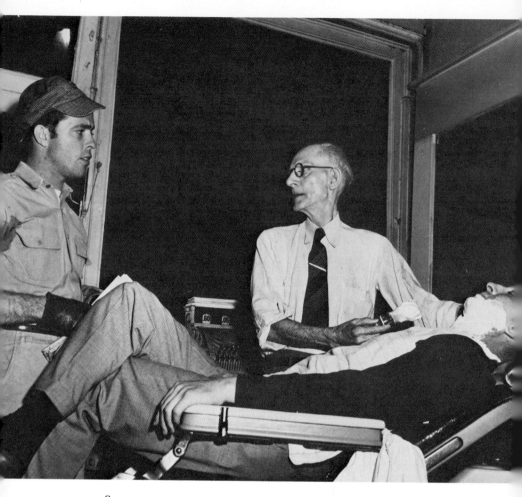

Scene 4.

the man's reaction to the news.

                                〈Barber〉 [Third Customer]

He was shot in the back - by a nigger.

MED. SHOT - THE CHURCH STEEPLE

Instead of a cross, the spire is crested by a great iron
hand, forefinger pointing to heaven. The bells have just
stopped. We hear the SOUND of the first deep low
reverberation, and then very distant and high-pitched,
the SOUND of a police siren.

[Instead of an iron hand, a cross is used.]

MED. SHOT - THE CHURCH STEEPLE AND THE OPEN DOORS

as the rest of the congregation enters, the women
adjusting their hats, the men removing theirs and stamping
out their cigarettes as they disappear in the cool gloom
of the church. Siren continues.

MED. SHOT - SEVERAL MEN [SEVEN ELDERLY MEN]

seated on the wall around the monument. Back of them,
across the Square, are the courthouse and the jail. The
SOUND of the auto siren, although still far away, has
become more emphatic. One of the men gets up to listen.

[The lettering on the monument reads: ERECTED 1907]

MED. SHOT - CHURCH STEPS

They are empty. The outer doors are just shutting.
Inside the church a hundred or so untrained voices begin
to sing the opening hymn. The siren of a police car is
more insistent, more definite.

9   [Exterior of Square; the men around the monument react to
CONT'D   the off-stage siren.]

10   FULL SHOT - INT. OF THE BARBER SHOP

           The siren's louder now, loud enough to cut through the
           layers of conversation. The shop explodes into action.

                              Voices (ad lib)
                    It's him - it's the Sheriff.
                    Bringing him in?
                    Can't tell -
12-13-48   Never thought he'd do it -
                    ⟨Not keeping it quiet anyhow⟩

11-16   SEVERAL CLOSE SHOTS

           all performed with almost comic haste:

           (a) A patron, asleep in the barber chair while being
           shaved, wakes up, hastily searches for, finds, and puts o
           his steel-rimmed glasses.

           (b) One of the barbers locks the cash register, then go
           back and knocks loudly on the door of the bath. [Instea
           of knocking, the barber calls out.]

                              Barber
                    He's here - the Sheriff's got him!
                    Come on -

           (c) Another patron, his hair lathered for a shampoo,
           grabs his hat from the rack and is about to plant it on,
           but sees himself in the mirror, and begins to rub off th
           soap with a barber's cloth.

           102

16
CONT'D

[Close shot of truck driver's feet and legs which are seen under the swinging-door.]

(d) A truck driver emerges from a door marked "Bath", a towel around his waist and his feet dripping pools of water.

(e) The customers and the barbers, in a hurry to reach the jail before the Sheriff, crowd out of the door past the bootblack's stand and into the street.

(f) The truck driver is left looking disconsolately out from behind the shelter of the barber shop.

7 MED. SHOT - INT. DAY

The back portion of a church, as the siren of the Sheriff's car shrieks defiantly closer; people in the back rows, sharing the hymn books in pairs, turn to look at each other; but then don't stop singing.

8 MEDIUM SHOT

PAN WITH the Sheriff's car as it enters the Square by the street diagonally opposite the jail. It jolts, not too slowly, on one flat tire. The SOUND of the opening hymn can be heard from the church, mixing oddly with the Sheriff's siren.

9 FULL SHOT OF THE SQUARE

48 HIGH ANGLE as the Sheriff's car rocks across it, disregarding traffic lanes, as the fifteen or twenty or so men who have been inside the barber shop or lounging near it run toward the jail; and together with others who

19   appear from everywhere and nowhere, block the street
CONT'D before the Sheriff's car.

20   MED. LONG SHOT

From behind these people, bunched across the opening of
the street toward the Sheriff's car as it approaches.

21   MOVING SHOT

from behind Sheriff Hampton, a big bony man folded up
behind the wheel, and through the windshield as he drives
straight to the street corner where the jail is located.
We can see only the handcuffed, dark, gnarled hands of
his prisoner holding the ridge of the front seat as the
car jolts forward and is forced to slow down by the men
who now stand across the whole width of the street.

22   MOVING SHOT - CLOSER

The spectators are waiting for the Sheriff's car. Their
faces show no emotion, just a kind of vacancy that waits
to be rented by emotion. CAMERA MOVING as the car moves.
They give way slowly and reluctantly as the car passes
through the body of the crowd and comes to a stop before
the jail.

23   MED. SHOT - THE SHERIFF

unfolds himself and gets out of the car, reaching back
behind him as he faces the men in the street, to open the
rear door and let his deputy and his prisoner come out.
The deputy comes first, a decrepit, sun-dried bit of a
man with a brace of pistols and an ear-phone.

                    [Sheriff:

'D   Come on.]

For a second the prisoner, LUCAS BEAUCHAMP, doesn't move.

Then he gets up slowly and stiffly. He's a tall man,

strongly built, and he must bend to get out of the car.

He scuffs his hat off on the frame of the door. The

Sheriff retrieves it from the gutter, hands it back to

him.

[The deputy has no earphone in the film, but in the text

he has a "guttapercha eartrumpet" (T 37).]

MED. SHOT - HIGH ANGLE

OVER the heads of the crowd, toward the prisoner as the

Sheriff hands him his hat. The Negro using both hands,

dusts off his pale felt hat and puts it on again. The

angle at which he wears it, restores to him a certain

cockiness and pride, --almost arrogance.

                    Voices (in the crowd)

            Knock it off again, Sheriff.

            <Take his head too this time.> (T 44)

            [Take off his head next time.]

            Don't bother the Sheriff - the Gowries

            will do it for him.

Sheriff turns toward the voices.

CLOSE SHOT - SHERIFF

                    Sheriff (not disagreeably)

            You boys get out of here. Get back to

                                                    105

Scene 24

                    Sheriff (cont'd.)
'D   the barber shop.   (T 45)

MED. SHOT - SHERIFF, HIS DEPUTY, PRISONER AND SOME OF THE
CROWD

                    Man in Crowd (pointing
                to the flat tire)

        <Somebody try to slow you down, Sheriff?>
        [You got a flat tire, Sheriff. Somebody
        try to slow you up?]

                    Sheriff (easily; with confidence)
        Maybe. Somebody that don't know me anyhow.

                (then to his prisoner)
        All right, Lucas. Come on.

They begin to move up the path toward the jail.

MED. CLOSE DOLLY SHOT

PAST the heads of the crowd in the f.g., CAMERA MOVES WITH
the Sheriff and Lucas Beauchamp as they go up the walk.
They mount the steps of the jail porch, the Sheriff now a
little ahead; the Negro pauses as he reaches the last
step, and stops and faces around to the crowd.

                            INTERCUT WITH:

MED. CLOSE DOLLY SHOT

CAMERA MOVES ACROSS the faces in the crowd seen from
Lucas Beauchamp's angle. They are quite ordinary simple
people, but moving across the f.g., some faces appear as
they seem to the prisoner: death-pale skin, an ice-cold

28
CONT'D
eye behind a steel-rimmed lens, or an ear with tufts of
hair growing out of it, or a hook nose like a hawk or an
owl. Among them, between two such gargoyles, is the
tense face, mouth set and eyes staring, not quite hostile
and almost afraid, of a sixteen year old boy.

29   CLOSE SHOT - PRISONER
on the top step of the jail porch as he turns and looks.

30   CLOSE SHOT OF BOY
CHICK MALLISON, dressed somewhat more carefully than the
other spectators, perhaps because he was supposed to go
to church or Sunday school. Seeing the prisoner look at
him, he involuntarily pulls back a little.

31   MED. CLOSE SHOT - LUCAS BEAUCHAMP
                         Lucas (addressing the boy)
                    You, young man. Tell your uncle I
                    wants to see him. (T 45)

32   MED. CLOSE SHOT - THE BOY
He doesn't move, doesn't reply.
                         Voices in the Crowd
                    Wants to see who?
                         Another Voice
                    Lawyer Stevens -- John Stevens.

33   MEDIUM SHOT
From Lucas Beauchamp's point of view toward the crowd.
12-13-48   Voices in the Crowd
                    Wants to see a lawyer?
                         Another Voice
                    Lawyer! He won't even need an
                    undertaker. (T 45)

108

The Sheriff steps into the f.g., looking down at the crowd

'D   not angry, not even disturbed.

>   Sheriff
>
>   I told you folks once to get out of
>
>   here. I ain't going to tell you again. (T 45)

MEDIUM SHOT - THE CROWD

watching, not enraged, nor even sullen, just watching and

not moving. Only the boy turns, pulls out of the crowd

and begins to run across the empty Square.

>   DISSOLVE TO:

MEDIUM LONG SHOT - EXT. - DAY

In front of Chick's house, of large simple proportions, as

Chick swings open the gate, goes up the flower-decorated

walk, up the steps across the porch and through the front

door.

MEDIUM SHOT - INT. DAY - THE GROUND FLOOR HALLWAY OF

CHICK'S HOUSE

CAMERA PANS CHICK THROUGH THE FRONT DOOR AND FOLLOWS

BEHIND him as he turns through the open door of the dining

room, and sits down in the vacant chair at the Sunday

dinner table, set for four. CAMERA REMAINS FAR BACK

ENOUGH FOR A:

FULL SHOT OF THE TABLE

Opposite Chick, in a chair with arms, is Chick's father,

a short round man with nervous rapid gestures. At the

left is seated Chick's mother, with the serenity and

37
CONT'D

almost smugness of a woman in a house with three men. To
the right is her brother, Chick's uncle, the lawyer John
Stevens, tall, sallow, talkative, ironic. The table
gleams with silver and starched linen. All three are
already eating; as Chick sits down, only Mrs. Mallison
puts down her knife and fork.

12-9-48

>   Chick's Mother
>   Chick. You're perspiring. You're wet
>   through.

>   Chick's Father (gesturing
>   with his knife)
>   Where've you been? You missed Sunday
>   school, and the picture show doesn't
>   open until six --

>   Stevens
>   Perhaps there are other attractions.

All three grownups now look at Chick who gazes down
toward his empty plate.

>   Chick
>   Gosh, I'm hungry.

His father lifts the bread basket to pass it to him, then
withholds it.

>   Chick's Father
>   Is that a proper way to behave?

>   Chick
>   Sir?

110

                    Chick's Father

D   <Come in here and not a word of greeting?>

            [Coming in here without a word of greeting?]

                        Chick

        No, sir.

                    Chick's Father

        <This is your home, not a restaurant.>

        [This is your home.]

                        Chick

        Yes, sir.

                    Chick's Father [o.s.]

        Well?

CLOSE SHOT - CHICK

He has a different intonation for each greeting.

CLOSE SHOT - CHICK'S MOTHER

                        Chick [o.s.]

        Hello, Mom -

CLOSE SHOT - CHICK'S FATHER

                        Chick (o.s.)

        'lo, Father --

CLOSE SHOT - STEVENS

                        Chick (o.s.)

        'lo, Uncle John.

Stevens winks gravely at him.

FULL SHOT - THE TABLE

but TOWARD Chick's father as he shouts toward the kitchen
door behind him and to the right.

Chick's Father

Paralee!

Paralee (from the kitchen

door, opening it an inch or two)

⟨Ye-e-e-s?⟩

[Yes, sir?]

Chick's Father

⟨You can bring in the chicken again⟩

[Bring the chicken in again.]

Paralee

I don't know if there's any left.

Kitchen door closes again.

Chick's Mother

Paralee is upset today.

Chick's Father

I don't see why. She's not related to

that murderer - or is she?

Stevens

No. But neither is Chick.

Paralee brings in a platter of food for Chick; her son,

Aleck, comes in behind her with a tray and a white apron

to help clear the dishes. Chick looks at him, then

quickly back to his plate.

                    Chick's Father

D   Now, Chick - suppose you explain

        where you've been.

                        Chick

        Nowhere in particular.

                    Chick's Father

        Nowhere in particular is ⟨an

        extremely⟩ [a mighty] large place. I

        reckon you can do better than that.

                    Chick (looking at his

                full plate; not touching it yet)

        ⟨May I have the salt?⟩

        [May I please have the salt?]

Stevens passes the salt.

MED. CLOSE SHOT - CHICK'S FATHER

                    Chick's Father

        [More coffee, Paralee.] You waited

        outside the jail with that riffraff

        from the pool hall and the barber shop,

        didn't you? ...Well? Did you see what

        you expected to see?

MED. CLOSE SHOT - CHICK

                    Chick (looking at his uncle)

        They didn't do anything. They just

        stood there. That's all.

He's eating now, but slowly.

45   MED. CLOSE SHOT - CHICK'S FATHER

                    Chick's Father

          I want you to stay home until this thing

          is cleaned up, over, finished and done

          with. It's happened before and it's

          bound to happen again. There's nothing

          for any of us to get excited about. I've

          got to run up to Memphis for a couple of

          days, and business the way it is, I don't

          want to have to worry about you too.

          Understand?

46   MED. CLOSE SHOT - CHICK

        He nods; he's having difficulty swallowing his food.

47   MED. THREE SHOT - CHICK'S FATHER, PARALEE AND ALECK

        as Aleck moves behind him, taking empty plates into the

        kitchen.

                    Chick's Father (to Paralee)

          That applies to Aleck too.

                    Aleck (going out)

          Yes, sir.

12-13-48   Paralee (holding the door

                    open as she goes out after him)

          I tole him but he don't listen to me.

          He listen to Chick. I ain't no friend

          of his. I'm just his maw.

        114

'D

                    Chick's Father

          Everybody's going to stay right here at

          home. All this fuss and nonsense -

          just because - (he spears himself another

              piece of chicken)

MED. TWO SHOT - CHICK AND HIS MOTHER

She strokes back a stray lock of hair on Chick's head,

takes his folded napkin, unfolds it and tucks it under his

chin.

                    Chick's Mother

          Your friend, Lucas Beauchamp, really

          seems to have done it this time. (T 31,

          Stevens' line)

                  Chick   (his voice full

              of mixed anger and confusion)

          Yes. They're going to make a nigger

          out of him once in his life anyway. (T 32)

                  Chick's Mother (shocked)

          Chick!

CLOSE SHOT - CHICK

gets up suddenly, leaves the table.

FULL SHOT - THE WHOLE ROOM

as Chick leaves the table, he pulls the napkin out of his

collar and aiming for a nearby chair, misses and leaves

the room.

50   Stevens (getting up)
CONT'D   Let me talk to him.

                            Chick's Father (his mouth full)
                What in heaven's name --

                            Chick's Mother
                ⟨He hasn't even finished his --⟩

                [Why, he hasn't even finished his dinner.]

                            Stevens (going toward the

                    door and picking up the napkin)

                It's terrifying, I know. But we've got

12-14-48   to face it. He just doesn't like his

                napkin up here. Makes him feel as though

                he were not quite grown up.

51   MED. SHOT - PAST MOTHER AND FATHER TO STEVENS
        at the door.

                            Chick's Mother
                But he isn't.

                            Chick's Father
                And he better not be.

                            Stevens
                Let me go up and talk to him.

                            Chick's Father
                Tell him I said to come down and finish

                his dinner, whether he's hungry or not.

                            (he half-turns, MED. CLOSE INTO

                    CAMERA)

        116

Chick's Father (cont'd.)

D   Paralee! Some more gravy! -- And tell

          Aleck to put my suitcase in the car --

FULL SHOT - INT. - DAY - CHICK'S ROOM UPSTAIRS

It is decorated with all the elaborate disorder of a boy's

life: two high school pennants, a salamander in a jar, a

first baseman's glove on the floor, and on one wall, a

hunting rifle on a rack. Chick comes in and sits down on

his cot. There is a baseball between his feet and he

leans down and gets it and picks with his fingers at the

loose stitching. There are footsteps coming up the

staircase. Chick reaches out with one foot, closes the

door hard and lies back on the cot. Footsteps come closer

and now there is a knock on the door. Chick doesn't reply,

doesn't get up. He examines even more minutely the worn

stitching on the ball. The door opens and Stevens enters,

closes it behind him, and stands there lighting his pipe.

[The set of Chick's bedroom is decorated with an airplane,

hanging from the ceiling, photographs on the wall of a

Confederate soldier, and of another plane; a sword,

probably from the Civil War also, hangs on the wall along

with a Jefferson High School pennant and those of Southern

universities: Ol' Miss., Vanderbilt, and most prominent

of all, the University of Tennessee (Clarence Brown's alma

mater). Next to an old-fashioned heating register,

Chick's hunting rifle is propped up against the wall.]

53   MED. CLOSE - STEVENS

            without looking at Chick, he picks up the baseball glove

            and tries it on.

12-9-48

54   MED. CLOSE - THE BOY

            watches him; he is toying with the ball. Suddenly he

            throws it across the room.

55   MED. CLOSE - STEVENS

            catches the ball. After a second he tosses it back to

            Chick underhand.

56   TWO SHOT - PAST STEVENS TO CHICK

            Chick takes a two-finger hold and returns the ball, a

            little harder this time. Stevens takes the impact, toss

            it back, still gently. The boy stands up, grips the bal

            a third time, returns it hard and viciously. It socks

            into the leather. The uncle receives it into his glove,

            but doesn't return it this time.

                              Stevens
                      Tell me what happened.

                              Chick (bursting out)
                      Why did he have to go and do a thing
                      like that?

                              Stevens
                      Who knows? We'll never really know.
                          (calmly, with exasperating calm)
                      Your friend, Lucas Beauchamp --

       118

                    Chick

He's not my friend!

                    Stevens

Chick - you mustn't take this so

seriously.

                    Chick

I'm not -- (he turns away, sitting down

        again on the cot)

I can't help it.

                    Stevens

But why? -- tell me why?

                    Chick

I don't know.

                    Stevens (more quietly)

You must tell me.

                    Chick

I don't know if I can.

                    Stevens

Try. You're old enough to try.

Chick looks at him and looks quickly away. Stevens sits

down beside the boy. CAMERA MOVES FORWARD with him.

                    Stevens

And maybe I'm old enough to understand.

MED. TWO SHOT - TOWARD THE BACKS OF CHICK AND STEVENS

                    Chick

It was quite a while ago. I went

Chick (cont'd.)

hunting with Aleck Sander.

Stevens

On the old Edmonds' place? Yes -

The CAMERA BEGINS TO MOVE PAST Chick's face and TOWARD

the opposite wall of the room.

Chick

It was November. Pretty cold.

CAMERA MOVES IN TOWARD THE WALL in front of them, on w

Chick's hunting rifle hangs in its wooden rack.

<Chick (o.s.)

Aleck and the dogs were running

ahead of me.>

DISSOLVE T

58   LONG SHOT - EXT. - DAY

A pasture in late Autumn, the long weeds blackened and

then sprayed with frost. In the middle distance two b

are crossing a field. The sky is low, even, gray, fri

Chick's Voice

We were hunting rabbit --

[We hadn't jumped one all morning.]

59   MEDIUM SHOT

CAMERA PANS WITH the two boys as they cross the pastur

and vault the pasture fence. Chick Mallison has a dif

ent, longer haircut, carries a gun. And Aleck, the Ne

boy, a little taller but the same age, is carrying a t

stick: a nut of railroad steel screwed onto a broomstick.

D Their mouths and the mouths of their dogs breathe white in

the November weather. CAMERA CONTINUES TO PAN with them

as Aleck, following the dogs, runs easily over a foot log

thrown across the creek at the bottom of the pasture.

MED. SHOT - TOWARD CHICK

as he runs toward the foot log slippery with frost. It

connects the two banks of the creek, each a good deal more

than a man's height above the milky skim-ice covering the

water. His first step skids, his second tries to recover,

with his third he is falling.

MED. SHOT - FROM CHICK'S POINT OF VIEW

as the willow tree growing out of the other bank of the

creek tips to one side. CAMERA TILTS DOWN, the sky rushes

away at a crazy angle and the creek, with its surface of

ice, rushes forward and up. Chick cries out as he falls.

                    [Chick

          Alexander!]

CLOSE SHOT - ALECK

turning, to see what is happening.

MED. SHOT - LOW ANGLE

TILT DOWN with Chick as he falls eight or nine feet,

through the paper-thin ice and into the water below. With

the weight of his fall, he goes under completely.

MED. SHOT - ALECK

runs back and pulls off the top rail of the fence, a long

heavy pole.

                                        121

65   MED. SHOT - CHICK

rises from the water, gasping. He thrashes under the

soaking leaden weight of his clothes.

                         Chick

                My gun --!

He deliberately goes under again, dragging up his gun fr

the bottom of the creek.

66   MED. SHOT - ALECK

advancing with the rail.

67   MED. SHOT - CHICK

rises with the gun in one hand and with the other grabs

for the tips of a leafless willow hanging over the water

With this grip he begins to pull himself toward the edge

then Aleck in his excitement drives down at him with the

fence rail, intent at rescue. But the awkward thrust hi

Chick's feet and he loses his footing and goes under

again.

68   MED. CLOSE SHOT - CHICK

as he comes up again, choking and gasping. Then a deep,

sober man's voice takes command of the situation.

                    Lucas Beauchamp's Voice

                Get the pole out of his way so he can

                get out. (T 6)

69   MED. SHOT

as Aleck draws back the fence pole, looking across the

creek to the man who had given this order.

122

0   MED. CLOSE SHOT - CHICK

pulls himself up, inch by inch, grasping the willows, and

getting a foothold on the underwater slope of the bank.

He too looks up at the owner of this serene, imperious

voice.

INTERCUT WITH:

4-48

1   MED. CLOSE - CHICK'S ANGLE

TILT UP FROM the man's feet, wearing gumboots, to his legs

in their heavy overalls, then to the thick sheep-lined

coat, with an axe carried on the shoulder, and then the

pale felt hat, set at a jaunty angle over a dark Negro

face with narrow eyes and aquiline nose. (T 6)

Chick's Voice

That was just about the first time I

saw Lucas Beauchamp.

MED. SHOT - CHICK, LUCAS AND ALECK

as Chick, unaided, climbs to the firm ground of the bank.

Lucas

Come on to my house. (T 7)

And as Chick hesitates, Lucas turns to order Aleck too.

Lucas

Tote his gun. (T 7)

Aleck obeys. And now, so does Chick, relinquishing the

gun to Aleck. Lucas has turned his back to them and is

leading a way along the path. CAMERA PANS WITH THEM as

72
CONT'D
they go past, Chick last of all, shivering in the still
November air, his clothes heavy and icy-wet.

73   MED. LONG SHOT - THE THREE

walking up the path which becomes almost a gash in the
earth, a gully. They go up toward a fence enclosing the
land around a house.

                    Chick's Voice
          Then I realized: We were hunting on
          his land. I remembered you told me
          the story. His grandfather was a slave.
          And he got this land as a gift. And you
          told me why: Because his grandfather
          was first cousin to the man that owned
          him.

74   MEDIUM LONG SHOT

as all three climb the last of the hill and through the
gate and up the path, lined with two borders, improvised
of tin cans, bits of glass and broken china, that leads
an unpainted one-story cabin.
[This border detail found on page nine of the novel does
not appear in the film.]

                    Chick's Voice
          So, grandfather to father to son, it
          came to Lucas Beauchamp. It was ten
          acres, all his own, smack in the middle
          of the whole plantation. It was Lucas

D   Beauchamp's land, and Lucas Beauchamp

proved it, every step he took. --His

land and his house --

                                 DISSOLVE TO:

FULL SHOT - INT. DAY - LUCAS BEAUCHAMP'S CABIN

In the f.g., part of the four poster bed with its dark

patchwork quilt; on the right, a large photograph framed

and set on an easel, Lucas in coat and waistcoat, and his

wife, Molly, much younger and without her usual head-cloth.

Now much older and almost shriveled in appearance, she's

taking Chick's boots, coat and sweater out to the kitchen,

visible through an open doorway. Centered in the b.g., is

the fire on the hearth, which Aleck feeds now with fat

pine slivers, and then two full logs laid into the blaze.

Chick puts his wet hands out toward the fire. Lucas

Beauchamp stands opposite him, his back to the fireplace,

his hands clasped behind him, rocking back and forth on

his heels, calm and impassive.

MED. CLOSE TWO SHOT - LUCAS AND CHICK

Chick is still shivering. His wet shirt and trousers

cling to his wet skin.

                     Lucas (to Chick)

        Strip off. (T 11)

                <Chick

      No, I --> (T 11)

Scene 76.

Strip off. (T 11)

[There are six cross-cuts in this interchange of dialogue.]
Chick obeys, taking off his shirt, and then beginning on
his wet underwear. Molly crosses in front of the CAMERA,
coming into the room.

MEDIUM SHOT - THE BED

with the quilt, in the f.g., toward Chick, undressing. His
-48   shoulders and back in the firelight are in glaring contrast
to the three Negroes in the room: Lucas, with his back to
the fire; Aleck, kneeling with firewood, and Molly, shrunk
down by age until she seems rather a large-sized doll than
a woman, now lifting the quilt from the bed and advancing
toward the fire with it. Then she lifts it up and
envelops Chick's body.

MED. CLOSE - CHICK

as the dark quilt encloses his body.

<Chick's Voice

And then, when my clothes were dry, -->

                                        DISSOLVE TO:

CLOSE SHOT - TOWARD A TABLE

in the kitchen as Molly's dark, withered hands set down a
plate of steaming hot greens and sidemeat and pale
biscuits. CAMERA TILTS UP to SHOW Chick at the table
alone. He raises the glass of buttermilk, tiny lumps of
buttermilk floating at the top, and puts it to his lips.

Scene 79.

NT'D

--there was something else: just what

I expected; sidemeat and greens. He

made me eat the dinner that was cooked

for him.

Beyond Chick, through the doorway, into the front room,

are Lucas, Aleck and Molly.

MED. CLOSE SHOT - LUCAS

reaching behind him to take the gold toothpick out of its

glass on the mantel and mouthing it and fingering the gold

watch chain looped across the bib of his overalls.

MED. CLOSE SHOT - MOLLY

rocking in her chair, that extends a good twenty inches

above her head.

CLOSE SHOT - THE PHOTOGRAPH OF LUCAS AND MOLLY

enlarged, retouched, set in its gilt frame on a gilded

easel. (T 14)

MED. SHOT - CHICK

eating the meal with growing distaste. We see past him,

through the kitchen doorway to the interior of the front

room. Chick stands up from his meal, only half eaten.

His back to the doorway, he thrusts his hand into his

pocket and draws out a half dollar; searches again and

finds more coins, a total of seventy cents.

MED. SHOT

CAMERA MOVES WITH Chick as he turns into the front room,

84   the coins held in his hand, and walking between and past
CONT'D Lucas and Aleck, hands the coins to Molly in her rocking
        chair.

85   CLOSE SHOT - CHICK'S HAND

        spread out with the coins on the palm; Molly's thin hand,
        all bone, skin and nerve, disentangles itself from the
        shawl she wears, and reaches out to take the money.
        [Chick's and Molly's hands almost touch.]

86   MED. THREE SHOT - LUCAS, IN THE F.G.

        taking the toothpick out of his mouth, as he looks at
        Chick and Molly.

                          Lucas
                What's that for?   (T 15)

87   MED. CLOSE SHOT - CHICK

        with the coins in his hand.

                          <Chick's Voice
                I was so angry, I was so awful ashamed.>

88   MEDIUM CLOSE SHOT - LUCAS
        watching him.

                          <Chick's Voice
                He knew what I didn't know -->

89   CLOSE SHOT - CHICK

        His rage and embarrassment inside him begin to show on
        his face.

                          <Chick's Voice
                --what I didn't have sense enough to
                understand.>

        130

MED. CLOSE SHOT - LUCAS

CAMERA MOVES UP TOWARD HIM, so his face looks even darker,
more arrogant and more overbearing.

                    Chick's Voice

        And he knew all the time, and I didn't--

CLOSE SHOT - CHICK

                 ⟨Chick's Voice

        --that I was his guest.⟩

He looks at Lucas, his anger bursts inside him. He looks
down and away, toward his hand, CAMERA SWINGS DOWN,
FOLLOWING his glance to the open hand, CLOSE. Then the
palm turns over suddenly, and the four coins drop and
spread and roll, gleaming white on the dark floor. CAMERA
PANS TO FOLLOW the last coin, rolling into silence in a
corner of the room.

CLOSE SHOT - LUCAS BEAUCHAMP

calm, intractable, undisturbed.

CLOSE SHOT - CHICK

More out of shame than anger and not wanting to shout at
all:

                    Chick [to Lucas]

            Pick it up!   (T 16)

FULL SHOT - LUCAS

dominating, but showing the whole room with Chick, Aleck,
Molly, the fire, the bed, the quilt, the photograph.

94   Lucas [long pause; points
CONT'D   to Aleck]
                    Pick up his money.
          Aleck obeys, finding and picking up each coin and holding
          them up toward Lucas, when he has them all.
                                    Lucas
                    Give it to him.
          Aleck touches Chick's clenched hand with his own, and at
          last, Chick takes the money.
                              [Chick's Voice
                    I was so angry. I was so awful ashamed.
                    He knew what I didn't know. What I
                    didn't have sense enough to understand.]
95   CLOSE SHOT - CHICK
          as he takes the money.
96   MED. CLOSE - LUCAS
                              [Chick's Voice
                    He knew all the time and I didn't,
                    that I was his guest in his home.]
          restoring the gold toothpick to his mouth. He is still
          ease, still calm, imperturable, and in command.
                                    Lucas
                    Now go on and shoot your rabbit. And
                    stay out of that creek. (T 16)
          [CLOSE SHOT - MOLLY
          rocking in her rocking chair.]

          132

DISSOLVE TO:

7   MED. CLOSE SHOT - INT. - DAY

A Christmas tree, inside a cigar store window, thick with
tinsel and spotted with colored bulbs, flashing automatically off and on.

                    Chick's Voice

        Then I could hardly wait 'til Christmas.

        I went downtown --

CAMERA MOVES PAST the display, into the store and toward
the little counter. Chick, wearing a heavy mackinaw
against the wet weather outside, is paying for and
receiving four cigars and a tumbler of snuff.

0-48   Chick's Voice

                --and bought Lucas Beauchamp four of
                their best cigars and a package of
                snuff for his wife, Molly. (T 22)

CAMERA MOVES INTO:

8   CLOSE SHOT - FOUR CIGARS

as Chick picks them up.

                    Chick's Voice

            That was to pay him his seventy cents
            with interest. But the next day -- (T 22)

                              DISSOLVE TO:

                                        133

Scene 97.

134

CLOSE SHOT - EXT. DAY

A gallon bucket of molasses.

                    Chick's Voice

          --he made me take it back again.

CAMERA MOVES BACK INTO:

MEDIUM SHOT

revealing Chick, in front of his own house, receiving the

bucket of molasses from a white boy, mounted on a mule.

The boy and the mule begin to ride away. (T 23)

                    Chick's Voice

          A batch of home-made molasses. A

          gift from him to me. And it was

          worse this time - because he had a

          white boy bring it to me.

Chick moves forward, up the walk, and TOWARD THE CAMERA.

                    Chick's Voice

          And this time it had to be finished,

          once and for all.

                              DISSOLVE TO:

MEDIUM SHOT - EXT. - DAY

CAMERA MOVING UP AND TOWARD the second story window of a

building on the Square. It's lettered:

          JOHN STEVENS, ATTORNEY AT LAW

Stevens in inside, back to the CAMERA. Chick is in the

f.g., seen through the lettered window, methodically

sharpening a handful of pencils, adding one by one to the

neat row along the desk.

101   Chick's Voice

CONT'D   Out of what you paid me, I saved a

                         quarter a week -- 'til finally there

                         was enough. Enough so he couldn't pay

                         me back, enough so he wouldn't even if

                         he could. Mother helped me --

                                                    DISSOLVE TO:

102   CLOSE SHOT - INT. - DAY

         A woman's dress held up, across the whole screen. It's a

         silk or rayon, with polka dots. The saleslady's hand

         holding the metal hanger, supporting the dress, lets it

         down in folds into a tissue-lined box. As the dress fold

         down it reveals Chick and his mother. Chick is taking ou

         and counting his money.

                              Chick's Voice

                         --we bought a dress, good enough to

                         wears on Sundays, and had it sent to

                         his wife, Molly. And I thought Lucas

                         would have to come now, and take off

                         his hat, and say "Thank you, Mr.

                         Mallison".

         CAMERA MOVES TOWARD the box as it is closed and begun to

         be wrapped.

                                                    DISSOLVE TO

103   MED. CLOSE MOVING SHOT - EXT. - DAY

         Behind Chick as he walks down the sidewalk along the edg

         of the Square. In the middle distance, Lucas Beauchamp

         136

approaching. He wears his usual gray felt hat and black

'D   broadcloth suit. He gives no sign of recognition, but

walks steadily on toward Chick.

[Chick and a group of boys are exiting from a parked bus;

Chick wears a baseball suit with letters JHS on the

shirt.]

Chick

But he didn't. I saw him in town

just once after that --

THE CAMERA STOPS as Chick stops, and Lucas comes past him,

looking through him rather than at him. CAMERA PANS

AROUND TO FOLLOW Lucas as he goes away, down the street.

His face is sombre, he wears the gold chain across his

vest, but the gold toothpick is missing.

Chick's Voice

--and he didn't even see me. I wasn't

there. He didn't even see I wasn't there.

CAMERA STILL TURNS TO WATCH Lucas walk away, down the

street. [The Confederate monument comes into view.]

Chick's Voice

I thought, now it's finished, it's all

over. -- And then, I heard you say,

his wife was dead; had been dead when

I sent her the dress. --And he was

grieving. And I reckon you can be sad,

or proud, or even lonely, inside a black

skin too.

Scene 103.

138

MEDIUM LONG SHOT - CHICK

mounted on his horse Highboy, cantering along a country

road, approaching a store at the crossroads. [It is

spring.]

                          Chick's Voice

          I went to see him. Not to his house.

          I wasn't going to be caught that way

          again. I picked neutral ground --

          [this time] Fraser's store --

                                          DISSOLVE TO:

MEDIUM LONG SHOT - INT. FRASER'S STORE

<crammed with counters, and displays of cloth; harness,

canned goods, barrels of cabbage, potatoes, sugar, rice,

flour.>

                          Chick's Voice

          --he came by there any Saturday after-

          noon.

There are little knots of men, mostly white [including

Vinson and Crawford Gowrie], talking and smoking and

drinking soda pop, rather than buying. In the f.g., a

small counter with Chick leaning upon it, opening one by

one, the six or seven various tools and blades of a

folding knife. Chick turns around. [Men are pitching

coins on the floor.]

105   [Ad Libs

CONT'D   Uh oh.

                        That wasn't so good.

                        I can do better than that just any time.]

106   MEDIUM SHOT - A PART OF THE STORE FURTHER FRONT

        On the right is a group of brawling drunken men, rolling

        and lighting their cigarettes. Through the outside door,

        in the b.g., Lucas comes forward into the store; his dres

        the manner of his walk, and the way he wears his hat, the

        very angle of his gold toothpick, are the height of

        arrogant dignity. One of the white men, short, scrawny,

        furious, all the uglier because he looks so young, leans

        forward toward Lucas.

                            [Ad Libs

                Move over.

                Uh oh. That wasn't so good either.]

                            Chick's Voice

                <They were watching him. The Gowrie boys.

                One of them was Vinson Gowrie.>

                [They were watching him -- two of the

                Gowrie boys. One of them was Crawford

                Gowrie. The other was Vinson, the younger

                brother.]

                            [Ad Libs

                Uh oh.

                You ain't holdin' your mouth right.

        140

T'D   Come on, boy.

That was awful close.

All right?

Yeah.

Hm. Uh oh. They got you.

All right.

Too hot to play any time.]

MED. SHOT - PAST THE ANGRY GOWRIE, TOWARD BEAUCHAMP

Lucas passes him in silence, turns aside to one of the

counters, close by, picks a box of ginger snaps from a

display, throws down his nickel, then turns around

deliberately. Lucas tears open the end of the paper box,

puts the toothpick back in his pocket, calmly shakes out

a ginger snap, feeds it to himself and going past Vinson

Gowrie, chews slowly and methodically.

Vinson Gowrie

⟨You lousy biggity burr-headed --!⟩

[You crummy, biggity, burr-headed....]

Vinson lunges forward, grabbing a single-tree from a

counter at his right. Lucas half turns, looking back at

him scornfully and calmly, as though he were a helpless

and contemptible drunk. Gowrie lunges. Behind him,

Fraser's son is jumping the counter. Vinson strikes down

at Lucas with the solid pole, ⟨ringed at either end⟩

[Chick is standing in the doorway in the background.]

Scene 107.

CLOSE SHOT - CHICK

The knife, with its multiple blades still open,
fan-shaped in his hand. Pulled a dozen ways in the
conflict of his feelings, he can't move at all.

MEDIUM TWO SHOT

CAMERA FOLLOWS as Fraser's son grabs Vinson from behind,
deflecting the blow(so it rings down on a cold iron stove,
half knocking it loose from its pipe.) Now others come to
help Fraser's son, struggling to hold back the furious
Gowrie.

> [Vinson

...nigger!]

> Fraser's Son

Get out of here, Lucas!

MED. CLOSE SHOT - LUCAS

half looking back. Having swallowed the ginger snap, he
watches and sucks at a tooth.

MED. SHOT - PAST THE STRUGGLING GROUP AROUND VINSON AND
TOWARD LUCAS

> Fraser's Son

Get the blazes out of here, you fool.

> [Ad Libs

Take it easy, there, Vinson.

Oh, don't be a fool!

Wait a minute now!

Come on, take that thing away from him!

CONT'D   It ain't worth it!

                          Take that away from him!]

112   MED. SHOT - PAST LUCAS TOWARD THE SPECTATORS AND CHICK AND

          THE LITTLE GROUP AROUND VINSON GOWRIE

          Lucas turns slowly around TOWARD CAMERA which MOVES BEFORE

          him, as he goes through the aisle and leaves the store,

          still eating, still chewing, still feeding his Saturday

          luxury with unshakable, calm insolence.

          [Throughout the scene, Crawford Gowrie watches with a

          matchstick in his mouth. He strikes the match.]

113   MED. CLOSE SHOT - CHICK

          still looking after Lucas, he slowly, almost automatically

          closes the several blades into the handle of the knife.

                              Chick's Voice

                    I didn't go after him. I couldn't.

                    I don't know why. Maybe because Vinson

                    Gowrie was white, and I was white and

                    Lucas Beauchamp was not.

114   MED. LONG SHOT - FRAMED BY THE DOORWAY OF THE STORE

          TOWARD the twisted path through the woods, as Lucas goes

          away. The color of his hat, the thrust of his arm,

          shaking out another ginger snap, can still be seen.

                              Chick's Voice

                    <And right in these woods - on a Saturday

                    afternoon - just yesterday - he killed

                   144

                    Chick's Voice (cont'd.)

        Vinson Gowrie. Shot him in the back.>

        [Right in these woods, on a Saturday

        afternoon, a few weeks later, he killed

        Vinson Gowrie. Shot him in the back.]

                                    DISSOLVE BACK

                                    TO:

CHICK'S HUNTING RIFLE

on the wall of his room. CAMERA MOVES AWAY to REVEAL

Stevens and Chick, still seated on Chick's cot.

                    Chick

        And yet he still thinks I'm his friend.

Stevens gets up.

MED. CLOSE SHOT - STEVENS

standing now above Chick.

                    Stevens

        Well, go on.

CLOSE SHOT - CHICK

                    Chick (more quietly)

        He wants a lawyer.

                    Stevens (o.s.)

        Is that all?

                    Chick

        He asked for you.

CLOSE SHOT - STEVENS

CAMERA MOVES WITH him as he goes toward the window, pulling

118
CONT'D   the baseball glove off his hand. He is frowning and
serious. He came upstairs to solve a boy's problem and
now it's been thrust back at him.

119   MED. TWO SHOT - PAST STEVENS
          DOWN TOWARD Chick.

                         Chick (standing up)
                 Uncle John, can't you go right now?

                         Stevens
                 What's the hurry?

In answer, Chick goes and opens the door to go out but h
stops when Stevens speaks:

[The following dialogue occurs in the hall outside
Chick's bedroom.]

                         Stevens
                 Chick. Nothing's going to happen.
                 They never start anything in the daytime.
                 They'd be ashamed to see each other's
                 faces.

                         Chick
                 Suppose they're not?

120   MED. SHOT - PAST CHICK TO STEVENS
          who crosses the room toward him.

                         Stevens
                 They'll wait for the Gowries. They
                 won't do a thing without the Gowries,
                 and the Gowries have got to bury Vinson

          146

                          Stevens (cont'd.)

          before they do anything about anybody

          that isn't a Gowrie.

Stevens has come up to Chick and now he puts his hand

affectionately on Chick's shoulder.

                          Chick

          Then they'll come and pull him out of

          jail and hang him up --?

                          Stevens

          No. The Gowries are not much good.

          Except to fish and fight and raise

          enough corn to boil up some whiskey.

          But it's Sunday, -- even for a Gowrie --

          and they'll wait 'til Sunday is past.

          Until midnight at least. (T 80)

                          Chick

          Suppose they don't?

                          Stevens (harshly, taking

                    his hand off Chick's shoulder)

          Then there's a steel door and there's

          Sheriff Hampton. It's his job, not

          yours, and not mine.

Stevens turns to go past, toward the staircase a couple of

feet away.

MED. SHOT - PAST CHICK

DOWN THE STAIRCASE, TOWARD Stevens as he descends.

121   Chick

CONT'D   But you are going to see him, aren't
                          you?

                                             Stevens
                          There's not much I can do for him now.

                                             Chick
                          Uncle John --

                                             Stevens
                          All right, I'll go --

                                             Chick
                          --I want to go with you.

                                             Stevens
                          <--after supper.>
                          [All right. After supper.]

                                             Chick
                          <But suppose --?>
                          [But suppose they come --]

Stevens has come to the bottom of the stairs, and he
turns to answer Chick.

                                             Stevens
                          Suppose it then. Lucas should have
                          thought of that before he shot a
                          white man in the back. (T 40)
                          [Come on. Finish your dinner.]

                                                  DISSOLVE TO

MED. SHOT - EXT. - NIGHT

CAMERA MOVING along the houses in a mixed residential and business street that leads into the Square. There's an occasional light in one of the rooms, and pools of light from the street-lamps, but very few people.

MED. TWO SHOT

CAMERA MOVING BEFORE Chick and Stevens as they walk along this street on their way to the jail. Into the f.g., as the CAMERA MOVES, appears a man standing inside the front gate to his house and next to the wall of his grocery, closed for the day. He is Mr. Lilley.

>   Stevens

Evening, Mr. Lilley.

>   Lilley

Little early, ain't you, Lawyer?

Them Gowrie folks have got chores to

do before they can get into town.

Stevens and Chick slow down for a moment, but don't actually stop.

>   Stevens

Maybe they'll decide to stay at home

on a Sunday night.

---

*Much of the dialogue in this sequence can be found in the pp. 47-49.

123   Lilley

CONT'D   Sho now. It ain't their fault it's

                      Sunday. He ought to thought of that

                      before he taken to killing white men

                      on a Saturday afternoon.

                              Stevens (half to

                            Lilley, half to Chick)

                      I agree.

          They've passed Lilley now. He's in the b.g., illuminate

          by light from an upstairs window of his house.

                              Lilley (raising his voice)

                      My wife ain't feeling good tonight --

                      but tell um to holler if they need help.

                              Stevens

                      I expect they know they can depend on

                      you, Mr. Lilley.

          They turn a corner and go into the Square.

124   MED. CLOSE TWO SHOT

          CAMERA MOVING behind them as they turn the corner. We s

          the Square beyond them, the lighted tower of the

          courthouse, circles of light from the lamps. light

          spilling from the entrance of the jail far opposite.

          [The Confederate monument is visible.]

                              Stevens (to Chick)

                      You see? He has nothing against Lucas.

                      He'll probably tell you he likes him

                              Stevens (cont'd.)

D   better than he does a lot of white

              folks, and he'll believe it.

MED. CLOSE TWO SHOT - FROM STEVENS' SIDE

CAMERA MOVING with them as they go past the shadowed

columns of the courthouse.

                              Stevens

              All he requires is that Lucas act

              like a Negro. Which is what he

              believes must have happened: Lucas

              blew his top and murdered a white man.

MED. CLOSE TWO SHOT - FROM CHICK'S SIDE

CAMERA MOVING with them as they pass a number of cars

parked along that side of the Square, each of them filled

with indistinguishable pale faces or hands, waiting and

perhaps passing a pint from hand to hand.

                              Stevens

              And now the white folks will take

              him out and burn him. And no hard

              feelings on either side.

They've begun to cross the street toward the jail.

                              Stevens

              In fact, Mr. Lilley will probably be

              one of the first to contribute cash

              money toward Lucas' funeral and the

              support of his widow and children, if

              he had any.

126   Then Stevens puts out a hand and stops because a car is
CONT'D   coming directly toward them.

127   MED. LONG SHOT - A CAR

packed with six or seven men, circling the Square with a
roar and now rushing straight TOWARD CAMERA, CLOSE,
headlights glaring. As it goes by, as close as possible
there's a collective human cry, six or seven voices, no
special words but more like a terrifying snarl of
excitement and even exultation.

                         [Ad Libs

              Yippee!

              Yay!

              Get out of the way!]

128   MED. TWO SHOT - PAST THE BACKS OF STEVENS AND CHICK

as the car rushes away and out of the Square. Stevens a
Chick begin to cross the street, CAMERA FOLLOWING.

                         Chick
              What's that?

                         Stevens
              Some of Mr. Lilley's friends.

Beyond them, we can see the dark bulk of the jail. But
the front door is open, and the hall illuminated by a
single bulb, casting a fan of light out into the yard a
bright enough for the whole Square to see: a deputy
leaning back in a hard chair, reading the Sunday comics
and with a double-barreled shotgun against the wall. T

Scenes 128–29.

128   room, with its shelf of knick-knacks on the wall, and it
CONT'D   arm-chairs, its linoleum floor, is the jailer's living

         room as well as the entrance to the jail.

129*   MED. SHOT - CAMERA MOVING IN

         Chick's angle, toward this tableau in the entrance of th

         jail. Mr. Tubbs, the jailer, a harassed, irritable man,

         is coming out of a door on the right, which he shuts

         behind him. To his heavy cartridge belt are attached a

         45 Colt and a ring of keys. As the CAMERA MOVES IN, the

         deputy in the chair lowers his paper just enough to see.

         He's a farmer, with a farmer's weather-cured skin and

         narrow, almost Indian eyes.

                              [Stevens

                    Evenin', Mr. Legate.

                              Legate

                    Evenin'. (Legate nods)]

                              Tubbs

                    Mr. Stevens? -- So you had to get

                    mixed up in it, too. You can't let

                    well enough alone.

12-14-48

130   MED. SHOT - PAST THE DEPUTY, MR. LEGATE, IN THE F.G.

         Stevens and Chick are coming in the front door.

         _____

         *Much of the dialogue, descriptions of the setting and

action from this point through Shot 161 can be found in the tex

pp. 52-73.

'D

                         Stevens

        I'm his lawyer, Mr. Tubbs.--

        〈Evening, Mr. Legate.〉

                          Tubbs

        〈He won't even shut and lock the

        front door!〉 [Will, here, won't even

        shut or lock the front door.]

                          Legate

        I'm just doing what the Sheriff said.

        He's paying me five dollars a night

        to resist, and that's just what I'm

        going to do.

                          Tubbs

        Does the Sheriff think that 〈damn〉

        [darn] funny paper's going to stop the

        Gowries?

                          Legate

        I don't expect to stop them all by

        myself. I got you, and you got a

        pistol.

                          Tubbs

        Me? Me get in their way for seventy-

        five dollars a month?

MED. SHOT - DOWN JAIL CORRIDOR

TOWARD Chick, Tubbs, and Stevens as they approach the

stairway in the immediate f.g.

131   Tubbs (leading the way)

CONT'D   Better for everybody if them folks

                         had took him as soon as they laid

                         hands on him yesterday.

                                    Stevens

                         But they didn't. And I don't think

                         they will.

CAMERA PANS LEFT AND TILTS UP to see them turn and climb

the staircase toward the iron-and-oak door at the top.

                                    Tubbs (higher-pitched)

                         Don't mind me. I'm going to do the

                         best I can. I taken an oath of office,

                         too. And how'm I going to live with

                         myself if I let a passel of no good

                         Gowries take a prisoner away from me?

132   MED. CLOSE - FROM INSIDE THE SECOND FLOOR OF THE JAIL

         as Tubbs reaches and unlocks the heavy door.

12-11-48   Tubbs

                         But don't think nobody's going to make

                         me admit I like it. I got a wife and

                         two children; what good am I to them

                         if I get myself killed protecting a

                         goldurn stinking [nigger] --

He snaps on a light switch in the hall, looking toward

the left, toward the bull-pen, as Stevens and Chick come

up beside him.

         156

MEDIUM SHOT

CAMERA PANS, through the netting of the bull-pen as the

light goes on overhead, revealing the tiered bunks against

the farther wall, occupied by ⟨five⟩ [six] Negro prisoners,

lying absolutely motionless and with ⟨eyes shut⟩ [open].

As the CAMERA PANS, in the f.g., appear first Tubbs, his

hands gripping into the wire mesh of the cage, then Chick

and Stevens.

                    Tubbs

          Look at them. They ain't asleep. Not

          a one. And I don't blame them, with a

          mob of white men going to bust in here

          with pistols and cans of gasoline. It

          won't be the first time that all black

          cats look alike. -- ⟨Come on.⟩

MED. CLOSE THREE SHOT - STEVENS, CHICK & TUBBS

as the jailer leads them toward a cell at the end of the

corridor.

                    Stevens

          You put him in the cell, did you?

                    Tubbs

          Sheriff's orders. I don't know what

          the next white man that figgers he

          can't rest good till he kills somebody

          is going to think about it.

CAMERA MOVES with them as they reach the dark cell and

134   Tubbs unlocks the door.
CONT'D   Tubbs
                        I taken all the blankets off the cot
                        though.

                                Stevens
                        Maybe because he won't be here long
                        enough to have to go to sleep.

135   CLOSE SHOT - TUBBS
        He laughs, a high-pitched, strained, hysterical laugh.
        reaches over to turn on the light in the cell. The semi
        darkness on his face turns into sharp, pitiless light an
        shadow.

136   FULL SHOT - THE INT. OF THE NARROW CELL
        Lucas Beauchamp is asleep on the bunk, fully dressed
        except for his coat and hat on a nail in the wall. He h
        spread a layer of newspaper between his body and the nak
        springs, and is using one of his shoes as a pillow. CAM
        MOVES IN as Stevens and Chick enter. Stevens stands nea
        the bunk, looking down at Lucas, and after a second his
        eyes open and he looks at the lawyer and then at Chick,
        without moving.

                                Stevens
                        Well, old man, -- you played the devil
                        this time.
        Then Lucas moves, sits up with a grunt from the familiar
        pain in his stiff back. He bends down and finds one sho

Scene 136.

136   on the floor under the bunk, and his hands grope for the

CONT'D   other.

137   MED. CLOSE SHOT - CHICK

         standing near the door of the cell.

138   MED. TWO SHOT - HIGH ANGLE

         past Stevens and down toward Lucas.

                         Lucas Beauchamp

              Then you can take my case?

                         Stevens

              Take your case? What do you mean,

              defend you before the Judge?

         Stevens reaches down and picks up Lucas' other shoe from

         the head of the bunk.

                         Lucas Beauchamp

              I'm gonter pay you. You don't need to

              worry.

                         Stevens

              I don't defend murderers who shoot

              people in the back.

         And he drops the shoe on the floor beside the other.

         Lucas disregards them.

                         Lucas Beauchamp

              Let's fergit the trial. We ain't come

              to it yet. (pausing)

              I wants to hire somebody. It don't

              have to be a lawyer.

                    Stevens

        To do what?

                Lucas Beauchamp

        Are you or ain't you going to take the

        job?

                    Stevens (angrier)

        I'd already taken your case before I

        came in here. I'm going to tell you

        what to do as soon as you have told me

        what happened.

                    Lucas Beauchamp

        Nemmine that now. [Stevens: Never mind

        that?] What I needs is --

                    Stevens

        <Nemmine that!> Tell the Gowries to

        never mind it when they bust in here

        tonight --!

CLOSE SHOT - LUCAS

                    Lucas

        So you don't want the job.

CLOSE SHOT - STEVENS

                    Stevens

        No!

MED. SHOT - CHICK, IN PROFILE IN THE F.G.

looking toward his uncle and Lucas Beauchamp. Stevens

turns and looks at the boy, then turns back to Lucas,

141   <taking a notebook and a fountain pen out of his pocket.>
CONT'D   Stevens
                    But I'll do it, just the same. (more
                        calmly)
                    Now tell me exactly why you killed
                    Vinson Gowrie.
            Lucas is silent.

                               Chick
                    Wasn't it --'count of that trouble in
12-14-48   Fraser's store? Two months ago? I
                    was there, Uncle John, I can be your
                    witness.
            Lucas shakes his head in silent negation.

                               Stevens
                    <Lucas, let's get to the facts!>
                    [That's Lucas' trouble now. He's got
                    too many witnesses, already. (to
                    Lucas: Well?)]

142   MED. CLOSE TWO SHOT - STEVENS AND LUCAS
         Lucas is still silent, working his mouth as though he we
         tasting something. Finally he speaks, looking away from
         Stevens.

                               Lucas
                    They was two white folks, partners in
                    a sawmill. Leastways, they was buying
                    the lumber as the sawmill cut it --

         162

                            Stevens

Who were they?

                            Lucas

Vinson Gowrie was one of um.

                            Stevens <gesturing with

        his pen>

Lucas, has it ever occurred to you that

if you just said Mister to white people

and said it like you meant it, you might

not be sitting here now?

                            Lucas

So I'm to commence now. I can start off

by saying mister to folks that drags me

out of here and builds a fire under me.

                            Stevens

Nothing's going to happen to you. Nobody

takes liberties with Sheriff Hampton.

                            Lucas

Shurf Hampton's home in bed now.

                            Stevens

He appointed Mr. Will Legate to sit

downstairs with a [twelve gauge]

shotgun.

                            Lucas

[Will Legate?] I ain't 'quainted with

no Will Legate.

142   Stevens

CONT'D   The deer-hunter? The man that can hit

                          a running rabbit with a thirty-eight

                          rifle?

                                            Lucas

                          Hah. Them Gowries ain't deer. They

                          might be catty-mounts and panthers but

                          they ain't no deer.

143   MED. THREE SHOT - CHICK IN THE F.G.

          toward Lucas and Stevens

                                            Stevens

                          All right. I'll stay here with you.

                          Till morning -- if it'll make you feel

                          any better! Now, go on. Vinson Gowrie

                          was partner in a lumber deal. Who was

                          the other man?

                                            Lucas

                          Vinson Gowrie's the only one that's

                          public yet.

                                            Stevens

                          And he got public by being shot in broad

                          daylight in the back. Well, that's one

                          way to do it. -- All right, who was the

                          other partner? What was his name?

                                       Lucas (stubbornly)

                          Some other man, he was stealing a load

                          of lumber every night or so.

                    Stevens

How do you know?

                    Lucas

I seen um. Watched um.

                    Stevens

All right. Then what?

-11-48   [Lucas

Now you answer me some questions.

Is you or ain't you gonna take the

case?] ⟨That's all.⟩

                    Stevens

⟨That's all! So you took a pistol

and went to straighten out a wrong

between two white men! What did you

expect? What else did you expect?⟩

[You haven't got a case. You, Lucas

Beauchamp, took a pistol and went to

straighten out a wrong between two

white men. What did you expect? What

else did you expect?]

                    Lucas

Nemmine expecting. I wants --

                    [Stevens

You don't want justice. You want mercy.

Well?

143   Lucas

CONT'D   Well what?

                                 Stevens

                  The rest of it. What happened?

                                 Lucas

                  That's all.]

                                 Stevens

                  <I see.> [Then I'll tell you.] You

                  went to Fraser's store again. You met

                  Vinson Gowrie and told him somebody was

                  robbing him and he cursed you, called

                  you a liar whether it was true or not,

                  naturally he would have to do that,

                  maybe he even knocked you down and walked

                  on and you shot him in the back --?

                                 Lucas

                  Never nobody knocked me down.

                                 Stevens

                  So much the worse. It's not even self-

                  defense.

             Stevens walks up and down in the narrow, seven-foot

             length of the cell.

144   MED. THREE SHOT

             PAST Lucas in the f.g., toward Stevens and beyond him

             to Chick.

             166

Stevens

Now you listen to me. I'll get you

tried in another county and persuade

the District Attorney out there, --

since they don't know you, -- that

you're an old man and never been in

trouble before. You'll plead guilty

and ask the mercy of the court. And

hope they'll send you to the peniten-

tiary, where you'll be safe from the

Gowries. (going to the door, and

    turning before he leaves)

I made this offer once, but I'll make

it again. Do you want me to stay in

here with you tonight?

Lucas

I reckon not. They kept me up all

last night and I'm gonter try to get

some sleep. If you stay here you'll

talk till morning.

Stevens

Right!

He turns away abruptly, dropping his ⟨fountain pen⟩

[pipe] to the floor.

Stevens (over his

    shoulder, to Lucas)

144   Stevens (cont'd.)

CONT'D

How do you expect to get any help

from anybody --!

Lucas

I don't want help. I pays my own way.

Stevens (shutting

and locking the cell door)

You won't pay your way out of this.

Chick turns and looks back at Lucas through the bars

of the cell door.

[Chick (standing in

the doorway, bends over to pick

up Stevens pipe and hands it to

him)

You broke it.]

Lucas (to Chick)

You might bring me a can of tobacco.

145   MED. SHOT - THROUGH BARS

to Lucas, still seated on the springs of the cot.

Lucas

If them Gowries leaves me time to

smoke it.

146   MED. SHOT - STEVENS AND CHICK

outside cell.

Stevens (harshly)

Tomorrow. We don't want to keep you

awake tonight.

168

CAMERA PANS with them as they go toward the door of the staircase.

MED. SHOT - THROUGH BARS

out to corridor, where Chick, walking away with his uncle, looks back for a moment. Stevens reaches out to flick the light switch in the wall.

MED. SHOT - THROUGH BARS

toward Lucas, CAMERA MOVING AWAY from him. The bulb overhead is switched out, leaving him in darkness, except for part of his face and perhaps one hand, caught by the light from the dismal corridor.

DISSOLVE TO:

MED. LONG SHOT - EXT. - NIGHT

Chick and Stevens coming down the walk <toward the gate in the picket fence around the jail.> Will Legate, armed with his funny paper and his shotgun, is still illuminated in the open doorway. As the gate swings open, Chick hesitates. [Chick follows his uncle; their strides are alike.]

<Stevens

Well?>

[Chick

You are going to help him, aren't you?

Stevens

Of course I am, whether he wants me to or not. Ask for a change of venue - plead 'im guilty.

149   Chick

CONT'D   Then maybe he'll tell you what really

                           happened?

                                        Stevens

                           I know what happened. He killed Vinson

                           Gowrie. No matter what the provocation,

                           and he probably had plenty -- nevertheless,

                           he's killed a man.

                                        Chick

                           But there was somethin' he wanted to -

                           started to tell ya!--

                                        Stevens

                           I know the answer to that, too. He

                           was going to tell me a lie he knew I

                           couldn't believe, and being his lawyer,

                           I'd have to pretend I did. No, I know

                           what happened and I know the only cure

                           for it. Come on. Let's go home.]

                                        Chick

                           <Maybe I might take him some tobacco.>

                           [I might take him that tobacco.]

                    CAMERA BEGINS TO MOVE IN toward them.

                                        <Stevens

                           Chick -- the stores are all closed.

                                        Chick

                           I imagine I'll find Skeets McGowan around

Chick (cont'd.)

'D

here somewhere. He must have a key to

the drugstore.>

Stevens

It can wait till morning.

<Chick (not moving)

Yes.>

Stevens goes though the gate and when Chick doesn't

follow, he closes the gate and half-turns back toward

him. CAMERA HAS MOVED INTO:

CLOSE TWO SHOT - STEVENS AND CHICK

Stevens

<Your mother doesn't want you here and

your father expressly told me, before

he left, to see you didn't go anywhere,

till this is over>

[Chick, your father told me before he

left to see you didn't go anywhere.]

Chick

I know.

Stevens

Then just get home as soon as you can.

<After all, a man ought to be kind now

and then, even to his parents.> (T 33)

Chick

Yes, sir.

150   Stevens leaves, and after a moment, the boy turns to
CONT'D   run back up the path to the jail.
151   MED. THREE SHOT - CHICK, LEGATE AND TUBBS
             as he comes out of his quarters again, opening his door
             at the right of the hall.

                              Tubbs
                 Again?

                              Chick
                 I forgot something.

                              Tubbs
                 Let it wait till morning.

                              Legate
                 <Let him get it now. If he leaves
                 it here till morning it might get
                 tromled on.>
                 [No, let him get it tonight. I'm
                 afraid if he leaves it till mornin',
                 it might get trompled on.]

             Tubbs leads the way back toward the staircase.
152   MED. LONG SHOT - LEGATE'S ANGLE
             toward the street. In the f.g., the comic section in
             his hands is slowly lowered, revealing beyond it the
             front yard of the jail and the obscure street, both
             apparently empty. And then on the street, there's the
             flash of a match being struck, and held, and a cigarette
             lit, and then the match is thrown away and is burnt out,

leaving the street still empty with its dangerous

shadows.

MED. SHOT - CHICK AND TUBBS

as Tubbs opens the staircase door.

> Chick

>> Never mind the other one. I can
>> attend to it through the bars.

Tubbs shuts the door behind him, locks it, goes down the

staircase. CAMERA MOVES IN CLOSE to Chick as he looks

toward Lucas' death-cell.

MED. LONG SHOT - DOWN THE CORRIDOR

toward the cell. The single light left on in the hall

throws odd, half-recognizable shadows into the cells.

CLOSE SHOT

CAMERA MOVES before Chick as he walks through the silent

second story of the jail.

>> INTERCUT WITH:

MED. SHOT

CAMERA MOVES along walls, past the wire-mesh of the

bull-pen, past angles of bars and empty cells, one with

door ajar.

MED. CLOSE SHOT

seeing Chick advancing, through the bars, as if from

Chick's angle. Now Chick looks through the bars into

the cell, and Lucas' hands come out of the darkness to

grip the bars in the unshaded light from the hall. [Both

Chick's and Lucas' hands grasp the bars. One CLOSE UP
shows only one of Lucas' eyes, followed by a CLOSE UP of
Chick's eye. A little later, Chick puts his ear to the
bars to hear Lucas' whisper.]

                    Chick (imitating his
                uncle's harshness)
        All right. What do you want me to do?

                        Lucas (part of his face
                leaning forward in the f.g.)
        Go out there.

                    Chick
        Go out where?

                    Lucas
        The Gowries buries at the Chapel.

                    Chick (in horror)
        What?

                    Lucas
        That's nine miles to the bridge and
        then first right hand up into the
        hills, and all you got to do is go
        and look at him.

                    Chick
        Me? Why should I do such a thing?

                    Lucas
        C'mere.

Chick leans closer, takes hold of the bars, his hands
gripping above Lucas' hands.

MED. CLOSE TWO SHOT

PAST Chick to Lucas seen through the bars.

                    Lucas

        Because my pistol is a fawty-one Colt.

                    Chick

        All right. Suppose it is. Then what?

                    Lucas

        He wasn't shot with no fawty-one Colt.

                    Chick

        What was he shot with?

Lucas turns away, goes back into the darkness of the
cell.

                    Chick

        What gun was he shot with, Lucas?

Lucas returns, grasps the bars again.

3-48   Lucas

        I'm gonter pay you. Name your price
        at anything within reason and I will
        pay you.

CLOSE SHOT - THE TWO PAIRS OF HANDS

clasping the same bars, the boy's and the old man's,
the white and the dark.

                    Chick (o.s.)

        But why me? Why do you pick on me?
        What can I do about it?

159   Lucas (o.s.)

CONT'D   You ain't cluttered. You can listen.

                But a man like your uncle, he ain't

                got time. <He's too busy with facks.>

                [He's too full of notions.]

                                Chick (o.s., after a

                        pause)

                Tell me what you want me to do.

160   CLOSE TWO SHOT - PAST LUCAS TO CHICK

        the bars in between.

                                Lucas

                They buries at Caledonia Chapel --

                                Chick (incredulously)

                Up in that part of the county? What

                they call Beat <Four> [Nine]? Even

                the Sheriff can't go up there unless

                they send for him. And you want me --?

                Anyway, I'd have to get back by midnight.

                Or the Gowries -- [they might --]

                                Lucas

                <I knows about them.>

                [I knows about the Gowries.]

                                Chick

                And even midnight will be too late.

                I don't see how I can do it.

161   CLOSE SHOT - LUCAS [then, one of Lucas' eyes]

                        Lucas
'D   I'll try to wait.

                                        DISSOLVE TO:

1   MED. SHOT - EXT. NIGHT - THE SQUARE

        Chick coming out of the gate in front of the jail and

        turning into the street. CAMERA MOVES IN front of him,

        passes a man in denim pants, open shirt, and heavy shoes.

        He's leaning against a telephone pole, with one knee

        bent and the sole of this foot resting against the pole.

        As Chick comes by, the man extends this foot across

        Chick's path.

                        Man

            Wait.

        Chick stops and looks at him.

                        Man (glancing up at

                    the jail)

            What'd he tell you?

                        Chick

            Nothing, Mr. Gowrie.

        MED. CLOSE TWO SHOT - CHICK AND THE MAN

                        Man

            You been up to see him. Twice.

                        Chick

            Why not? Why shouldn't I?

                        Man

            He killed my kid brother. -- I'm here

Scene 161.

Man (cont'd)

to see they don't nobody sneak him

over the county line where we can't

get at him. Now tell me what you

went up there for?

Chick

He asked me to bring him tobacco.

Man

Tobacco! -- We buried Vinson this

<afternoon> [morning]. You know how

he was killed?

He takes out an ordinary kitchen match, strikes on his

denim pants, holds it lit as he searches in his pocket

for a loose cigarette.

Man

You tell me what he told you.

63   CLOSE SHOT - CHICK

Chick

He said it wasn't his gun.

4-48

4   CLOSE SHOT - THE MAN - CRAWFORD GOWRIE

Man (drawing in, then

exhaling as he speaks)

He's a smart nigger. I'd say the

same thing.

As if it were Chick's glance, the CAMERA SWINGS AWAY

164
CONT'D
from the Man's face and TILTS UP to the Courthouse
tower, just opposite. The two visible faces, lit from
behind the translucent dial, warn that it is already
past eight o'clock.

                                                    DISSOLVE TO:

165
<FULL SHOT - EXT. - NIGHT
CAMERA MOVES RAPIDLY PAST a road, past a pick-up truck
parked near a pasture gate, and then through a screen
12-11-48
of trees to Chick's house. Two rooms are lit, one
upstairs, one downstairs. As the CAMERA APPROACHES, w
see Chick's mother and father in the living room
downstairs; but as the CAMERA CONTINUES TO MOVE, it
lifts toward the half-open library window upstairs, an
entering the room, becomes a>
[EXT. SHOT
of Chick running down the street, crossing the lawn ar
running up the steps to his house. CAMERA PANS up to
lighted window.

                                                    DISSOLVE TO

166
FULL SHOT OF THE LIBRARY
[The library shows a framed engraving of a Confederat
officer, rows of legal books, a high-backed desk chai
and a desk with more books on it and a glass filled w
tapers for lighting a pipe. Miss Habersham sits in a
alcove, beside a table with a Tiffany glass lamp on i

    180

Stevens' framed degrees line one of the walls of the
alcove.]

in the midst of a conversation between Chick and his
uncle.

                    Stevens (seated behind
               a desk at the far wall)
          So he told you it wasn't his gun? (he
               stands up from his chair)
          If I were Lucas -- or any other ignorant
          murderer (T 79)
          <that's exactly what I'd claim myself.>
          [...I'd claim exactly the same thing
          myself.]

                    Chick (still breathing
               hard from having run most of the
               way, and one hand resting on the
               open door of the library)
          That's just what Crawford Gowrie said.

                    Stevens
          Where?

                    Chick
          Outside the jail.

Stevens moves from behind the desk, frowning not at
Chick, but at himself.

MED. CLOSE SHOT

167   CAMERA PANS with Stevens.

CONT'D   Stevens

                    So the Gowries are there already --

                    and you come to me, and I say no more

                    than what a Gowrie says. Well, it's

                    true. In matters of life and death --

                              (he's come to the window and is

                              looking out at the moonlit road)

                    --a man's vocabulary is almighty small.

168   <CLOSE SHOT - ALMOST AN INSERT

                    A sharp click of a gold watch opened in a woman's gloved

                    hand. It is some twenty minutes later than the time

                    indicated on the courthouse clock.>

169   MED. SHOT - STEVENS

                    with his back to the boy; Chick, turning to look at the

                    portion of the room concealed by the open door. In the

                    f.g., the figure of MISS HABERSHAM, sitting on the

                    straightest chair in the room, holding the watch open as

                    far away from her as the chain will permit.

                                   Chick

                    Oh. Excuse me..Evening, Miss Habersham.

                              [Miss Habersham

                    Good evening, Chick.]

                    She nods in reply. Her watch is fastened by a gold cha

                    to her mail-order print dress. She wears expensive

                    gloves and prim custom-made shoes, and a hat some forty

9
NT'D

years old, sits squarely and precisely on top of her
head. (T 75-77)

>Stevens

Whereas --

0

MED. CLOSE SHOT - STEVENS

Below and beyond him, the light from the window barely
silhouettes the pick-up truck down there at the pasture
gate.

>Stevens

--in the matter of Miss Habersham's
truck, in dreadful collision two
hours ago with a worn-out rooster --

Stevens turns back toward the room, walking in front of
the high, book-lined shelves. CAMERA PANS with him.

48

>Stevens

--which her neighbor, Mr. Winston,
swears and contends, is a scion of
high-pedigreed stock, worth at least
seven dollars - there are all the
words in the world --! (he gestures
behind him to a row of black and
gilt bound volumes of the Law on
Torts)

MED. CLOSE SHOT - MISS HABERSHAM

closes her watch-case with a snap, thus closing Mr.
Stevens sentence as well.

172   FULL SHOT - THE ROOM

with Chick, Stevens, Miss Habersham. Stevens directs
his argument as much to the silent Miss Habersham as to
Chick.

> Stevens (the anger and
> harshness of early this evening
> returning to his voice)

Why, if he had to shoot a white man, did
he do it up there in Beat <Four?> [Nine?]
He couldn't have picked a worse place for
himself in this whole county, maybe not
in the whole world. But if he had to do
it there, why did he pick a Gowrie? And
if he picked a Gowrie, why did he have to
shoot him in the back?

> Miss Habersham

Maybe he didn't.

> Chick [standing in doorway]

Maybe we might find out about that, if we
went up to where he was buried.

> Stevens (approaching Chick)

Chick, now tell me -- what did Lucas
ask you to do?

CAMERA MOVES SLOWLY TOWARD THEM to become, by the end
of the scene, a

173   MED. CLOSE TWO SHOT - CHICK AND STEVENS

184

Scene 172.

173   Chick

CONT'D   Maybe the Sheriff could do it.

                             Stevens

Do exactly what?

                      Chick (hesitating)

Dig him up.

                 Stevens (violent reaction)

What?

                             Chick

To get the bullet out and look at it.

                             Stevens

Why, in heaven's name!

                             Chick

To see did it come from a .41 Colt.

174   MED. CLOSE SHOT - MISS HABERSHAM

There is the barest flicker of reaction on her face.

175   MED. TWO SHOT - KEEPING CHICK, AS MUCH AS POSSIBLE, I'

THE F.G.

CAMERA PANS as Stevens walks up and down.

                             Stevens

Dig up Vinson Gowrie out of ground he's

been prayed and consecrated into?

Violate a Gowrie grave to save a black

from punishment? I'd a heap rather tell

old man Gowrie I wanted to exhume his

boy's body to get the gold out of its

186

Stevens

teeth! (T 80)

> (he is shouting now, to cover
>
> his anger and disturbance)

Even if Lucas' story were true, even

if every word were true, even then we

couldn't do it. Not you, not me, not

Sheriff Hampton --

Chick is retreating, beginning to close the door as he

leaves the room. CAMERA MOVES BACK with him.

Stevens

--not the Governor, not the President

of the United States - !

Chick shuts the door, <directly into CAMERA>.

[Chick leans against the door for several seconds,

looking discouraged.]

MED. SHOT - DOWN THE UPSTAIRS HALL

as Chick moves toward CAMERA, [hurries downstairs and

exits.]

<CLOSE SHOT - CHICK

Chick's Voice

I can't stay here. I'll saddle Highboy

and ride and ride and by the time I

come back, it will be all over!

VERY CLOSE SHOT - THE BACK OF CHICK'S HEAD

He plunges down and away from the CAMERA, going down the

178
CONT'D
179

180

181

back stairs, opening the door into the back yard, and slamming that shut too.>

MED. SHOT - EXT. NIGHT

<from behind Chick as he crosses the narrow back porch, then vaults the rail, landing in the dust of the back yard. He starts for the stable at the left. At the right are the two windows, gleaming in the moonlight, of the darkened cabin where Paralee and her son, Aleck, live when they're not working for the Mallisons.>

[Chick is running across the lawn in the background.]

MED. LONG SHOT - FROM INSIDE THE DARKENED SANDER CABIN through the shutters of one of the windows, as Chick crosses the moonlight of the yard. In black profile, with a white head-kerchief, Paralee turns to watch him pass. Rising into silhouette, as if he were standing up from a chair, is the figure of her son, Aleck. Chick has already gone into the stables.

                    [Aleck

          It's Chick!]

                    Paralee (whispering)

          Aleck! You're not going nowheres

          tonight!

                    Aleck

          I didn't say I was.

MED. LONG SHOT - <INTO THE STABLES> [EXTERIOR OF STABLES]

as Chick leads his horse, Highboy, out toward the yard,

'D   a white blaze on the horse's forehead appearing first

in the darkness of the stable doorway. Though Chick

has just managed to put the saddle on him, he can't get

to tighten the girth-straps. <Highboy's wild, unruly,

frightened behavior is a kind of picture of the turmoil

inside the boy's mind.>

MED. SHOT - INSIDE THE SANDER CABIN

looking toward the yard, Paralee and Aleck outlined

against the shuttered window.

                    <Aleck

        It's Chick.

                    Paralee

        Leave him be.

MED. LONG SHOT - THE SOFT PASTURE ROAD

leading from the stables, alongside the house, toward

the pasture gate that opens into the county road. Chick

struggles with Highboy, still rearing and snorting.

MED. SHOT - ALECK AND PARALEE - INSIDE THEIR DARKENED

CABIN

toward the moonlit window, looking into the yard. We

hear the whinny and commotion of Highboy outside. Aleck

opens the door of the cabin, stands half-way into the

moonlight.>

                    Aleck [leaving window
                and going to the door]

                                        189

184   Aleck (cont'd.)

CONT'D   It's Chick with Highboy.

                                       Paralee

                   [Leave him be.] Go 'head - go 'head

                   if you want to! - That Lucas think he

                   so smart. What he have to go and do

                   a thing like that? - Go 'head, go on,

                   do just what you want to do --

                                       Aleck

                   I ain't going nowheres. Least, not

                   very far.

185   MED. SHOT - CHICK, STRUGGLING WITH THE HORSE

               [NEAR THE GATE]

               ⟨He's more than halfway down the pasture road, toward

               the gate.⟩ Beyond him, a library window upstairs,

               projects an oblong of light across the pale road and

               the dark foliage on either side. On the other side of

               Highboy, a dark face emerging out of darkness, appears

               Aleck, soothing, quieting, murmuring to the horse. Now

               they both begin to tighten the girth-straps.

                                       Aleck

                   Where you going?

                                       Chick

                   Far enough.

                                       Aleck

                   Where's that?

                              Chick

          Where I don't have to see or hear

          anything that ever happens tonight.

                              Aleck

          Highboy ain't had enough feed to go

          ⟨stereo⟩ that far.

As if in answer, Chick mounts the horse.

MED. LONG TWO SHOT

DOWN the pasture road. TOWARD Chick and Aleck. Chick

has just mounted. Aleck walks alongside as Highboy

starts nervously forward. They cross the patch of light

in silence. And then look back and up at the library

windows. They arrive at the pasture gate, bars of wood

dark across the f.g. Suddenly Aleck stops moving, and

Chick almost in the same motion, stops the horse and

leans forward to look into the darkness. Pasture gate

begins to swing open toward them.

                    Miss Habersham (o.s.)

          Chick --

⟨Miss Habersham's hand appears on the top rail of the

gate, and then her whole figure in the f.g., straight,

thin and erect, with the ancient hat set directly on

top of it.⟩

MED. THREE SHOT - TOWARD MISS HABERSHAM [AS SHE MOVES

TOWARD CAR]

Behind her is the outline, black without detail, of her

                                                  191

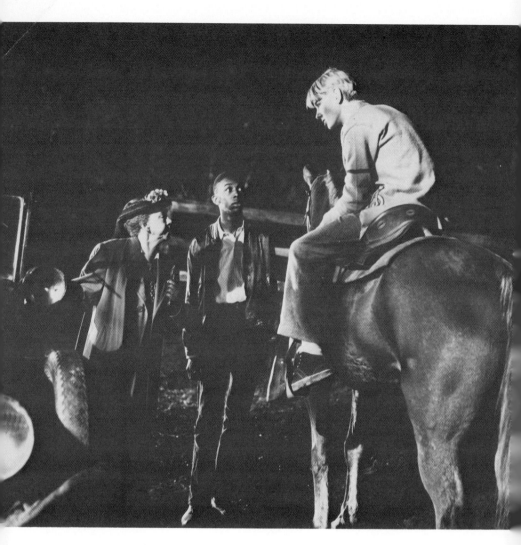

Scene 187.

battered pick-up truck.

T'D
                    Miss Habersham

          What did Lucas tell you?

               Chick [mounted on Highboy]

          He said it wasn't his pistol.

                    Miss Habersham

          I know -- But then what?

                    Chick

          He wants me to dig up the body.

<Across the f.g., Aleck tussles with Highboy who wants
to rear and strike at imaginary dangers.>

MED. THREE SHOT - PAST HISS HABERSHAM TOWARD THE BOYS

                    Miss Habersham

          Well?   .

                    Chick

          I can't! -- even if I could, you
          heard what Uncle John said.

                    Miss Habersham

          I've got a flashlight in my car. (she
               turns to Aleck)
          Can you get some tools, a pick and a
          shovel?

                    Aleck (walking away, obeying
               her, but murmuring to himself)
          Do no good. He be burned just the same.
          Just exactly the same, 'fore you get to
          dig anything up out of any place.

                                             193

189   MED. CLOSE TWO SHOT

<PAN with Miss Habersham as she goes back to her truck
and Chick, still mounted, follows her.>

                         Miss Habersham
         How far is it?

                    Chick
         Caledonia Chapel. It's on the hill,
         right beyond the Nine-Mile Bridge.

                         Miss Habersham
         Then we do need the horse.

                    Chick [close up]
         We? You expect to go, Miss Habersham?

                         Miss Habersham (getting
              into her car)
         We'll park the truck at the bottom of
         the hill, and then use Highboy. He'll
         make less noise.

190   CLOSE SHOT - CHICK
         He turns as Aleck comes up.

191   MED. THREE SHOT - PAST MISS HABERSHAM
         in the truck, to Chick and Aleck as he arrives with the
         tools.

                         Miss Habersham (to Aleck)
         Can you drive?

                    <Aleck> [Chick]
         I ain't supposed to go.

194

TWO SHOT - PAST ALECK TO MISS HABERSHAM

                    Miss Habersham

        I know. And neither is Mr. Stevens,

        and neither is the Sheriff, or the

        Governor, or the President of the

        United States. For that matter, neither

        am I. But somebody's got to do it.

In answer, Aleck puts the tools gently and noiselessly,

into the back of the truck.

MED. CLOSE SHOT - CHICK

turns Highboy toward the darkness of the road.

MED. CLOSE - MISS HABERSHAM AND ALECK

as Aleck swings up to take the wheel.

                                        DISSOLVE TO:

MED. CLOSE MOVING SHOT FROM THE SIDE - CHICK

riding through the country on Highboy. Dark fields,

houses, trees, occasional close leaves and branches of

a tree go by the CAMERA.

MED. CLOSE TWO SHOT - MISS HABERSHAM AND ALECK

riding.

MED. LONG SHOT - BETWEEN MISS HABERSHAM AND ALECK,

THROUGH THE WINDSHIELD

as the headlights of the truck pick up Chick and Highboy,

overtake and pass him. Miss Habersham puts up one

gloved hand to greet him.

198   MEDIUM SHOT - CHICK

riding in the moonlight, but receding as if seen from the truck.

199   LONG SHOT - THE LIGHT OF THE CAR

as they make a turn in the road, discovering a group of cabins.

200   MED. LONG SHOT - THE CAMERA STATIONARY - THE LIGHTS OF THE CAR

illumine a cabin near the road, flash across the windows

201   FULL SHOT - INT. CABIN

as the lights of the truck move across the wall and illuminate the scene inside. There are three Negro children lying awake in bed. Their mother, sitting rigidly in a chair beside the bed, reaches over as the lights swing through the room, and pulls the blanket for a second over the children's faces. The lights swing out and the cabin is in darkness again.

202   MEDIUM SHOT - THE HEADLIGHTS

travel across the front of the second cabin.

203   FULL SHOT - INTERIOR ANOTHER CABIN

The light swings through the room, revealing an old Negro couple facing one another across a table on which rest two cups of steaming coffee. [Two men and a woman are seated at the table.]

204   MEDIUM SHOT - THE HEADLIGHTS MOVE

across some trees and then to a third cabin, setting a little apart.

196

MEDIUM SHOT - TOWARD THE CABIN

as the turning headlights, for a second or two, pick up

the eyes and head of a young Negro man about twenty,

<looking out behind the half-shuttered window. The

SOUND of the truck moving by. The lights swing off.

Now we see only the barest outlines of the young man's

head and the glint of his eyes. He slowly swings open

the shutter.> Moonlight pours on his hands and face,

then he stops moving again, holding his position utterly

still at the SOUND of a horse. [The young Negro man

opens the door and looks through the crack.]

MEDIUM LONG SHOT

through the half-shuttered window TOWARD the road. It's

the apparition of Chick on Highboy, racing on up the

road and Highboy's own nervous pace.

                                    DISSOLVE TO:

<just behind and past Chick's shoulder, toward the road

ahead. They race along beside a small stream. Now he

turns the horse to the right and his hooves ring on the

hollow planking of the Nine-Mile Bridge.> Suddenly, on

the other side of the bridge, a figure appears,

disengages itself from the shadow of a tree. Highboy

snorts as Chick halts him. The figure has come out of

the darkness: It's Aleck putting a hand out to touch

and quiet the horse.

208   <MEDIUM SHOT - PAST ALECK UP TO CHICK

as he turns the horse down the bank and toward the
stream.

Aleck

Now what?

Chick

I want to water him.

CAMERA PANS with them as Highboy descends the bank with
stiff fore-legs. At the edge, three feet before the
glitter of running water, the horse refuses, rearing up
and away.>

[Aleck

Don't go across the bridge. You'll

make too much noise. Go down and

ford the creek.]

Chick

What's the matter now?

209   MEDIUM CLOSE SHOT - THE STREAM OF WATER
reflecting the moonlight and the sky, and flanked by
black, wet, glistening sand.

210   MEDIUM SHOT - HIGHBOY
rearing with Chick, nearly unseating him, until Aleck
gets hold of the rein and turns him around.

Aleck

He smell quicksand. (T 97)

DISSOLVE TO:

MEDIUM LONG SHOT - EXTERIOR - MOONLIGHT

the lower slope of the hill. In one part of the f.g.,
the silhouette of the pick-up truck, lights out, parked
among the bushes. The figure of Miss Habersham waits
beside it, recognizable mostly by her stance and the
shape of her hat. Down below, in the b.g., the stream,
the bridge, and Chick and Aleck climbing up toward the
hill with Highboy. In the f.g., Miss Habersham's hand
comes up and then down to open her watch and snap it
shut, the gold case flashing in the pale light.

MEDIUM CLOSE SHOT - MISS HABERSHAM

looks around, as if trying to see every shadow,
distinguish every sound.

                                    DISSOLVE TO:

MED. SHOT - THE TOPS OF PINE TREES

glittering and hissing in the night wind. CAMERA TILTS
DOWN TO:

MED. THREE SHOT

Miss Habersham is now mounted on Highboy, and Chick and
Aleck each carry a tool, and with a free hand, clutch
the leather strap under the saddle, holding on as the
horse climbs the slope of a hill, through the whips of
the underbrush. CAMERA ON Aleck's side, PANS TO FOLLOW
them.

CLOSE SHOT - CAMERA FOLLOWING

with Aleck. He stops. The horse goes on a single pace,
and then stops too.

199

215   <Aleck (listening)

CONT'D   Hush.

216   CLOSE TWO SHOT - PAST CHICK, UP TOWARD MISS HABERSHAM
       They're listening too.>

217   MED. CLOSE THREE SHOT - CHICK, ALECK, MISS HABERSHAM,
       [LISTENING]

                              Aleck (barely breathing
                          the information)
                   Mule coming down the hill. (T 99)
       CAMERA PANS AWAY to the left, past the screening
       underbrush and scraggly trees, to the crude road that
       goes up the hill. An indeterminate shadow is coming
       down. It's a horse or a mule, mounted by the shadow of
       a man, and with another hump of shadow, across the
       animal's back, in front of the rider. It goes by, CAMEI
       PANNING TO FOLLOW. With a shuffle of hooves, and a
       creak of leather harness, the shape passes down, and int
       the blackness and disappears.

                                          INTERCUT WITH:

218-221   SEVERAL CLOSE SHOTS:

          (a) Aleck

          (b) Miss Habersham

          (c) Chick

          (d) Highboy, his head turning, and <Chick's> [Aleck's]
12-17-48   hand coming out to press over the horse's nostrils,
               in case he should call out to the other animal.

          200

THREE SHOT - CHICK - ALECK - MISS HABERSHAM

all perfectly still, [silence, except for the sound of
crickets chirping] and watching down hill toward the
road.

> Aleck (whispering)

Who was that on the mule?

> Chick

I couldn't even see it was a mule.

> Miss Habersham

I couldn't see anything.

> Chick

But suppose he saw us. Suppose he

comes back and catches us --

> Miss Habersham

Maybe Aleck will hear him in time.

Miss Habersham turns the horse and, moving close by the
CAMERA, they begin to climb the steeper pitch of the
hill.

> DISSOLVE TO:

MED. SHOT - EXT. - NIGHT - A CRUDE, CABIN-LIKE WOODEN
CHURCH

Silence. <Then a sudden hurry of wings, and several
night birds fly off the eaves, and across the sky.>
CAMERA TILTS DOWN AND OFF to the slanted, thin slabs of
gravestones in the burying ground near the church. The
flashlight plays on one after another.

223   [Extreme long shot of Chick, Aleck and Miss Habersham
CONT'D   entering the cemetery and walking among the headstones.
224   MED. CLOSE - CHICK

is examining a gravestone by flashlight. The
coffin-shaped stone, with the letters weathered rather
than incised into it, reads:

AMANDA WORKITT GOWRIE

WIFE OF NUB GOWRIE

1899-1926

Chick

<Here --.>

[Here it is.]

CAMERA PANS as the flashlight moves down and to the
right, and illumines a fresh mound of raw earth,
scattered with a few flowers, and a single wreath.

12-14-48

225   MED. THREE SHOT - LOW ANGLE

All three, as Miss Habersham takes the flashlight, hood
it in her folded handkerchief. No one has made a move
toward the mound of earth in the f.g.; then Miss
Habersham stoops down and lifts the wreath off the
grave. After her taking courage, Aleck steps forward
and swings down with the pick.

Aleck

This don't need any pick. (T 102)

Chick thrusts his shovel into the earth.

Scene 224.

226   MEDIUM CLOSE SHOT - LOW ANGLE - MISS HABERSHAM
       looking like some sort of spinster angel, with the
       withering wreath in one hand, and a sword of light in
       the other.

                        Miss Habersham
                So much the better. Get a plank or
                something, and help him.
       Dirt from the first shovelful leaps up across the f.g.
                                              DISSOLVE TO:

227   MEDIUM SHOT - OVER MISS HABERSHAM'S SHOULDER TOWARD
       the three-foot depth of the grave, where Chick is at
       work with a shovel, and Aleck with a board which he
       uses as a shovel.

                     <Aleck (in rhythm, each time
                he lifts up and deposits a load of
                earth.
                Hah. -- Hah. -- Hah.>

228   CLOSE SHOT - ALECK
       sweating.

229   CLOSE SHOT - CHICK
       sweating.

230   CLOSE SHOT - MISS HABERSHAM
       turns at a SOUND far away, perhaps a pine cone falling
       in the darkness.
       [SOUND of birds' wings, flapping loudly; medium shot
       of bird flying off. Shot of Miss Habersham's reaction.]

<CLOSE SHOT - LOW ANGLE

a weathered figure, carved into a tombstone. A shadow

moves on it and is gone.

CLOSE SHOT - MISS HABERSHAM

turns her head ever so slightly.

MEDIUM CLOSE SHOT - MOVEMENT OF A PINE BRANCH

waving back and forth across the moon.>

CLOSE SHOT - MISS HABERSHAM

looks down again toward the grave.

CLOSE SHOT - PILE OF EARTH

as first from Aleck's plank, and then from Chick's

shovel, more earth is piled upon it.

MEDIUM SHOT - THE OPEN GRAVE

with Miss Habersham at the head of it. Chick and Aleck

are invisible below the level of the ground where we

see the black plank and the flash of Chick's shovel, as

they raise the earth up and pile it to one side. There's

an animal screeching somewhere in the grove.

<CLOSE SHOT - LOW ANGLE - HIGHBOY

turns his head, nostrils dilating, one huge, liquid,

almost human eye moves close to the CAMERA.

CLOSE SHOT - MISS HABERSHAM

She turns to look.

CLOSE SHOT - THE FIGURE IN THE GRAVESTONE

ghastly white. The animal sound is repeated, but much

further away by now. The light on the gravestone begins

239
CONT'D
to change and darken.>

240   THE MOON

very large on the screen, is beginning to be shaded

over by a patch of running clouds.

241   CLOSE SHOT - MISS HABERSHAM'S FACE

as the moonlight changes and diminishes.

DISSOLVE TO:

242   LONG SHOT - THE WHOLE GRAVEYARD

as the moonlight disappears and the figures and shape

of the gravestones go into shadow. The SOUND of the

earth being piled on earth continues rhythmically.

DISSOLVE TO:

243   MED. TWO SHOT - ANGLES FROM THE BOTTOM OF THE GRAVE

now almost dug, toward Miss Habersham, who at her

height, seems especially thin and elongated, still

standing in the same position with her wreath and her

flashlight.

Chick (o.s.)

All right, Aleck. Give me some room. (T 103)

Aleck climbs up into the scene, turns around and looks

down. Chick's shovel is pitched up after him from the

depth of the grave. Miss Habersham stoops, <taking the

hood of her handkerchief off the flashlight> [pointing].

244   THREE SHOT - LOOKING DOWN PAST ALECK AND MISS HABERSHAM

A heap of fresh earth on each side, toward Chick, in

the pit of the grave. He scrapes the last earth from

'D   the corners of the pine coffin with the flat of his shoe.

                         Miss Habersham

          We'll need a crowbar.

                         Aleck

          And rope. We forgot the rope.

                         <Chick

          Wait - !>

CLOSE SHOT - MISS HABERSHAM

looking down.

CLOSE SHOT - ALECK

looking down.

MED. CLOSE SHOT - CHICK

[CAMERA SHOOTS DOWN on Chick, then PANS UP as he reacts.]

as he stands astride the coffin, stoops and with both

hands, lifts away the loose unfastened cover. The circle

of light moves to center on what he is doing. Except for

a few threads of earth, sifting down from Chick's shoes,

the coffin is empty.

[CLOSE SHOT - EMPTY COFFIN

                         Chick

          It's empty.

All three look down at empty coffin.]

                                        FADE OUT

248   FADE IN:

       FULL SHOT - INT. SHERIFF'S KITCHEN

       Chick, Miss Habersham and Stevens are all facing the

       Sheriff, and Aleck moves uneasily in the b.g., near the

       kitchen window slowly growing pale in the first faint

       daylight. CAMERA MOVES FORWARD INTO:

249   MED. CLOSE SHOT - SHERIFF

                         Sheriff Hampton

                 You wouldn't come here at four o'clock

                 in the morning with a tale like that if

                 it wasn't so. (T 109)

                 [Looks like he might be innocent. He

                 could have killed Vinson Gowrie, but he

                 never dug him up, because Vinson wasn't

                 buried till Sunday afternoon. By that

                 time, Lucas had been locked up in that

                 cell for almost - uh - six hours.]

       The Sheriff is dressed in his undershirt, pants and

       socks. He was interrupted while getting breakfast on

       the stove behind him.

                         Miss Habersham (o.s.)

                 Sheriff Hampton -- [if we don't ---]

                              <Sheriff (interrupting)

                 You say he ain't there. But officially

                 he is. By the county records he is.> (T 109)

       208

MED. SHOT - PAST THE SHERIFF TOWARD THE GROUP

in the kitchen. Miss Habersham sits down on a kitchen

chair, folding her gloved hands in irritated patience.

                    Sheriff

    <So we got to tear that grave open

    again - officially. And it best be

    done with Gowrie's kind permission.

    It's their boy and it's their ground.>

    [So Vinson isn't in that grave? But

    officially he is. By the county records

    he is. So you want me to dig him up

    again officially? Mm. Gowrie grave and

    Gowrie ground -- hmph! Who's gonna get

    old Nub's permission?]

                    Stevens

    <Who's going to talk to old man Gowrie?>

    [Aren't you the Sheriff?]

Stevens is standing with his arm on Chick's shoulder.

His nephew, worn out with the day's excitement, with the

night's riding and digging, is falling asleep on his

feet. He fights it though, trying to hear and understand

what's being decided. The Sheriff has taken up a

butcher knife, and at the kitchen table, begins to cut

slices off a side of bacon.

                    Sheriff <(to Stevens,

        gesturing with the knife)

Scene 250.

Sheriff (cont'd.)

I was hoping you would.>

[But you're the lawyer. You're the

talker.]

Stevens

And tell him what? That we're trying

to save the black skin of a man who's

found with a fired pistol in his pocket?

Standing over a dead Gowrie? <With a

reason like that, to drive up in those

lily white hills, -- practically the

Gowries' back yard, -- and convince the

dead man's father --?> [It'll take more

than a lawyer to do that.]

Miss Habersham gets up impatiently, goes toward the

Sheriff, taking off her gloves.

Sheriff

<Well, if we're going up into Beat

Four without permission, --we're going

to wait till broad daylight.> [Well,

if we're going up to that graveyard

without permission, we'll wait until

it's broad daylight.]

Miss Habersham takes the knife from the Sheriff's hand.

Miss Habersham

We didn't. (T 112)

251   MED. CLOSE SHOT - MISS HABERSHAM

She begins to cut the bacon with clean, rapid strokes.

                    Miss Habersham

          And what's to happen to Lucas Beauchamp

          in the meantime?

She waves the knife at them.

252   FULL SHOT - PAST MISS HABERSHAM - TOWARD THE OTHERS

                         Sheriff

          <There's an iron door.>

          [That's an iron door, Miss Eunice.]

                    Miss Habersham

          <Jailer Tubbs has the key to the door.>

          [There's a key to it.]

                    Stevens (drily)

          <And, of course, Tubbs is only a man.>

          [Meaning Tubbs is only a man.]

Coffee is boiling over; Stevens advances to pull it away

to a cooler part of the stove. Sheriff takes down some

cups from a shelf, gives them to Stevens, who begins to

pour coffee.

                         Sheriff

          <I place my confidence in Will Legate.

          And a brand new shotgun.> [Will Legate

          and that twelve-gauge shotgun ain't

          only a man.]

Miss Habersham

<That's fine, far as it goes. But if

enough Gowries, or their kin, enough

Ingrums and enough Workitts get to

town, by two, three hours of daylight

they'll be quite enough of them -->

[If enough Gowries and their kin, enough

Workitts and their kin --]

Stevens (putting a cup

of coffee down on the table where

she's slicing the bacon)

<--Enough of them you mean, to make up

their collective minds -- because they'd

never do it one by one - to pass even

Will Legate and a double shotgun?>

[She means, if enough of them get together

to make up their collective minds, they'll

pass even Will Legate and his twelve-gauge

shotgun.]

Sheriff

<We'll be back by then.>

[Oh, we'll be back before then.]

Miss Habersham

And if you're not?

Stevens

<We'll do our best, Eunice. You can't

                                        Stevens (cont'd.)

CONT'D   ask better than that.>

                 [He's doing the best his judgment tells

                 him to, Miss Eunice. You can't ask

                 more than that.]

                             Miss Habersham

                 <I don't ask anything. It's Lucas you've

                 got to account to. Alive or dead.>

                 [If you mean these two children and me,

                 we're not asking anything. It's Lucas

                 you've got to account for --]

                             [Sheriff

                 Now --

                             Miss Habersham

                 -- or account to.

                             Sheriff

                 Now, Miss Eunice, ain't none of us up

                 to doin' anything before we've had some

                 breakfast.

                             Miss Habersham

                 Ha!

                             Stevens

                 Drink your coffee. That's the quickest

                 way to get Mr. Hampton started.]

12-16-48

253   MED. TWO SHOT - STEVENS AND MISS HABERSHAM

Stevens

What I'd like to know is how the same

Lucas Beauchamp could convince me he

was guilty, and convince you -- (turning

    to Miss Habersham)

-- he was innocent.

        <Miss Habersham

Pah!>

        Stevens (turning from

    Miss Habersham toward Chick)

And you too.

CAMERA FOLLOWS HIM as he picks up another cup of coffee

and gives it to Chick, who opens his eyes just wide

enough to see and take it.

        [Sheriff

What I would like to know is what Chick

and his buddy would have done if there

had been a body in that coffin.]

        <Stevens

Or didn't you believe him 'til you saw

the coffin was empty? And remembered that

Vinson was buried Sunday noon, just about

the time Lucas was being locked up in

the Sheriff's cell? So even if he killed

Vinson, he couldn't very well have dug

him up?>

Chick

I didn't think about it. Or I'd never

               have done it. [I don't know. I hadn't

               thought about it.

                         Aleck

               Uh - I did.]

     Chick tests the coffee, grimacing at its bitterness.

                         Miss Habersham (o.s.)

               Put some sugar in it, child.

     Chick obeys: three or four spoonsful, and it tastes

     more horrible to him than ever.

                         Stevens (now turning to

                         Aleck; the CAMERA FOLLOWING him

                         again)

               <Or you, don't you think you can get out

               of this discussion just because your mama

               can't vote. Because you're the one. You

               went out there in the dark, and helped

               dig up a white man's grave.> Why? Was

               it because Miss Habersham made you?

               [And you -- you were out there too, helping

               to dig up a white man's grave.]

                         Aleck

               Never nobody made me. I didn't even

               know I was going [until all of a sudden,

               there I was.] (T 113)

after

<Stevens

'D   You're all lying.

CAMERA MOVES IN TOWARD him.>

4-48

MEDIUM CLOSE - STEVENS

                    Stevens

<Why didn't I believe Lucas Beauchamp?

Why not? Why didn't he trust me, his

lawyer, with the fact he was innocent?

Answer me that!>

[Why didn't I believe Lucas? Why didn't

he trust me, his lawyer, with the truth?]

MED. CLOSE SHOT - MISS HABERSHAM

                  Miss Habersham

You're a white man. Worse than that:

You're a grown white man.

MED. CLOSE SHOT - STEVENS

                    Stevens

<I'm sorry about that.>

[Oh, yes, I've heard that before, too.

I heard Aleck's grandfather tell Chick

and Aleck that once. If you want to

get anything done, don't bother the

men folks with it. They're too

cluttered up with facts. Get the women

and children to working on it. Is that

what you meant?

257   MEDIUM CLOSE SHOT - MISS HABERSHAM

                        Miss Habersham

        <So there's a wall grown up between you.

        Lucas can't see through it, and neither

        can you.>

        [Why don't you drink your coffee yourself

        so we can get started?]

258   CLOSE SHOT - STEVENS

                          Stevens

        <I'm really sorry about that.>

        [It's more than that. There's a wall

        grown up between us. Lucas can't see

        through it and I won't. Well, maybe

        that's wrong. We're the ones who can't

        see through it, because we're the ones

        who are blind.]

He turns his head toward the kitchen doorway. Someone's

coming in the front way, and now the screen door bangs

shut again. [There are two medium close shots of the

closed door.]

259   FULL SHOT - THE GROUP IN THE KITCHEN

Stevens, Chick, Miss Habersham, Aleck, the Sheriff, as

they turn toward the SOUND of footsteps coming slowly

through the front room and toward the kitchen.

260   MED. CLOSE SHOT - MISS HABERSHAM

        <She doesn't drop the knife; she merely opens her hand

and lets it go.> [There is a long silence. Everyone
'D   watches closely.]

Miss Habersham

Will Legate.   What are you doing here?

MED. SHOT - PAST THE GROUP IN THE KITCHEN TOWARD THE

KITCHEN DOORWAY

as Will Legate comes in with his shotgun, bending down

as he enters.   He looks around and waits a second before

replying:

Will Legate

<I said I'd work Sunday night, not
Monday morning.>
[Oh, morning, Miss Habersham.   It's
about daylight.   I've got two miles
to walk before I can feed and milk.]

Miss Habersham (to Stevens)

You see?

<Will Legate (putting down
the gun)
The Sheriff's got other deputies.

Stevens

But Miss Habersham's right.   They'd be
no help.   They're just men with guns.   (T 17)

Sheriff (to Will Legate)

I'll pay you another five dollars -- for
the day.

                            Will Legate (pleading his
                                case to Stevens)
I'm a farmer, not a Sheriff's man. Sun
be up in an hour, and I got to milk and
. feed, don't I?

                            Stevens (pouring himself
                                some coffee, and walking slowly
                                toward Chick)
They'd pass you, anyhow, sooner or later,
when there's enough of them to whip each
other up.>

                            [Sheriff
Who's on guard?

                            Will Legate
I woke Tubbs and give him the shotgun.
Aw, it's all quiet over there. I
wouldn't've left if it hadn't been.

                            Miss Habersham
But you shouldn't --

                            Sheriff
Now, Miss Eunice, let's finish breakfast
and get started.

                            Stevens
Mr. Hampton is right, Miss Eunice, and
so are you. They'd pass even Will
Legate sooner or later, when there was
enough of 'em.]

2   MED. CLOSE TWO SHOT - CHICK AND STEVENS

                         Stevens

            But there's one thing would stop

            them. Long enough, anyway.

       Chick looks at his uncle.

                         Stevens (sipping his

                    hot coffee)

            And that's somebody without a gun.

                    (he sips) A lady. (T 117)

                    (he sips again)

3   MEDIUM CLOSE SHOT - MISS HABERSHAM

                         Stevens (o.s.)

            A white lady. (T 117)

-48   Miss Habersham reaches behind her for a towel and wipes

       her hands on it.

                         Miss Habersham

            All right. But I'm not going to sit

            there all morning doing nothing. So

            the jailer's wife will think she has

            to talk to me. I'll go home and get

            some mending to do. And feed my

            chickens. Maybe Aleck can drive me -- (T 118)

       FULL SHOT - THE KITCHEN - PAST THE SHERIFF AT THE STOVE -

       TOWARD MISS HABERSHAM AND THE REST OF THE GROUP

       Aleck opens his mouth to object.

                                                    221

264   Aleck

CONT'D   <I don't know if Paralee -->

                 [Oh, I don't know if Mom'd want me --]

                                 Stevens

                 You've gone this far, you can go a

                 little further. You and me both.

                                 Aleck

                 I reckon so. (to Miss Habersham)

                 Yessum.

The Sheriff heaves a prodigious sigh. Turning around

into CAMERA he throws a lump of butter onto the hot

skillet.

                                 Sheriff

                 Who can eat more than two eggs?

                                          DISSOLVE TO:

265   LONG SHOT

         from the slope of the field down toward the county road.

         In the f.g. is a plow abandoned in a half-turned furrow.

         Along the road is an endless line of cars and slatted

         trucks, all going by in one direction, toward town.

         SOUND of a siren. Driving fast, in the opposing direc-

         tion, the CAMERA PANNING with them as they pass the

         traffic are two cars, the Sheriff's and Stevens'. [The

         Sheriff drives a 1949 Ford.]

266   MEDIUM SHOT

         from the front of the Sheriff's car, toward the Sheriff

in the front seat, jerking the wheel over for the turns
without slackening speed. In the rear seat are the two
Negro convicts, silent, looking straight ahead, holding
the tools, pick and shovel, stiff and upright, in both
hands. ⟨The faces in the cars passing by crane back to
look at them, but caught in the forward traffic, can't
stop their cars.⟩

MEDIUM CLOSE TWO SHOT - CHICK AND STEVENS
Chick in the f.g., Stevens driving, and the procession
of cars going swiftly by in the b.g.

                    Stevens (glancing at Chick)
           Well, there's one half the county has
           sense enough to stay home -- the darker
           half.
Chick arouses himself to turn and look at the people
going by.

                         Chick
           We're too late. They're going to get
           him.

                        Stevens
           No. Not these people. And I don't
           see anything of the Gowries. Not
           yet, anyway.

                    Chick (looking across at
                       the blur of faces going by)

267   Chick (cont'd.)

CONT'D   But suppose they -- [co --]

268   MEDIUM CLOSE SHOT - STEVENS DRIVING

                              Stevens

         I reckon not. They're just going to

         town to see something happen. To wait

         for the Gowries. Just to wait:

         that's all.

269   MEDIUM CLOSE SHOT - CHICK

                              Chick (drowsily)

         But [but] suppose --

270   MEDIUM CLOSE SHOT - STEVENS

                              Stevens

         The best way to stop supposing, -- or

         denying, either -- is just to get out

         there and do what we have to do. (T 143)

271   CLOSE SHOT - CHICK

         His head nodding, his eyes at last falling shut.

                                              DISSOLVE TO:

272   MEDIUM LONG SHOT - PAST CHICK AND STEVENS

         through the windshield of Stevens' car, toward the road

         ahead of them, as they reach the crest of the hill and

         turn in before Caledonia Chapel. Chick starts, fully

         awake. At the right of the wooden church, is the

         graveyard; it is enclosed by a wire fence overgrown

         with a tangle of vines; and going through a gate and

then toward the raw mound of earth in the right hand

$'$D   corner, are Sheriff Hampton and his two convicts carrying

pick and shovels.

MEDIUM SHOT - CAMERA PANS

with Chick and Stevens as they get out of their car and

walk toward and through the fence gate, listening and

looking around them.

<MEDIUM LONG SHOT - CAMERA PANS

showing first the gray, silent, wooden church, the

stones tilted by the action of time and weather, and

then the still, breathless pines in a grove all around

the church and the graveyard.

MEDIUM THREE SHOT

as Stevens and Chick join the Sheriff. They turn to

look down hill.

MEDIUM LONG SHOT

down hill toward the bridge, the stream and the road,

all empty.>

FULL SHOT - STEVENS, THE SHERIFF, CHICK AND THE CONVICTS

Sheriff (to the convicts)

All right, boys, jump to it.

They move, slowly taking their positions near the grave,

one at the head, the other at the foot. The taller,

---

*Much of the dialogue and action from this point to
329 can be found in the text, pp. 159-178.

225

277
CONT'D

thinner convict has the pick, the heavier, stockier man has shouldered both shovels and now puts one of them down against the nearby fence.

> Sheriff
>
> Let's get our work done and get out
> of here.

278   MEDIUM TWO SHOT

PAST the convict with the shovel in the f.g. and TOWARD the man with the pick. He raises his arms. The calm, still grove of pines is behind him. Suddenly he stands frozen with the pick lifted in mid-air.

279   MEDIUM SHOT - CHICK'S FACE IN THE F.G.

the others behind him. The Sheriff and Stevens still look toward the church, but the convicts look steadily away, and, slowly, almost in slow motion, lower their tools and let them rest against the graveyard fence, as though the pick and shovels were there but they had nothing to do with them. Then - we see it on his face and a slight widening of the eyes -- Chick hears something move within the trees: a dry, even SOUND of hooves scuffling in the dust and the pine needles.

280   MEDIUM LONG SHOT - THE CHURCH AND GROVE OF TREES

From behind the church, down out of the pines, comes first a small white mare with an old man mounted on it.

281   MEDIUM CLOSE SHOT - THE SHERIFF - STEVENS AND CHICK

282   MEDIUM SHOT - THE OLD MAN

Scene 282.

282 using one hand, because a sleeve of the other is empty

CONT'D and fastened cuff to shoulder with a safety pin,

dismounts near the graveyard fence. Behind him appears

a black mule without a saddle and mounted by his twin

sons, somewhere over twenty, identical except for

somewhat different clothing. This silent procession is

followed by two gaunt fox hounds, just far enough behind

to respect the intentions of the mule.

> Old Man (in the high-pitched,
> almost falsetto voice of a mountain
> folk-singer)

What's going on around here, Shurf?

283 MEDIUM SHOT

as the old man looks toward the group for the new grave.

> Sheriff

I'm going to open this grave, Mr. Gowrie.

Old man Nub Gowrie vaults the fence lightly and easily

and advances six feet toward the Sheriff. The twin sons

on their mount, ride forward and stop in the f.g.

> Nub Gowrie

No, Shurf, not that grave.

284 MEDIUM CLOSE SHOT - THE SHERIFF

> Sheriff

Yes, Mr. Gowrie, I'm going to open it.

285 MEDIUM CLOSE SHOT - NUB GOWRIE

His face is sharp, old, bitter, with pale blue eyes and

228

skin weathered with sun and wind. Very deliberately, he reaches down and unbuttons the lowest two buttons on his shirt, puts his hand inside and draws out a heavy, nickel-plated pistol and lifts it under the stub of his left arm. He rebuttons his shirt before he takes up the weapon again, not pointing it particularly, just holding it.

MEDIUM SHOT - BETWEEN THE CONVICTS

on either side of the f.g. and past the Sheriff and the others toward Nub Gowrie with the gun in his hand. The Sheriff half-turns to the two Negroes.

> Sheriff

Get back in the car. [...boys.]

But they don't move.

> Nub Gowrie

[Never mind] ⟨He's right,⟩ boys, I
ain't going to hurt you. I'm talking
to the Shurf here.

> Sheriff

Your boy ain't in that grave.

Nub Gowrie says nothing. He doesn't move either. Somewhere back in the grove, there's the high-pitched, hoarse voice of a blue-jay; then silence again.

> Nub Gowrie (in a flat,
> conversational tone)

Don't tell me the name of the fellow

Scene 286.

230

                    Nub Gowrie (cont'd.)

          that proved my boy ain't there, Shurf.

          [long silence]

Chick moves slightly.

MEDIUM CLOSE SHOT - CHICK

opens his mouth but doesn't quite manage to speak.

MEDIUM CLOSE SHOT - NUB GOWRIE

with the pistol.

CLOSE SHOT - CHICK

                       Chick

          <It's empty. I saw it last night.>

          [I-i-i-it's empty. I-I saw it last

          night.]

MEDIUM CLOSE SHOT - NUB GOWRIE

In the b.g. are his twin sons, still mounted on their

mule. Gowrie raises his pistol. There is no sign on

his face either of anger or disturbance or any other

emotion for that matter.

MEDIUM CLOSE SHOT - CHICK

MEDIUM SHOT - PAST CHICK TO NUB GOWRIE

He looks away from Chick, back to his sons, and with the

pistol signals them to dismount.

MEDIUM SHOT

Just outside the graveyard, toward Nub Gowrie as his

twin sons turn the corner of the fence into the f.g. and

climb over. Their father points to the shovels with his

                                              231

293   gun. They each take over.
CONT'D   [Nub

             Grab those shovels, sons. They belong

             to the county. If we bust one, ain't

             nobody's business but the Grand Jury's.]

294   LONG SHOT - THE WHOLE CEMETERY
        as the twins come up to the naked grave and first one,
        then the other, thrust into the soft earth.

                                          DISSOLVE TO:

295   MEDIUM SHOT - STEVENS AND THE OLD MAN,
        Nub Gowrie, standing near the graveyard fence. Before
        them is the heap of clay excavated from the grave. The
        twins, almost with one movement, plant the two shovels
        askew into the lifted earth and leave them there. The
        two convicts wait in the b.g. Chick turns and faces
        away -- down hill to the tangled undergrowth. Nub
        Gowrie still has the pistol in his one hand and he looks
        away from the grave and turns the gun from side to side
        in his grip.

                        Nub Gowrie (in a flat
                     voice, almost without emotion)
                  What have they done with my boy?

                           Stevens (quietly)
                  Mr. Gowrie -- I think you knew last
                  night that something was wrong.

        232

MEDIUM CLOSE SHOT - GOWRIE

doesn't answer. He slowly puts the gun under the stub

of his left arm.

MEDIUM CLOSE SHOT - STEVENS

                    Stevens (more strongly)

        You knew: or Lucas would've been dead

        sometime after midnight, or as soon as

        you could get to town.

Gowrie reaches down and unbuttons his shirt.

MEDIUM CLOSE SHOT - STEVENS

                    Stevens (pressing the

              point home)

        But you stayed home -- why?

MED. SHOT - PAST CHICK IN THE F.G.

standing close to the fence, and toward Nub Gowrie and

Stevens. Gowrie puts the gun back in his shirt, slowly

buttons it again.

                    Stevens (repeating

              the question)

        Why, Mr. Gowrie?

In the f.g., Chick points down hill.

MEDIUM LONG SHOT - UP THE HILL

toward the whole group of men.

                    Chick

        <Uncle John, look! (pointing) - The

        tracks - !> [Uncle John! I found

        some tracks. Come on.]

300
CONT'D
Nub Gowrie vaults the fence and crashes down TOWARD
CAMERA, turning for a moment to call back to his dogs.

<Nub Gowrie

Hi! Hi! Hum on, boy!>

The dogs and then the twins come down toward him and
TOWARD CAMERA.

DISSOLVE TO:

301
MEDIUM SHOT - CAMERA PANS

with the dogs as they work slowly through the brush.

DISSOLVE TO:

302
FULL SHOT - THE TREES AND UNDERBRUSH

covering the lower part of the hill. SOUND of dogs
working, a hundred yards or so away. CAMERA TILTS DOWN
to discover Chick in the f.g. examining the muddy flat
at the foot of the hill and just beyond the stream.
CAMERA TILTS up again as Chick stands up and yells.

Chick

Here! I found 'em again!

The SOUND of men and dogs now comes toward him, closer.

303
MEDIUM SHOT - OVER CHICK'S SHOULDER

as he turns and runs, the CAMERA FOLLOWING him. Beyond
him we can see the tracks plainly. They're the prints
of a mule, and they're rather small, almost delicate,
but deeply stamped into the mud below the bank, and
long enough ago to have been refilled with seeping
water. The SOUND of men and dogs comes louder and
closer.

234

MEDIUM LONG SHOT - THE CAMERA MOVING

in front of Chick as he follows the tracks in the f.g.
The others burst into the trail, out of the tangle of
bushes just above it. Nub Gowrie is first, then the
twins, then the Sheriff and Stevens, then the two Negro
convicts. The dogs in the front, passing Chick now, are
frantic with excitement. Suddenly, in the f.g., the
tracks rise over a slope in the bank and stop in a
welter of footprints around a sapling.

MEDIUM SHOT - AROUND THE SAPLING

as Stevens, the Sheriff, Chick and old man Nub Gowrie
come up, the twins holding the dogs, and the Negro
convicts ill-at-ease and restless in the b.g. The
Sheriff reaches the sapling and touches a bit of abraded
bark at the first low fork.

                    Sheriff
    [Here...] Here's where the animal
    was tied.

                    Stevens
    And here's where he stopped.

                    Chick
    Aleck said it was a mule.

                    Sheriff
    Aleck [who]? Oh, sure. The other
    detective. (He scratches his chin)
    Yes, did he say who it was? Somebody

305   Sheriff (cont'd.)

CONT'D   that couldn't or wouldn't let Vinson

                              rest? --

12-15-48

306   MEDIUM THREE SHOT - PAST STEVENS AND THE SHERIFF

           toward old man Gowrie.

                                       Sheriff

                              But had to take him out and hide him?

                              Somewhere -- anywhere? So we couldn't

                              look at the bullet and name the gun?

                              Somebody who knew that Vinson was never

                              shot with Lucas Beauchamp's 41 Colt?

                                       Stevens

                              Well, there's Vinson's partner in the

                              lumber deal, whoever that is. Because

                              Lucas won't tell. At least - not to

                              his lawyer.

                                       Sheriff (to Stevens)

                              So you think his partner --? (to Gowrie)

                              Who was Vinson's partner?

307   MEDIUM CLOSE SHOT - NUB GOWRIE

           as he raises his head, his mouth is drawn open as though

           it were no longer easy to breathe. The sun glitters

           from the porcelain and the plastic gum of his false

           teeth. There's something almost like grief in his

           posture, in his open mouth and the narrowing of his eyes

236

307   Gowrie (stubbornly)

CONT'D   We ain't found Vinson yet.

308   MEDIUM SHOT - PAST GOWRIE

toward the Sheriff, Stevens and Chick.

                        Sheriff

Set your dogs to find him.

                        Gowrie

Never mind the dogs. They'll trail

and they'll ketch anything that ever

run or walked either. But my boy

never walked away from here and never

left no trail.

                    Sheriff (more softly,

            more kindly)

Hush now, Mr. Gowrie.

                        Stevens

But the man that carried him --

walked -- (pointing to the sapling)

- all by himself from here on. And

in a dreadful, terrifying hurry -

before two boys and an old woman

could come down that hill and discover

him at work. So he had to do it: hide

what he had to carry. And do it fast,

sure, and quiet. And where there would

be no trace. Not for a long time. A

river - or a well -

                                      237

308   Chick

CONT'D   Or sand.

                                       Sheriff

                          Here? What sand?

                                       Chick

                          Right there by the bridge. My horse

                          wouldn't <drink> [cross] last night -

                                       Stevens

                          Quicksand.

                                       Gowrie

                          No, lawyer. Put a man in quicksand?

                          My boy in quicksand? <Man do a thing

                          like that - ?> [A man'd do a thing

                          like that would --]

          He breaks out of the group. CAMERA PANS to FOLLOW him.

309   MEDIUM SHOT - DOWN TOWARD ALL THE OTHERS

          as they start after him.

                              <Sheriff (to the twins)

                          Come on.>

310*   MEDIUM SHOT - CAMERA PANS WITH OLD MAN NUB GOWRIE

          as he runs along the bank and onto the bridge, leaning

          on the rail to look down into the sand below.

_____

          *No emendations have been made from shot 310 through

shot 326. See the description on the pages of the continuity

script reproduced and included in the appendix.

          238

MEDIUM SHOT - THROUGH THICK UNDERBRUSH

as the others crash their way toward and just past the

CAMERA.

MEDIUM LONG SHOT - FROM BEHIND NUB GOWRIE

on the bridge in the f.g. grabbing the rail with his

hand and staring straight down. In the middle distance,

the others come along the bank toward the bridge.

                    Sheriff

     Grab him!

Nub Gowrie vaults over the rail of the bridge and jumps

straight down, feet first, into the wet, milky sand.

Rapidly, evenly, the sand begins to draw him down.

MEDIUM CLOSE SHOT - NUB GOWRIE

as he sinks into the sand. It rises past his knees,

climbs up to his thighs.

CLOSE SHOT - THE QUICKSAND

sifting around him as he sinks.

MEDIUM CLOSE SHOT - NUB GOWRIE

as he goes down into the sand. It has climbed almost to

the belt of his trousers and now he thrusts his hand

down into it. Almost at that moment, he stops sinking.

MEDIUM SHOT - PAST GOWRIE

up toward the others on the bridge and the bank. Gowrie

turns, pulling his hand out of the quicksand. It is

covered with a glove of clear white sand. He beckons to

them.

316   Gowrie (in a flat voice)
CONT'D   Here. I found him. Under my feet.

317   MEDIUM CLOSE SHOT - SHERIFF

                                       Sheriff (turning as he
                        gives these orders)
                   Get a rope! - you - cut some poles -
                   some branches - anything! - Get him
                   out of there!

318-325   SEVERAL MEDIUM CLOSE SHOTS - INTERCUT
           (a) The sides of the shovels used as blades, hacking
           branches out of the willows.
           (b) The two Negro convicts pulling loose brush up into
           the CAMERA.
           (c) One of the twins pulls a rope off the mule.
           (d) The other twin pulls the saddle strap off the mare.
           (e) The two dogs barking, hysterical with excitement.
           (f) Chick and Stevens getting a foothold on a clump of
           brush, reach old Nub Gowrie and draw him up out of the
           quicksand and onto safety of the bank. He is coated
           with wet sand from the waist down. He looks away from
           them, back to the quicksand.
           (g) First one crude pole and then another, is thrust
           into the sand.
           (h) The Sheriff makes a slip knot in the rope, tosses
           it forward from the bridge.

Scenes 318–25.

326   MEDIUM CLOSE THREE SHOT - CHICK - STEVENS AND THE OLD
       MAN

       all watching.

                         Sheriff (o.s.)

              Lower! - grab that pole! - pull him

              up now - easy, easy - that's it! Now.

              Put him down.

       Across the f.g. gripped and held by a Negro convict on
       one side, a Gowrie twin on the other, are first the
       shoes, then the trouser legs of the dead man, covered
       with the same fine coating of sand.

                         Chick

              Oh gee - Uncle John, oh gee, let's get

              him away from the road - at least let's

              get him back into the woods where they

              won't see him - !

                         Stevens

              Steady. They've all passed now, anyway.

              They're all in town now.

       Chick, Stevens and Gowrie look down as the body is
       lowered out of sight of the CAMERA.

327   CLOSE SHOT - OLD MAN GOWRIE

       Tears grow in his pale, cold blue eyes. His face is
       distorted between grief and the effort not to show grief

328   MEDIUM CLOSE SHOT - LOWER ANGLE UP TOWARD GOWRIE

       as, looking down, he wipes the glove of sand off his

hand, then fumbles at his hip pocket for a handkerchief

'D   and, finding none, pulls out one tail of his shirt.

With a gesture at once awkward, stiff and tender, he

stoops down TOWARD CAMERA to wipe the sand off his son's

face.

                                        DISSOLVE TO:

MED. CLOSE SHOT - THE DOUBLE CONE OF A LOUD SPEAKER

attached to an arcade column, and blaring a sentimental

tune, with heavy base emphasis, out of a radio store on

the Square. CAMERA PANS OFF AND ACROSS the roofs of

cars and trucks, come in from the town and countryside

to fill whole areas of the Courthouse Square, so closely

parked that it would be possible to walk on them, as if

on another roadway. CAMERA PANS, there's a radio,

invisible in a car, tuned to a different station, and a

different song, but with the same sweetness and gayety;

and then there's a portable somewhere too, with a third

tune, all of these nice enough by themselves, turn

garish and rude as they crisscross and roar against one

another. The PAN ENDS with a girl, sitting on the cab

roof of a truck, wearing blue jeans and glasses, and

aged nine or ten, but too big for her age, and adding to

the noise of music and human voices, by whirling a

wooden clacker.

                                        DISSOLVE TO:

                                                    243

330-336   DOLLY SHOT - MEDIUM OR CLOSER

CAMERA MOVES AT EYE LEVEL, among the crowd in the Square.
It's Monday morning, full sunlight, and usually stock
auction day. But it's become a holiday. In this close,
warm crowd of people and cars, cokes are being hawked,
sold, opened and swallowed. People are in no way extraordinary: women in faded print cotton dresses, and the
men often in surplus Army suntans, and wearing felt hats
or sweat-stained panamas. And in the f.g., THE CAMERA
PASSES details like these:

(a) A school bus pushing its way with difficulty to the
Square. It is filled, not with children, but with men
from the surrounding country. They pile out the door,
lighting pipes, cigarettes, or one of them tearing off a
chaw of tobacco with his bad teeth.

(b) A child with a yo-yo, legs dangling from the roof
of a truck.

(c) A very small child on her father's shoulders with a
great double, dripping ice cream cone.

(d) A very fat, very pleasant woman, passing a side
mirror of a car, and taking advantage of it to repair
her lip rouge.

(e) A triangle of men playing blackjack on the front
hood of what used to be a jeep.

                    [Man

        Oh, well, we had two hearts- just

            244

Man (cont'd.)

the three and the five.   That's

                   eighty cents you owe me.]

(f) A woman in a country sun-bonnet, carrying a crying

baby and walking it up and down trying to hush it.

The DOLLY SHOT slows down as the woman and the child

come opposite a small truck with a few planks of newly

sawed lumber and bearing the name: "GOWRIE."   She

stands opposite the cab of the truck and looks up at the

driver seated inside.   (The MOVING SHOT comes to a

stop.)   It's Crawford Gowrie, his eyes staring straight

ahead in a kind of stupor through the windshield.

7   MEDIUM SHOT - PAST CRAWFORD GOWRIE

toward the mother and other people in the crowd.

                       The Mother

           Well, Mr. Gowrie -- when do you

           reckon you'll get started?

Crawford Gowrie finds and strikes a match along his

trouser leg.   Holding it lit, according to his habit,

he looks for a cigarette in his shirt pocket.   A crowd

of curious people begin to turn and press in toward the

truck.

                   A Man (on the other

                   side of the truck but addressing

                   his remark to the mother)

           He's got to wait for his pop and his

           brothers to git here, don't he?

                                                          245

Scene 337.

Crawford puts the cigarette in his mouth.

D

> Another Voice
>
> Where they at, Crawford? Planting
>
> corn this morning?

Crawford Gowrie, in response to the baiting of the
crowd, flicks out his match without lighting the
cigarette.

> A Third Voice
>
> No, now don't say that. They're
>
> waiting to be called up for jury duty.

MEDIUM CLOSE SHOT - CAMERA PANS WITH CRAWFORD GOWRIE
as, cigarette still in his mouth, he gets out of the
truck in a sudden movement and reaches over the boards
of lumber to find and pull off an Army gasoline can,
and accompanied by some of the crowd, he pushes his way
about twenty feet toward the sidewalk.

MEDIUM SHOT - TOWARD CRAWFORD GOWRIE
as he comes forward. In the f.g. are the two pumps of
the gasoline station. The attendant, who has been
standing on an oil cart in order to see what's happening,
jumps down again and takes the can as Crawford sets it
on the cement between the pumps. There's a second's
pause. Then the attendant reaches over and unhooks the
hose from the gasoline pump, unscrews the cap from the
can, and inserts the hose. [The attendant is dressed
for the occasion in a white shirt, tie, and dark suit.]

247

340   MEDIUM CLOSE SHOT - PAST THE ATTENDANT

TOWARD Crawford Gowrie, as he takes out some money from

his grimy wallet.

<Attendant

There'll be no charge for this Mr.

Gowrie.

Crawford Gowrie nods.>

341   CLOSE SHOT - THE GASOLINE

pouring from the hose into the can.

342   SEVERAL CLOSE SHOTS OF FACES

in the crowd, some grim, some smiling ever so slightly

with anticipation.

343   MEDIUM CLOSE SHOT

The gas over-flows the can. The attendant's hand

reaches in to remove the hose, and starts to put on the

cap. CAMERA MOVES BACK as Crawford Gowrie reaches down

and takes the can without bothering with the cover.

CAMERA PANS to follow him as he pushes forward through

the crowd. It partly follows, partly makes way for him.

344   MEDIUM CLOSE SHOT - CAMERA MOVING

before Crawford Gowrie, going forward with the can of

gasoline. It spills up over his hand as he walks.

345   MEDIUM LONG SHOT - HIGH ANGLE

Down from the porch of the jail toward the bubble of

clear space that contains Crawford Gowrie advancing

through the crowd and coming steadily forward.

248

CLOSE SHOT - CAMERA MOVING

before Gowrie.

MEDIUM SHOT - BEHIND AND ABOVE CRAWFORD GOWRIE

as he crosses diagonally through the front yard of the

jail, begins to mount the porch.

MEDIUM SHOT - CAMERA MOVING

in front of Crawford Gowrie and the crowd accompanying

him, as he reaches the steps of the jail porch, mounts

them steadily, slowly, heavily. CAMERA PULLS BACK

before him, withdrawing into the open doorway of the

jail. Crawford Gowrie stops, puts the can of gasoline

down on the floor of the hall. His attention and that

of the crowd immediately behind him is fixed straight

forward. CAMERA CONTINUES TO MOVE SLOWLY BACK and away

from him. Into the f.g., as he looks toward CAMERA,

appears the straight, calm figure of Miss Habersham,

seated on her chair and blocking the hallway into the

jail, not so much with her position as with her presence.

MEDIUM SHOT - PAST CRAWFORD GOWRIE

In the hallway of the jail, and facing Miss Habersham,

straight and calm, seated with her basket of mending at

her side.

                    Crawford Gowrie

          Git out of the way, Miss Habersham.

                    Miss Habersham

          I'm very comfortable <where> [the way]

          I am.

                                                    249

Scene 349.

An arm is thrust forward from the crowd back of

D   Crawford, and points down toward Miss Habersham. [The

confrontation is edited into a series of alternating

close cross cuts of Crawford and of Miss Habersham.]

Voice (o.s.)

There's one way: you could take and

move her and her chair out in the yard.

Crawford Gowrie

Or else -- I could do this --

MEDIUM CLOSE SHOT - CRAWFORD GOWRIE

as he reaches forward and down and tilts the gasoline

can so a little of it spills on the wooden floor of the

hall.

MEDIUM SHOT - MISS HABERSHAM - LOW ANGLE

as the stain of gasoline reaches almost to her shoes,

planted firmly together as if on a chalked diagram.

She doesn't move.

MEDIUM SHOT - PAST MISS HABERSHAM TOWARD CRAWFORD

GOWRIE

and the others in the hallway.

Miss Habersham

[Will you] <please> step out of the

light so I can thread my needle.

She unrolls a length of white thread from the spool.

Crawford Gowrie

Miss Habersham, I'm not going to touch

251

352   Crawford Gowrie (cont'd.)
CONT'D   you now. You're an old lady, but you're

                   in the wrong. You're fighting the whole

                   county. You're bound to get tired, and

                   when you get tired, we're going to go in.

353   MEDIUM CLOSE SHOT - MISS HABERSHAM

                                    Miss Habersham
                   I'm going for eighty, and I'm not tired
                   yet.

354   MEDIUM LONG SHOT - CRAWFORD GOWRIE
         silent, in the f.g., the crowd watching and restless in
         the b.g., as far as the CAMERA can see.

355   ⟨MEDIUM LONG SHOT - TOWARD THE OPEN DOOR
         of the jail, the crowd in between. In the f.g.,
         standing on the roof of a truck, the little girl with
         glasses breaks the silence with a derisive sound of her
         clacker.

356   MEDIUM SHOT - PAST CRAWFORD GOWRIE AND MISS HABERSHAM
         The sound of the clacker.

357   CLOSE SHOT - THE WOODEN CLACKER
         going round and round with its infuriating noise.⟩

358   MEDIUM CLOSE SHOT - MISS HABERSHAM
         She stands up, the mending still in her hands.

                                    Miss Habersham (in a high,
                          clear voice trembling a little out
                             of fatigue and emotion)
                   Go home. Every one of you.

         252

MEDIUM SHOT - HIGH ANGLE - FROM OUTSIDE THE JAIL OVER
THE HEADS OF THE CROWD TOWARD MISS HABERSHAM

                    Miss Habersham

        Go on home. You should be ashamed.

The crowd doesn't move, doesn't answer. CAMERA BEGINS
TO PULL BACK.

MEDIUM LONG SHOT - CAMERA MOVES ABOVE THE FACES OF THE
CROWD

[They break up into smaller groups, moving about
nervously.] ⟨They are standing quite still.⟩ They're
not ugly or cruel or special in any way. Fat or thin,
tall or short, men, women and children, they are no
different in appearance than the audience that will see
them on the screen. CAMERA TILTS UP AND AWAY TOWARD
the face of the jail, in the upper story of which is
centered a window, closely barred with strips of iron.

                                    DISSOLVE TO:

MEDIUM SHOT - INTERIOR JAIL - DAY - PAST CHICK
In the doorway of Lucas' cell toward Stevens and Lucas.
Once more Lucas is seated on the springs of his bunk.
He stubbornly folds the newspaper that had been his
sheet and mattress.

                    Lucas

        I never see no man shoot Vinson

        Gowrie.

253

361   Stevens

CONT'D   But you must know who shot him.

362   MEDIUM CLOSE SHOT - LUCAS

           is silent, his face concentrated downward on folding

           the newspaper.

363   MEDIUM CLOSE SHOT - STEVENS

                                    Stevens

                   Don't you realize you'll never be

                   safe? Not 'till we know who he is.

                   Not till we find him? Not till we

                   put him right here -- in your place

                   -- on this bunk -- in this cell?

           He slams his hand down on the springs of the upper bunk.

364   MEDIUM SHOT - PAST STEVENS TO LUCAS

           Lucas holds the newspaper, folded now as though it were

           ready for sale again.

                                    Lucas

                   <You're the lawyer. You tell me.>

                   Can they put a man in jail if they

                   never see him fire no shot? [You're

                   a lawyer. You know the law.]

           Lucas gets up.

                                    Stevens

                   Your case was slightly different --

                                    Lucas (pointing to the

                          open door)

           254

Lucas (cont'd.)

Can they take him out of jail and maybe

burn him, if they only suspicioned he

maybe might have --

Stevens

<Wait. No. You were standing over a

dead man. You had a recently fired

pistol in your pocket. That was a

great deal more than suspicion.>

[Listen. You were standing over a

dead man. You had a recently fired

pistol in your pocket. Do you call

that just suspicion?]

MEDIUM THREE SHOT - PAST LUCAS IN THE F.G. TOWARD

Stevens, and toward Chick in the b.g.

Lucas

It was Sat'dy --

Stevens

I know that. But why did your carry

a pistol?

Lucas

[Well,...] Mr. Carrothers --

Stevens

--gave it to you?

---

*Much of the dialogue from this point to shot 386 can

ound in Chapter Ten of the text.

'D

365   Lucas

CONT'D   [He] --sold it to me.

                             Stevens

                 All right.

                             Lucas

                 He always carried it, Sat'dys --

                             Stevens

                 He was a white man! -- So that's why

                 you -- I see: When you dress up on

                 Saturday, you wear the pistol.

                 Exactly like old Carrothers did.

                 Just as simple as that.

                             Lucas

                 Downstairs in the office they got my

                 pistol and my hat and my toothpick.

                 <Do I gets them now or does I have to

                 wait till the Shurf --> [Does I get

                 'em now or does I --]

366   CLOSE SHOT - STEVENS

                             Stevens (passionately)

                 Lucas. Last night I was wrong. You

                 were right and Chick was right and I

                 was wrong. Today I am trying to save

                 your life. Not for your sake since

                 you're bent on throwing it away -- but

366   Stevens (cont'd.)

CONT'D   for my sake. So I won't have to

              carry it on my conscience.

367   CLOSE SHOT - LUCAS

                        Lucas

              All right. What'll you be sattersfied

              with?

368   MEDIUM SHOT - PAST CHICK IN THE F.G.

         to Stevens and Lucas.

                        Stevens

              The truth. Nothing more.

                        Lucas (sitting down

                  again slowly)

              They was two white folks, partners

              in a <lumber mill.> [sawmill.]

         [Close up of Lucas]

                        Stevens (with

                  excessive impatience)

              And one was Vinson Gowrie, yes. And

              the other -- ?

         The CAMERA BEGINS TO MOVE.

                        Lucas

              I don't sleep much, nights. I taken

              to walk --

                        Stevens

              Not because you suspected anything,

              of course.

368   The CAMERA HAS MOVED PAST Stevens and to a:
CONT'D

369   CLOSE SHOT - LUCAS

                              Lucas

                I taken to walk, and in the dark I

                comes near the sawmill -- and I seen --

          <He looks up at the bulb in the ceiling of his cell.

370   CLOSE SHOT - CAMERA MOVES IN TOWARD THE LIGHT

          in the ceiling of Lucas' cell.>

                              Lucas

                --a light --

                                        DISSOLVE TO:

371   LONG SHOT - EXTERIOR - NIGHT - BACKWOODS ROAD

          <The light becomes two lights,> the headlights of a

          truck advancing toward CAMERA.

                           Lucas' Voice

                --coming straight for me.

372   MEDIUM SHOT - EXTERIOR - NIGHT - PAST LUCAS

          TOWARD the truck as it rattles down the road, till its

          headlights outline the impassive figure of Lucas. The

          truck begins to brake to a stop. A hand goes up and

          flicks on the spotlight to the left of the windshield

          and swings it toward Lucas. The spotlight shines

          directly into CAMERA. Suddenly the truck starts again

          with a rush. CAMERA PANS with the truck as it goes by

          him into the darkness. The starting jolt hurls a plank

2   of lumber off the huge load behind.

NT'D

3   MEDIUM SHOT - TOWARD LUCAS

as he stoops and picks up the board.

                            Lucas' Voice

Just like I tole you. They was two

folks, partners in a sawmill. And one

of um --

4   LONG SHOT - THE LIGHTS OF THE TRUCK

disappearing down the road.

                            Lucas' Voice

--was stealing his share [of the lumber].

Ever night, maybe. Or ever night he

could.

5   MEDIUM CLOSE SHOT - LUCAS

holding the raw plank in his hands.

                            Lucas' Voice

And he seen me. So I knowed that wasn't

the end of it. (Lucas turns to look

            back, toward the road behind him)

Then I heared a mule --

6   MEDIUM SHOT - PAST LUCAS - TO THE ROAD BEFORE HIM

SOUND of hoof-beats. The eyes of a mule appear out of

the darkness and the gleam of metal of the animal's

harness, then the rider: Vinson Gowrie. Lucas lifts

the plank up towards him.

376
CONT'D

Lucas

This your lumber?

[Vinson] Gowrie takes the plank with one hand, holds it
and examines it, and then turns to Lucas.

Vinson Gowrie

Who drove that truck?

377   MEDIUM SHOT - PAST VINSON GOWRIE ON HIS MULE
down toward Lucas. Lucas does not reply.

Vinson Gowrie

You seen him! Who drove that truck?

Lucas shifts his gold toothpick to the other side of
his mouth. Then he steps aside as Vinson Gowrie hurls
the plank back at him, and slaps the mule, and goes past
him, racing down the road in vain, furious pursuit of
the truck.

378   MEDIUM CLOSE SHOT - LUCAS

Lucas' Voice

I knowed that wasn't the end neither

-- Next Sat'dy afternoon --

379   MEDIUM LONG SHOT - LUCAS

walking through the woods back of Fraser's store. He
wears his black broadcloth suit, his pale hat, and his
gold watch chain glints across his vest. The shape of
his Saturday pistol bulges in his coat pocket.

Lucas' Voice

<--I walks over to Fraser's store. And

260

Lucas' Voice (cont'd.)

'bout half-way down --> [--On my way

over to Fraser's store --]

Across the path, beyond Lucas, a white-tail rabbit

jumps toward the woods on the other side.

Lucas' Voice

--I seen my Sat'dy supper.

Lucas pulls his pistol out of his pocket and almost in

the same motion, fires at the rabbit. But it's too

late.

Lucas' Voice

But I missed him.

MEDIUM CLOSE SHOT - LUCAS

Lucas' Voice

Two miles later, when I comes in

sight of Fraser's store,--

DISSOLVE TO:

LONG SHOT - VINSON GOWRIE

seated on his mule, and directly across the path in the

woods. He carries a heavy club chopped from a sapling.

In the b.g. is Fraser's store in the cross-roads with

groups of men and animals milling around it. CAMERA

MOVES IN behind Lucas, approaching Vinson Gowrie.

Lucas' Voice

--there was Vinson Gowrie. He wanted

381   Lucas' Voice (cont'd.)
CONT'D   to know, 'fore he beat me, just who

                            been stealing their lumber. And I

                            tole him --

Lucas goes by him, and Vinson faces the mule around to

follow him. Lucas turns and stops. He now FACES THE

CAMERA while Vinson Gowrie has turned his back.

                                 Lucas' Voice

                      --I ain't decided yet. And he tole

                      me he reckoned he'd have to beat it

                      out of me then.

382   MEDIUM SHOT - PAST LUCAS

To Vinson on his mule as he slashes down with the club

-- Lucas not moving. There's a shot and Vinson falls

out of the saddle. A hundred yards beyond them, above

a flowering bush, a puff of smoke rises and disappears.

                                 Lucas' Voice

                      He never did. I don't know if it was

                      a rifle. $\langle$It was that far away$\rangle$ it

                      could have been a rifle. But I never

                      seen who fired it.

383   MEDIUM SHOT - HIGH ANGLE - LUCAS

standing over Vinson, fallen on his face into the road,

one hand still tangled in the reins of the mule, with a

bleeding hole in his back, dead.

Scene 382.

383   Lucas' Voice

CONT'D   He could have picked me off and shut

                  me up.

            <Lucas puts his hand to the bulge of the pistol in his

            pocket.>

                                              DISSOLVE BACK TO:

384   MEDIUM SHOT - SAME ANGLE - LUCAS

        in the same position, <with his hand on his pocket,

        empty now, of course, since> he is standing in his cell

        in the county jail.

                                Lucas

                  But he picked Vinson.

385   MEDIUM SHOT - PAST LUCAS AND STEVENS

        through the open door of the jail to the jail corridor

        beyond and Chick standing there.

                                Stevens

                  And do you know why? Because the

                  murderer watched you every step of the

                  way. He saw you fire at the rabbit,

                  and miss. So here was his chance: to

                  murder the man from whom he stole the

                  money, and to see you lynched for that

                  very same murder. So he'd be safe, and

                  you and Vinson would be dead. The scheme

                  should have worked, <in fact, it did

                  work,> --by every reason of geography

        264

                              Stevens (cont'd.)

          and psychology and the [past] two

          hundred years of this country's

          history. -- [in fact it did work.]

The Sheriff has come up the stairs and is walking toward

them across the cement corridor.

                              Stevens

          Except that once, --

                    (he looks at Chick)

          --a long time ago, and partly by chance --

                    (he looks back at Lucas)

          --a white boy fell into the creek on

          your property.

The Sheriff has reached the doorway of the jail.

                              Stevens

          Well, Sheriff?

MEDIUM CLOSE SHOT - THE SHERIFF

standing in the doorway. He has something wrapped in

tissue paper in his left hand.

                              Sheriff

          I don't know how you done with Lucas

          but we got something--(unfolding the

          tissue paper) -- out of Vinson Gowrie.

CLOSE SHOT - THE BULLET IN HIS HAND

                         Sheriff (o.s.)

          Lodged right up against the back of

387   Sheriff (cont'd.)

CONT'D   his breastbone. And fired out of

                          some kind of rifle.

388   MEDIUM SHOT - PAST LUCAS TOWARD STEVENS AND THE SHERIFF

                                    Stevens (turning back

                              to Lucas)

                          Who fired that rifle?

                                    Lucas

                          You fergit. I ain't seen no rifle.

                                    Stevens

                          But certainly you must know, -- or

                          suspect, -- or even guess --

                                    Lucas

                          Not pussonally. I don't wanter send

                          no man to jail I ain't seen pussonally.

                                    Stevens

                          Lucas. Why won't you trust me?

                                    Lucas (looking toward

                              the bullet) Ain't no need to.

                                    Stevens

                          Listen to me. It wasn't your pistol:

                          true. You didn't move that body down

                          to the creek: true. But try and

                          explain the truth to a mob who've been

                          waiting <all morning down there> [down

                          there all night] for something to kill!

                 266

                              Lucas

All right. I'll tell you how to

catch um. ⟨You git exactly the right

bait and exactly the right trap.⟩

[Put the right bait in the right trap.]

                           Stevens

How do you propose to do that?

                      Lucas (turning to

        the Sheriff)

⟨Let me git my hat and go home.⟩

[Gimme my hat and let me go home.]

                          Sheriff

We can't do that.

                          Stevens

Sure we can. (to Lucas) ⟨Go ahead.

You're free to go. (he walks toward

the doorway) On the strength of this

-- (indicates the bullet) -- I can get

you out in a couple of hours. But you

walk out of this jail and you won't be

alive more than ten minutes. And you'd

be lucky if it were less.⟩ [On the

strength of this, he's a free man now.

But you walk out of this jail and you

won't be alive ten minutes. And you'd

be lucky if it were less.]

389   MEDIUM CLOSE SHOT - THE SHERIFF

                    Stevens (o.s.)
          Shall I ask the Sheriff to get your
          hat?
                    Lucas (o.s.)
          And my pistol. [And my toothpick.]
     The Sheriff begins to pull the door shut.
                    Sheriff
          No. [Come on.] I think I got a better
          idea than that.
     <The CAMERA PULLS BACK as he closes the door of Lucas'
     cell and locks it shut.

                                   DISSOLVE TO:>

     [Close up on Lucas as the others leave. Dissolve to the
     exterior of the jail. The CAMERA PANS DOWN to a close-u
     of the keys to the jail in the Sheriff's hand. Dissolve
     from the keys to Crawford Gowrie's face.]

390   MEDIUM SHOT - PAST THE HEADS OF THE CROWD
     near the entrance of the jail. Crawford Gowrie is
     prominent among them, his back to the open doors,
     talking to a group of men. First Chick and then
     Stevens come through the hallway of the jail. Stevens
     turns back to Miss Habersham, whose feet and sewing
     basket are just visible.
                    Stevens
          <You won't have to wait much longer.

     268

                    Stevens

        We're going to settle this whole

        thing before dark.>

        [Well, you won't have to stay here

        much longer. We're gonna get this

        whole thing settled before dark.]

                    Miss Habersham (o.s.)

        Oh, I don't mind. I've had lots of

        company.

                    Stevens (crossing

            the porch)

        So I see.

Stevens and Chick go down the jail steps and across the

path disregarding Crawford Gowrie. He follows them.

CAMERA PANS to follow him as he overtakes them in the

street.

                    Crawford Gowrie

        Lawyer --! [Lawyer.]

MEDIUM SHOT - FROM ABOVE - CAMERA MOVING BACK BEFORE

THEM

As they cross the street, and then, pushing through the

crowd, go along the opposite sidewalk.

                    Crawford

        Lawyer [Lawyer] -- (keeping up with

            them) -- that's the second time

        you've been to see him.

                    Stevens (still walking,
                    pushing through as fast as he can)
Yes.

                    A Man in the Crowd
What you reckon you kin do for him,
Lawyer?

                    Another Man
That we can't do a lot better?

                    Stevens
Save his life.

                    Crawford Gowrie
<Lawyer, that's one thing you ain't
been paid enough to do.>
[You ain't been paid enough money to
do that, Lawyer.]

Stevens has reached the foot of the outside staircase
that leads to his office on the second floor.

                    Stevens
I've been paid nothing! There's some
things you don't do for money. I
intend to go up to my office and 'phone
the District Attorney and get him to
agree to release this man. Today. And
send him home. So he can finish his
planting.

MEDIUM SHOT - DOWN THE STAIRCASE

as Chick and Stevens go up. Gowrie and others of the
crowd are at the foot of the staircase.

>>>>>>>>>>>>>>>>>>>>>>>> Gowrie

Wait. -- So you taken the case and
are going to defend him? Talk for
him? Hope to get him out?

>>>>>>>>>>>>>>>>>>>>>>>> Stevens

Yes.

>>>>>>>>>>>>>>>>>>>>>>>> Gowrie

And you call yourself white folks? ✗ bigot

Stevens turns, close in the f.g. Gowrie is two or
three steps above the crowd that has followed him to the
lawyer's building.

>>>>>>>>>>>>>>>>>>>>>>>> Stevens

Mr. Gowrie --

>>>>>>>>>>>>>>>>>>>>>>>> Gowrie

My brother was killed by that nigger!

>>>>>>>>>>>>>>>>>>>>>>>> Stevens

Lucas Beauchamp is innocent.

>>>>>>>>>>>>>>>>>>>>>>>> Gowrie (gesturing to
>>>>>>>>>>>>>> the crowd)

Not in this court!

MEDIUM CLOSE SHOT - STEVENS

looking down, as Chick opens the office door behind him.

Scene 392.

MEDIUM CLOSE SHOT - GOWRIE

His face is set and rigid with anger.

MEDIUM SHOT - PAST GOWRIE

and the heads of the crowd in the f.g., up the staircase
toward Stevens at the top, halfway through the outer
door of his office.

> Stevens (furious)
>
> I've seen a piece of evidence -
> unearthed - that might convince even
> you.

He goes through the door and closes it.

MEDIUM SHOT - INTERIOR - DAY - STEVENS' OFFICE

as he enters, going toward Chick, already standing by
the window. CAMERA PANS with Stevens, moves in behind
him. The crowd below, including those that followed
him to the office, are clearly visible through the
lettered window.

> Chick
>
> They don't believe you.

> Stevens
>
> One of them does. The question is,
> which one?

> Chick
>
> He'll clear out of the county before
> you can --

396   Stevens

CONT'D   He might. But there's one thing he's

                     bound to do first.

397   MEDIUM CLOSE SHOT - STEVENS

                               Stevens

                     He was frantic last night, when he had

                     to dig out of his grave [the body of]

                     the man he shot, and carry him down

                     hill, and find a place to bury him

                     again. And all by himself, furiously,

                     in the dark. One man against the whole

                     weight of the earth: what a horror that

                     must have been! And now, today -- every

                     hour that's happened since Saturday noon

                     must be boiling together in his brain.

398   CLOSE TWO SHOT - STEVENS AND CHICK

                               Stevens

                     They don't know it out there, but he

                     does! He's lost. He's finished. He's

                     running through the last few pennies of

                     his freedom. And I reckon he's going to

                     spend them the only way he knows -- on

                     revenge -- (T 232)

                                           DISSOLVE TO:

399   MEDIUM LONG SHOT - EXTERIOR - DAY - A ROAD IN THE
         COUNTRY

99
ONT'D

The Sheriff's car comes TOWARD CAMERA, it PANS with him
as he goes by. As the CAMERA ANGLE MOVES to the right,
it reveals Lucas Beauchamp's cabin on its low hill.
The Sheriff's car pulls sharply off the road to the
right and comes to a stop behind a screen of underbrush
and trees.

16-48

00
MEDIUM SHOT - THE SHERIFF
leaves the car and emerges from the grove <walking>
[running] toward Lucas' house.

DISSOLVE TO:

01
MEDIUM SHOT - THE SHERIFF
climbs the porch, looks around him with slow, grim
caution, and begins to open the door. As usual, he is
unarmed.

2
FULL SHOT - INTERIOR FRONT ROOM OF LUCAS' CABIN
The Sheriff enters the front door, closes and bolts it.
CAMERA MOVES with him as he goes to the mantel, and
finding a spiral of paper, lights it with a match. His
back is now to the CAMERA and he kneels down in order
to start the fire in the hearth. <But suddenly he
pauses, without turning around, the paper burning in
his right hand.>
[Nub Gowrie's feet and legs are seen first as he
enters the door in the background. The Sheriff lights
the fire.]

Scene 402.

3   MEDIUM SHOT - THROUGH THE FRAME OF THE KITCHEN DOORWAY,

TOWARD THE SHERIFF

as he turns in that direction. In the f.g. is the

shoulder and the empty sleeve with its safety pin, of

Nub Gowrie. The Sheriff takes the bullet out of his

pocket, holds it out.

> Sheriff
>
> You don't carry a 30-30 rifle, do you
>
> Mr. Gowrie?

4   MEDIUM CLOSE SHOT - GOWRIE

He has the big nickel plated revolver in his one hand.

His clothes are stained with dust and sweat.

> Gowrie
>
> No.
>
> Sheriff (o.s.)
>
> Do you know anybody that does?
>
> Gowrie [eyes widen]
>
> Yes.
>
> [Sheriff
>
> Hm.]

7-48

5   MEDIUM SHOT - PAST NUB GOWRIE TOWARD THE SHERIFF

as Gowrie walks forward into the room, the Sheriff

deliberately turns his back again, thrusting what's

left of the burning spiral of paper under the sticks

of wood in the hearth. Gowrie walks to the front

window, looks out.

405   Sheriff

CONT'D   Sit down, Mr. Gowrie.

                                (Gowrie stares out of the window)

                        Don't sit down if you don't care to,

                        but at least get away from that window.

                                     Gowrie

                        You sent for me. You 'phoned me.

                        Said if I wanted to see who killed my

                        boy --

            He turns, still gripping the heavy revolver.

                                     Sheriff

                        He'll be here. Sooner or later.

                        Before the day's over, he'll come to

                        kill Lucas Beauchamp.

                                     Gowrie

                        I don't see Lucas Beauchamp neither.

            The Sheriff points to the fire, which is catching at

            last, with the crackling and hissing of new pine, of

            flame and smoke going up the chimney.

                                     Sheriff

                        Now you do.

406   MEDIUM SHOT - EXTERIOR - LUCAS' CABIN

            A twist of smoke rises from the chimney. The unpainted

            wood, the brick, the shingles, are sharply drawn in the

            sunlight.

                                                        DISSOLVE TO:

MEDIUM SHOT - INTERIOR FRONT ROOM - LUCAS' CABIN

The Sheriff has just lit the lamp and is lowering the
chimney, and now he lifts the lamp itself off the
mantel. Nub Gowrie is seated on the rocker, his gun
resting in his hand. He points before him with the gun.

Nub Gowrie

        That his wife?

MEDIUM SHOT BETWEEN THE TWO MEN - IN THE F.G. TOWARD
the double photograph of Lucas and his wife, in the
b.g. and illumined now by the light from the kerosene
lamp.

                          Sheriff

        Was his wife -- she's dead. Two
        years now, maybe three.

                          Nub Gowrie

        Mine been gone <twenty-two> [twenty-five]
        years. The day the twins was born.

                          Sheriff

        Raising all them boys by yourself is
        hard.

                          Gowrie

        Hard. (he looks down at the hand
              holding the gun)
        Hard. (he opens his hand, spreading
              out the fingers and letting the
              gun rest in his palm)
        Five boys.

Scene 407.

MEDIUM SHOT - PAST THE PHOTOGRAPH

on the easel, in the f.g. toward the Sheriff and toward

Gowrie as the Sheriff lifts the lamp to look at the

picture more clearly. Beyond and between them, the front

window seems to smash open. There's a report and then

the echoes of a rifle outdoors. The Sheriff has almost

automatically squatted down to the floor. He sets the

lamp down. [The picture falls to the floor. The

Sheriff blows out the lamp.]

                    Sheriff

        That wasn't shot with no 41 Colt.

Nub Gowrie is getting out of his chair slowly and

turning toward the door.

                    Man's Voice Outside (so

                    hoarse, so furious, it's hard

                    to recognize)

        Come on out here, you running black

        nigger!

The Sheriff stands up, starts to walk forward slowly

toward the door.

                    Nub Gowrie

        [Wait a minute.] Git out of the way.

                    Sheriff

        You'll need help.

                    Nub Gowrie

        I don't want no help. I'll do it myself.

410   MEDIUM CLOSE SHOT - THE SHERIFF

411   MEDIUM CLOSE SHOT - NUB GOWRIE

412   MEDIUM CLOSE SHOT - EXTERIOR DOORWAY FROM THE PORCH

          OUTSIDE

          as Nub Gowrie opens the door.   The CAMERA SLOWLY MOVES

          BACK before him as he crosses the porch, descends the

          steps and walks through the dust of the front yard.

          Then Nub Gowrie stops and the CAMERA STOPS too.

                              Man's Voice

                    Pa, you got no business here.

          Nub Gowrie comes forward another step.   The barrel of a

          rifle is lowered into the f.g.

413   MEDIUM SHOT - PAST NUB GOWRIE

          To the man with the rifle: his son Crawford.

          [Crawford springs up from behind stump.]

414   MEDIUM CLOSE SHOT - CRAWFORD GOWRIE

          The mouth of the rifle pointing straight at CAMERA,

          <so close it's almost out of focus.>

                              Crawford Gowrie

                    Pa, git out of the way.

415   MEDIUM SHOT - PAST CRAWFORD GOWRIE

          to his father.

                              Nub Gowrie

                    Put down that gun.

          Crawford doesn't move.   His father lifts up his one

          hand and grasps the barrel of the rifle.

16   CLOSE SHOT - NUB GOWRIE'S SINGLE GRIP

on the barrel of the rifle.

17   MEDIUM TWO SHOT - PAST NUB GOWRIE TO HIS SON

Nub Gowrie

Is this the gun --

(he pulls away the rifle. It is

easy: Crawford no longer has the

force to resist)

--killed your brother Vinson?

18   CLOSE SHOT - CRAWFORD GOWRIE

sweat stands on his face. He is silent. This sweat

and silence are his confession.

19   MEDIUM LONG SHOT -- PAST SHERIFF ON THE PORCH

in the immediate f.g., toward Nub Gowrie and his son

Crawford. Nub Gowrie, with a gesture almost of disgust

and loathing, pitches the rifle away from him into the

dust of the yard. The Sheriff walks down the steps

toward them.

20   MEDIUM THREE SHOT

as the Sheriff reaches the two Gowries and the old man

lifts his son's hands one by one to be clamped in

handcuffs.

DISSOLVE TO:

21   LONG SHOT - HIGH ANGLE - EXTERIOR DUSK -- THE COURTHOUSE
AND SQUARE

SOUND of the Sheriff's siren approaching. The open

Scene 420.

284

1   streets are still crowded with vehicles and faces.
NT'D   The Sheriff's car, entering the end of the Square, cuts

       diagonally through the crowd as fast as possible.

2   ⟨MEDIUM LONG SHOT - FROM INSIDE THE LIGHTED ENTRANCE

       TO THE JAIL

       Miss Habersham, seated in the f.g., her hands folded,

       gets up and goes to the open door. The Sheriff's car

       is coming straight for the jail, siren whining.⟩

3   MEDIUM SHOT - INTERIOR STEVENS' OFFICE

       Chick dozing in a leather chair, while Stevens, in the

       f.g., consults his watch. He turns at the SOUND of the

       Sheriff's car, but Chick hears the siren too and leaps

       up out of his chair and runs to open the door. The

       CAMERA FOLLOWS AFTER THEM as they look down from the

       top of the outside landing. Except for the siren, the

       Square gradually falls silent.

4   MEDIUM SHOT

       as the Sheriff arrives in front of the jail, opening

       the door of the car and leading the way for Crawford

       Gowrie, handcuffed and followed by his father. CAMERA

       PANS WITH THEM, PAST the heads of people clustered in

       the front yard of the jail. As they mount the porch

       steps, the Sheriff turns halfway around and then stops.

5   MEDIUM CLOSE TWO SHOT - STEVENS AND CHICK

       looking down from the landing outside Stevens' office.

425   <Chick

CONT'D   Look -- !

                          Stevens

                Yes. (indicating crowd) What will

                they do?>

426   MEDIUM CLOSE THREE SHOT - THE SHERIFF AND NUB GOWRIE

        looking down from the porch, Crawford Gowrie with his

        back to the crowd and the CAMERA. The Sheriff slowly

        surveys the Square.

                          [Man

                Is he the one, Sheriff?]

                          Sheriff

                That's right. He's the one.--

427   MEDIUM LONG SHOT - CAMERA PANS

        over the crowd. Now that it's nearly evening, it seems

        darker than ever, swollen by people who had been at

        work all day. Their faces are partly illumined by the

        lights in all the shop windows. It is not quite dark

        enough yet for the street lights. The faces are

        entirely silent, watching the Sheriff's drama on the

        porch.

428   CLOSE SHOT - SHERIFF

                          Sheriff

                The man that killed his brother.

429   MEDIUM CLOSE TWO SHOT - THE SHERIFF IN THE F.G.

        Crawford Gowrie with his back to the Square.

Scene 426.

429   Sheriff

CONT'D   Ask him!

He takes hold of Crawford's shoulder in his heavy grip.

                    [Man

        Is that right, Nub?

                 Nub (facing the crowd)

       That's right. He killed him.]

430   LONG SHOT - PAST THE SHERIFF - PAST CRAWFORD

who is facing the CAMERA, and toward the packed Square.

In the f.g., group by group, the crowd seems to melt

and flow away, going back quietly, without a word to

the Sheriff or to one another, toward their parked

cars. Headlights go on all over the Square, there's

the whine of vehicles turning over and starting and

then their roar as they begin to pull out. The crowd,

with a wordless gnashing of gears, abolishes itself

<as the Sheriff waits.>

[The CAMERA SHOOTS DOWN on the Square filled with cars

and with people getting into buses.]

431*   MEDIUM LONG SHOT - PAST CHICK AND STEVENS

on the outside landing down toward the Square, as the

crowd disappears.

                      Chick

      They're running away.

---

    *The dialogue in shot 431 is a simplified version of the
long discussion about the mob's running in the text, pp. 190-204.

Scene 430.

                              Stevens

It's more than that.

                              Chick

No. That's all. There's nothing
left for them to do but admit they're
wrong. So they're running away.

                              Stevens

It's worse than that.

                              Chick

Then they're running from Lucas
Beauchamp.

                              Stevens

No.

                              Chick

Yes! -- they won't even wait to buy
him a can of tobacco. To show they
forgive him for all the trouble he
caused.

                              Stevens

Then <why should they> [what's their
hurry? They know they've got the rest
of their lives to do that.

                              Chick

From Crawford then. So they won't
have to burn him. They're running
away from Crawford.

                    Stevens

        Not from Lucas and not from Crawford.

                    Chick

        They're running: you can't change

        that.

                    Stevens

        No. I can't change that -- They're

        running away from themselves.

Stevens turns toward the completely empty Square. A

pick-up truck drives briskly from the direction of the

jail and turns the corner in the street below Stevens'

office. It's driven by Miss Habersham, her hat still

fixed firmly on top of her head. She waves a prim hand

to them as she goes by, slowing down.

                    Stevens

        [Hi ya, Miss] Eunice! -- What's the

        hurry?

2   MEDIUM CLOSE SHOT - MISS HABERSHAM

at the wheel of her car. CAMERA PANS with her as she

goes by, more slowly now.

                    Miss Habersham

        I've got to get home to my chickens.

        But -- (looking back and up at Chick

                and Stevens)

        --if you ever get into trouble again

        -- let me know.

433   MEDIUM CLOSE SHOT - CHICK AND STEVENS

12-16-48

                         Stevens

You see? (turns to Chick with just

         the beginning of a smile)

We were in trouble, not Lucas Beauchamp.

Chick turns away from the Square, now entirely empty,

with a gesture of anger and disgust.

                         Stevens

It's all right, Chick.

                         Chick

Is it?

                         Stevens

It will be all right.

434   MEDIUM LONG SHOT - PAST CHICK AND STEVENS

TOWARD the empty Square. Miss Habersham's pick-up

truck can still be seen or heard as it leaves the

Square.

                         Stevens (to Chick)

So long as some of us -- you, and

Miss Eunice Habersham, and Aleck,

and maybe me, -- or even so long as

one of us -- some one of us --

doesn't run away.

                                     DISSOLVE T

435   FULL SHOT - SAME CAMERA POSITION - EARLY SATURDAY

AFTERNOON

Scene 435.

435   bright sunlight. Scores of radios are blasting out
CONT'D the cheerful Saturday afternoon programs. The Square is

        jammed with people, animals, cars, trucks, and all in

        motion. Only today over half the faces are Negro. In

        the f.g., leaning on the rail of the porch is Chick

        looking down toward the crowd. Chick recognizes

        something in the movement down below and he goes back

        through the screen door to his uncle's office.

436*   FULL SHOT - INTERIOR - STEVENS' LAW OFFICE
        as Chick comes in the door from the gallery.

                         Chick
             Uncle John --

                         Stevens (o.s.)
             Chick. It's a fine Saturday afternoon.
             Why don't you go to the ball game?

                         Chick
             <He's coming here.>
             [Lucas is coming here.]

                         Stevens
             Well! --

437   MEDIUM CLOSE SHOT - STEVENS AT HIS DESK
                         Stevens (closing a law
                    book with finality)
             Oh, he's a gentleman. He won't remind

        ───────────────────────────────────

             *The dialogue from this point to shot 444 is nearly
        identical to the text, pp. 240-247.

                    Stevens (cont'd.)

        me to my face that I was wrong.

FULL SHOT - CHICK - STEVENS - AND INCLUDING THE CLOSED

DOOR

leading to the outside staircase. There's a double

knock.

                    Stevens

        Come in, Lucas.

Lucas enters, closing the door carefully behind him.

He is dressed as before: coat, waistcoat, pale hat,

watch chain, toothpick. His left coat pocket has the

old suspicious bulge.

                    Lucas

        <Gentle-men.>

        [Well, young man, you ain't fell in

        no more creeks lately, has you?

                    Chick

        I'm waiting till you get some ice

        on yours.

                    Lucas

        You're welcome whether it's frozen

        or not.]

                    Stevens

        Have a seat   [Lucas.]

Instead of sitting down, Lucas puts his hat on the

straight chair near the door, takes his gold toothpick

438   out of his mouth and restores it to his waistcoat
CONT'D   pocket. He walks toward the desk.

                              Lucas
                  I believe you got a little bill
                  against me.

439   MEDIUM THREE SHOT - STEVENS - LUCAS AND CHICK
                              Stevens
                  Not me. I didn't do anything. That
                  boy there is the reason you're
                  walking around today.
                              Lucas
                  All right. I'll pay him.
                              Stevens
                  You can't. He'd be practicing law
                  without a license.
                              Lucas
                  <All right.> [Well, I'll --]   (he
                          takes out a worn purse with an
                          old-fashioned snap)
                  I'll pay your expenses then.
                              Stevens
                  The only expense I had -- (waving his
                          <fountain pen> [pipe] at him)
                  --was getting this fixed.
                              Lucas
                  How much?

          296

                          Stevens

                    Two dollars.

MEDIUM CLOSE SHOT - LUCAS

as he opens the purse, extracts a rolled crumpled one

dollar bill and a number of silver coins.

                          Lucas

      <Well, I'm a farming man and you're

      a lawing man and I don't reckon I

      can learn you anything. -->

      [Two dollars? That don't seem like

      much to me. But I'm a farming man

      and you're a lawing man. I don't

      reckon it's my business to try to

      learn you yours.]

He spreads the money on the desk before Stevens.

<Stevens' fountain pen points to the money.>

                     Stevens (o.s.)

      <Wait now.> That ain't but one dollar

      and four bits.

                          Lucas

      Nemmine that.

He puts his hand into the bulge of his left coat pocket,

extracts the 41 Colt, puts it on the desk, then fishes

in his pocket again to bring out a soiled tobacco pouch,

which he puts down on the desk with a solid clink.

                                              297

440   Lucas (putting the

CONT'D   pistol back in his pocket)

That makes it out. Four bits in

pennies. I was aiming to take them

to the bank but you can save me the

trouble.

441   MEDIUM CLOSE TWO SHOT - LUCAS AND STEVENS

Lucas (opening the

neck of the tobacco pouch)

You wanter count um?

12-17-48   Stevens (almost irritably)

Yes. But you're paying. You count

them.

Lucas (spilling out

the pennies)

It's fifty of um.

Stevens

This is business.

Lucas begins to count them out in groups of five,

murmuring the numbers under his breath.

[Lucas

Five --]

Stevens

⟨Lucas,⟩ as long as you're paying

your debts, go and see Miss Habersham.

298

Lucas (while he's

counting) [Fifteen, twenty.]

I ain't much of a visiting man.

Stevens

<Well then, take her some flowers.>

[You could bring her some flowers.]

Lucas

[Twenty-five, thirty.] I ain't had no

flowers to speak of since Molly died.

Stevens

<I'll call Chick's mother and she'll

cut you some out of her garden.>

[Chick's mother will cut you some out

of the garden. You owe her that much,

Lucas.]

Lucas hesitates a moment as he counts.

[Lucas

Thirty-five.]

Stevens

<Chick can take you out there in my

car. --She's the only lady in this

county, as far as the records go, --

that ever guarded a jail.>

[She's the only lady anywhere that

ever held a jail with a twenty-gauge

spool of thread.]

441   Lucas

CONT'D   <Well, if won't nothing else

                            sattersfy you.>

                            [Fifty. All right. If there ain't

                            nothing else'll satisfy her.]

                                    (CAMERA PANS with him as he

                                    gets his hat) <(to Chick)

                            You ain't fell in no more creeks

                            lately, have you?

                                          Chick

                            I'm waiting till you get some ice

                            on yours.

                                          Lucas

                            You'll be welcome without waiting

                            for a freeze.>

                Then, CAMERA PANNING BACK with him, he returns and

                stands before Stevens' desk.

                                          [Stevens

                            Just one thing more - why didn't

                            you tell me the truth? That night

                            in jail?

                                          Lucas

                            Would you have believed me?]

442   MEDIUM CLOSE SHOT - STEVENS [LOOKING DISGRUNTLED]

                He opens his drawer, sweeps the money into it, shuts

                it, <looks up at Lucas.> [puts his pipe into his

                300

mouth, picks up a book and begins to read.   Lucas
stands waiting.]

>   Stevens (angrily)

     Now what?   What are you waiting for

     now?

CLOSE SHOT - LUCAS

                     Lucas

     My receipt.

CAMERA BEGINS TO MOVE AWAY INCLUDING Chick and then
Stevens as Stevens gets out a receipt pad and begins to
write.

                                    DISSOLVE TO:

FULL SHOT - EXTERIOR - SQUARE

TOWARD the outer staircase down from Stevens' office as

-48   Lucas, waving the receipt to dry the ink, descends to

the level of the Square and makes his way through the

movement of the crowd.

MEDIUM LONG SHOT - PAST CHICK AND STEVENS

in the f.g., looking down from the railing of the upper

gallery, watching Lucas as he goes away, through the

crowded, seething Square.   Lucas' pale felt hat is lost

among the heads and faces of an ordinary Saturday

afternoon.

                     Chick

     They don't see him.   As though   it

     never happened.

Scene 445.

445   Stevens

CONT'D   They see him.

                            Chick

                No. They don't even know he's

                there.

                            Stevens

                They do. The same as I do. They

                always will. As long as he lives.

446   MEDIUM CLOSE TWO SHOT - CHICK AND STEVENS

                            Stevens

                Proud, stubborn, -- insufferable:

                but there he goes: the keeper of

                my conscience, --

                    <(Stevens has been looking down

                    toward the crowd but now he

                    looks up, INTO CAMERA, as if

                    toward the invisible audience)

                --our conscience.>

                            [Chick

                Our conscience, Uncle John.]

                            THE END

CAST OF CHARACTERS

John Gavin Stevens	David Brian
Chick Mallison	Claude Jarman, Jr.
Lucas Beauchamp	Juano Hernandez
Nub Gowrie	Porter Hall
Miss Habersham	Elizabeth Patterson
Crawford Gowrie	Charles Kemper
Sheriff Hampton	Will Geer
Vinson Gowrie	David Clarke
Aleck	Elzie Emanuel
Mrs. Mallison	Lela Bliss
Mr. Mallison	Harry Hayden
Mr. Tubbs	Harry Antrim

MUSIC REPORT

REEL 1
1. Anniversary Fanfare #2   Miklos Rozsa
2. Main Title   Adolph Deutsch, ASCAP
3. Chimes
4. The Morning Light Is Breaking   G.J. Webb; S.F. Smith

REELS 2, 3, 4, 5, 6
Nothing

REEL 7
5. Running Wild   Gibbs *et al.*
6. Raucous Ruckus   Deutsch
7. Hoe Down—Improvisation
8. Raucous Ruckus   Deutsch

REEL 8
9. Down in the Valley   Unknown
10. Doin' Away Train   Deutsch
11. Careless Love   Unknown

REEL 9
12. Tiger Rag   Original Dixieland
    Jazz Band
13. Raucous Ruckus   Deutsch
14. Hand Me Down My Walking
    Cane—Revised   Arr. Deutsch
15. Raucous Ruckus   Deutsch
16. End Title & Cast   Deutsch

Appendixes

APPENDIX A

APPENDIX B

PAGES FROM CONTINUITY SCRIPT

NO	FEET	FRAMES	DESCRIPTION	REEL 3 PAGE 14

40B - continued

                    Sheriff

Here? Huh? What sand?

                    Chick

Right there by the bridge. My horse wouldn'

    526   3   cross last night.

41B   CU - Stevens - Nub at left behind him - Twin

in b.g. - Stevens speaks - Nub reacts -

                    Stevens

Quicksand.

                    Nub

No, lawyer. Put a man in quicksand? My boy

    535   15   in quicksand? A man'd do a thing like that

would --

42B   LS - Convicts, Chick, Sheriff, Nub, Stevens,

    540   0   Twins, and dogs - Nub looks around - starts

to b.g. -

43B   LS - Nub, Twins, Sheriff, Chick, Stevens,

convicts, and dogs - CAMERA PANS right as

Nub runs towards rbg - exits rbg - others

    557   14   re-enter left, following him -

REEL 3 PAGE 14

310

FEET	FRAMES	DESCRIPTION	REEL 3 PAGE 15

	FEET	FRAMES	DESCRIPTION
4B			MLS - Nub runs in left - CAMERA PANS right with him - he runs up onto road - runs onto
	574	4	bridge in b.g. - stops and looks over railing -
5B			MLS - Chick, Stevens, and Sheriff running to
	577	10	right as CAMERA PANS right - Chick runs up onto road -
6B			ELS - Nub on right side of bridge - he turns
	583	14	and runs to opposite side - looks over railing -
7B			LS - Chick, Stevens, and Sheriff running up onto road and towards rbg - Twins, convicts, and dogs run in left and f.g. and follow -
	588	2	CAMERA PANS right - Nub seen on bridge at rbg -
8B			MCS - Nub standing by railing - he starts to
	590	0	jump over -
9B			MLS - Nub jumps over railing - Stevens, Chick, Sheriff, Twins, and convicts in b.g. running forward - CAMERA PANS down with Nub
	592	3	as he lands in quicksand under bridge -

50B   MLS - Stevens, Chick, Sheriff, Twins, and

                             convicts running forward - they look down

     595   9   over railing to right -

51B   MS - Shooting down on Nub in quicksand - he

     598   11   thrusts his hands down into quicksand and

                             feels around -

52B   MCS - Sheriff, Stevens, Chick, Twins, and

                             convicts looking down over railing to right -

                             Stevens climbs over railing - reaches down

                             o.s. and speaks -

                                           Stevens

     603   10   Nub, give me your hand.

53B   MS - Shooting down on Nub feeling around in

                             quicksand -

                                           Stevens o.s.

     605   12   Nub!

54B   MCS - Sheriff enters right and speaks -

                             CAMERA PANS left and down as he goes to end

                             of bridge - starts to climb down bank -

                                           Sheriff

                             Get the rope off the hound dogs. You! Cut

     613   3   some branches, poles, grapevines, anything.

3

                          MCS - Twins and dogs as Twins take ropes off

                          of dogs - raise up o.s. -

                                     Sheriff o.s.

616   4   Get him out of there. Hurry up here.

3

                          LS - Sheriff on bank at left - Nub at right

                          in quicksand - Chick, Stevens, and Twins on

                          bridge - Sheriff speaks as others come down

                          bank to him - all ad lib -

                                     Sheriff

Look out, boys. Watch it, boys.

                                     Stevens

Don't get too close now.

                                     Sheriff

Don't get in here till we get some branches.

Come on, boys.

                                     Stevens

626   1   Hurry up with that brush.

3

                          MCS - Convict with armload of branches - he

                          exits left -

                                   Stevens o.s.

628   3   Come on. Let's go. Bring those poles down

                          here.

58B   LS - Stevens, Twin, Chick, Sheriff, and Nub -

                           Sheriff holds his hand out to Nub and speaks -

                                        Sheriff

        631   5   Give me your hand, Nub.

59B   MCS - Nub reacts and speaks -

                                        Nub

        638   4   Here. I've found him. I'm standin' on him.

60B   LS - Stevens, Twin, Chick, Sheriff, and Nub -

                           Sheriff speaks - tosses end of rope to Nub -

                           convicts hurry in right on bridge with poles

                           and branches - hand them to others - they put

                           branches on top of quicksand -

                                        Sheriff

        651   2   Here you are, Nub.

61B   MCS - Nub hanging onto rope - he is pulled

        654   2   from o.s. left -

62B   655   13   MCS - Dogs on bridge barking -

63B   CS - Sheriff and Chick - Sheriff pulling on

                           rope - Chick leans o.s. right - Sheriff

                           speaks - takes pole from o.s. left -

                                        Sheriff

        659   9   Here, hurry along, fellows. Give me the pole.

MS - Twin pulls long branches down from tree -

664   9   hurries forward and o.s. rfg -

LS - Nub, Stevens, Sheriff, Chick, Twins, and

convicts - convict hands poles down to

Stevens and one Twin - Sheriff walks across

branches towards Nub -

                         Sheriff

670   1   Where are those.....

MS - Convicts enter left with grapevines -

lower them over railing - CAMERA PANS down to

Nub - Sheriff and Stevens partially seen at

left - Sheriff pulls grapevines down to Nub -

he loops them under his arms - takes hold of

branch - he is pulled up from o.s. -

                         Sheriff

.....grapevines? Here you are, Nub. All

685   0   right. Go on - pull. Pull.

MS - Stevens, Twin, Chick, and Sheriff -

other Twin at lbg - all pull -

                         Sheriff

688   11   Take it easy, boys. There now.

MS - Convicts on bridge leaning over railing -

they pull up on grapevines -

NO	FEET	FRAMES	DESCRIPTION	REEL 3 PAGE 20

Sheriff

691 4   Pull.

69B   LS - Twins, Stevens, Chick, Sheriff, and

convicts pulling Nub from quicksand -

Sheriff

696 7   Easy, boys.

70B 699 0   MCS - Dogs on bridge barking -

71B   LS - Twins, Stevens, Chick, Sheriff, and

convicts pulling Nub from quicksand -

Sheriff

703 3   That's it. There.

72B 706 7   MCS - Dogs barking -

73B   MS - Stevens and Sheriff lifting Nub from

quicksand - Chick and Twins at left - CAMERA

PANS left as they bring Nub up onto bank -

convicts partially seen in b.g. - Nub speaks -

Sheriff

That's it, boys. Easy. Ah. There we are.

Nub

My boy. Get my boy out of there.

LAP DISSOLVE TO:

74B   CS - Vinson's body being pulled from quick-

sand - CAMERA PANS up - Chick leans down

into scene at left - Stevens, Sheriff, and

Twins partially seen - PAN left as they

carry Vinson's body to left and put it down

on ground -

     Sheriff o.s.

All right, boys, pull. Pull now. Pull.

Easy, boys. Right over here, boys. Here.

There we are. Put him right here. There we

758 6 are. That's Vinson, all right.

B   CS - Nub kneels down beside Vinson's body,

seen in f.g. - he reacts - others partially

seen - dogs howl o.s. - Nub wipes off

Vinson's face with end of his shirt -

     Chick o.s.

778 9 Gee, Uncle John,.....

B   CS - Chick and Stevens - convicts in b.g. -

Chick speaks -

     Chick

.....let's get him away from the road -- at

least, get him back in the woods where they

won't see him.

317

                              Stevens

                    Steady. They've all passed by now, anway.

                    They're all in town by now.

       791   12   FINISH

77B   END OF PART THREE -

REEL 3 PAGE 22*   V.B.

APPENDIX C

Page of the Director's Shooting Script

12-14-48 P.52

MED. SHOT - INSIDE THE SANDER CABIN   182

looking toward the yard, Paralee and Aleck
outlined against the shuttered window.

                        Aleck
It's Chick. *With laugh busy*

                        Paralee
Leave him be.

MED. LONG SHOT - THE SOFT PASTURE ROAD   183

leading from the stables, alongside the house,
toward the pastured gate that opens into the
country road. Chick struggles with Highboy,
still rearing and snorting.

alie leaves the window goes to door —

MED. SHOT - ALECK AND PARALEE - INSIDE THEIR   184
BOLTED CABIN

toward the moonlit window, looking into the
yard. We hear the whinny and commotion of
Highboy outside. Aleck opens the door of the
cabin, stands half-way into the moonlight.

It's Chick with Highboy.

                        Paralee
Go 'head - go 'head if you want to! - That Lucas
think he so smart. What he have to go and do a
thing like that? - Go 'head, go on, do just what
you want to do --

                        Aleck
I ain't going nowheres. Least, not very far.

MED. SHOT - CHICK, STRUGGLING WITH THE HORSE   185

NEAR He's more than halfway down the pasture road,
toward the gate. Beyond him, a library window upstairs, projecting oblong of light
across the pale road and the dark foliage
on either side. On the other side of Highboy,
a dark face emerging out of darkness, appears
Aleck, soothing, quieting, murmuring to the
horse. Now they both begin to tighten the
girth-straps.

319

CLARENCE BROWN
FILMOGRAPHY

THE FOLLOWING FILMOGRAPHY lists in chronological order the films directed by Clarence Brown. The dates following the titles of the films are taken from the volumes published by the Copyright Office of the Library of Congress and represent the date of film publication. It has been necessary to limit the information to the names of the production companies, the producers, the writers, and the players. In the case of the latter, only the leading actors are listed, with the exception of films in which extremely well-known players appear in supporting roles.

Clarence Brown first used sound in two of the eleven reels of *Wonder of Women* (5 Sept. 1929). After that date, all of his films employed sound. Except when noted, the films were shot in black and white.

In addition to directing fifty complete films and one of the six parts of *It's a Big Country* (16 Nov. 1951), Brown produced two films: *The Secret Garden* (1949), directed by Fred M. Wilcox, and *Never Let Me Go* (1953), directed by Delmer Daves. He also received writing credit for *The Light in the Dark* (1922), and was listed as an actor in *The Signal Tower* (1924).

The following abbreviations and symbols have been used:

sp	screenplay
adpt	adaptation
titl	titles
dia	dialogue
b/o	based on
( )	doubtful credit

1. *The Great Redeemer*, Metro, 11 Sept. 1920; Producer: Maurice Tourneur; Writers: sp, Jules Furthman, John Gilbert; b/o story by H.H. Van Loan; Players: House Peters, Marjorie Daw, Joseph Singleton.
2. *The Last of the Mohicans*, Associated Producers, 16 Nov. 1920; co-directed with Maurice Tourneur; Producer: Maurice Tourneur (Clarence Brown); Writers: sp, Robert A. Dillon; b/o novel by James Fenimore Cooper; Players: Wallace Beery, Albert Roscoe, Barbara Bedford.
3. *Foolish Matrons*, Associated Producers, 7 June 1921; co-directed with Maurice Tourneur; Producer: Maurice Tourneur; Writers: sp, Wyndham Gittens; b/o novel by Brian Oswald Donn-Byrne; Players: Hobart Bosworth, Doris May, Mildred Manning.
4. *The Light in the Dark*, Assoc. First Nat., 28 Aug. 1922, tinted film; Producer: Joseph M. Schenck; Writers: sp, W.D. Pelley, Clarence

Brown; b/o story by William Dudley Pelley; Players: Hope Hampton, Lon Chaney, E.K. Lincoln.

5. *Don't Marry for Money*, Weber & North Productions, 30 Aug. 1923; Producer: B.P. Fineman; Writers: story by Hope Loring/Louis D. Lighton; Players: House Peters, Rubye de Remer, Aileen Pringle.

6. *The Acquittal*, Universal, 30 Oct. 1923; Producer: Carl Laemmle; Writers: sp, Jules Furthman; adpt, Raymond L. Schrock; b/o play by Rita Weiner; Players: Norman Kerry, Claire Windsor, Richard Travers.

7. *The Signal Tower*, Universal, 29 Apr. 1924; Producer: Carl Laemmle; Writers: sp, James O. Spearing; b/o story by Wadsworth Camp; Players: Virginia Valli, Rockliffe Fellowes, Wallace Beery.

8. *Butterfly*, Universal, 12 Aug. 1924; Producer: Carl Laemmle; Writers: sp, Olga Printzlau; b/o novel by Kathleen Norris; Players: Laura La Plante, Ruth Clifford, Norman Kerry.

9. *Smouldering Fires*, Universal, 25 Nov. 1924; Producer: Carl Laemmle; Writers: sp, Sada Cowan, Howard Higgin, Melville Brown; titl, Dwinelle Benthall; b/o story by Margret Deland, Sada Cowan, Howard Higgin; Players: Pauline Frederick, Laura La Plante, Malcolm MacGregor.

10. *The Goose Woman*, Universal, 18 July 1925; Producer: Carl Laemmle; Writers: sp, Melville Brown; titl, Dwinelle Benthall; b/o story by Rex Beach; Players: Louise Dresser, Jack Pickford, Constance Bennett.

11. *The Eagle*, Art Finance Corp./United Artists, 16 Nov. 1925; Producers: John W. Considine, Jr./Clarence Brown; Writers: sp, Hans Kraely; titl, George Marion, Jr.; b/o story "Dubrovsky" by Alexander Pushkin; Players: Rudolph Valentino, Vilma Banky, Louise Dresser.

12. *Kiki*, First National, 26 Mar. 1926; Producer: Joseph M. Schenck; Writers: sp, Hans Kraely; titl, George Marion, Jr.; b/o play by Andre Picard, David Belasco; Players: Norma Talmadge, Ronald Colman, Gertrude Astor.

13. *Flesh and the Devil*, MGM, 10 Jan. 1927; Producer: Clarence Brown; Writers: sp, Benjamin F. Glazer; titl, Marian Ainslee; b/o novel *The Undying Past* by Hermann Sudermann; Players: John Gilbert, Greta Garbo, Lars Hanson.

14. *A Woman of Affairs*, MGM, 10 Dec. 1928; Producer: Irving Thalberg; Writers: sp, Bess Meredyth; titl, Marian Ainslee, Ruth Cummings; b/o novel *The Green Hat* by Michael Arlen; Players: Greta Garbo, John Gilbert, Lewis Stone.

15. *The Trail of '98*, MGM, 29 July 1929; Producers: Irving Thalberg/Clarence Brown; Writers: sp, Benjamin Glazer, Walderman Young; titl, Joe Farnham; adpt, Benjamin Glazer; b/o novel by Robert W. Service; Players: Delores Del Rio, Ralph Forbes, Harry Carey.

16. *Wonder of Women*, MGM, 5 Sept. 1929; Producer: Clarence Brown; Writers: sp, Bess Meredith; titl, Marian Ainslee; b/o novel by Hermann Sudermann, "The Wife of Stephen Trumholt"; Players: Lewis Stone, Leila Hyams, Peggy Wood.

17. *Navy Blues*, MGM, 2 Jan. 1930; Producer: Clarence Brown; Writers: dia, J.C. Nugent, Elliott Nugent, W.L. River; adpt, Dale Van Every;

b/o story by Raymond L. Schrock; Players: William Haines, Anita Page, Karl Dane.

18. *Anna Christie*, MGM, 10 Feb. 1930, lavender; Producer: Clarence Brown; Writers: adpt, Frances Marion; titl, Madeleine Ruthven; b/o play by Eugene O'Neill; Players: Greta Garbo, Charles Bickford, George F. Marion, Marie Dressler.

19. *Romance*, MGM, 28 July 1930; Producer: Paul Bern; Writers: sp, Bess Meredyth, Edwin Justus Mayer; b/o play by Edward Sheldon; Players: Greta Garbo, Lewis Stone, Gavin Gordon, Elliott Nugent.

20. *Inspiration*, MGM, 9 Feb. 1931; Producer: Clarence Brown; Writers: sp, Gene Markey; b/o novel *Sapho* by Alphonse Daudet; Players: Greta Garbo, Robert Montgomery, Lewis Stone, Marjorie Rambeau.

21. *A Free Soul*, MGM, 3 June 1931; Producer: Clarence Brown; Writers: sp, John Meehan; adpt, Becky Gardiner; b/o play by Willard Mack and novel by Adela Rogers St. John; Players: Clark Gable, Norma Shearer, Leslie Howard, Lionel Barrymore.

22. *Possessed*, MGM, 27 Nov. 1931; Producer: Clarence Brown; Writers: sp, Lenore Coffee; b/o play *The Mirage* by Edgar Selwyn; Players: Joan Crawford, Clark Gable, Wallace Ford.

23. *Emma*, MGM, 18 Jan. 1932; Producer: Clarence Brown; Writers: sp, Leonard Praskins, Zelda Sears; b/o story by Frances Marion; Players: Marie Dressler, Richard Cromwell, Jean Hersholt, Myrna Loy.

24. *Letty Lynton*, MGM, 6 May 1932; Producer: Clarence Brown; Writers: sp, John Meehan, Wanda Tuchock; b/o novel by Marie Belloc Lowndes; Players: Joan Crawford, Robert Montgomery, Nils Aster, Lewis Stone, May Robson.

25. *The Son-Daughter*, MGM, 29 Dec. 1932; Producer: A (Albert?) Lewin; Writers: sp, John Goodrich, Claudine West; dia, Leon Gordon; b/o play by George M. Scarborough and David Belasco; Players: Helen Hayes, Raymond Novarro, Lewis Stone, Warner Oland.

26. *Looking Forward*, MGM, 10 Apr. 1933; Producer: Clarence Brown; Writers: sp, Bess Meredyth; b/o play *Service* by C.L. Anthony [pseud. of Dorothy Gladys Smith]; Players: Lionel Barrymore, Lewis Stone, Benita Hume.

27. *Night Flight*, MGM, 2 Oct. 1933; Producer: David O. Selznick; Writers: sp, Oliver H.P. Garrett; b/o novel by Antoine de Saint Exupéry; Players: John Barrymore, Lionel Barrymore, Clark Gable, Robert Montgomery, Helen Hayes, Myrna Loy.

28. *Sadie McKee*, MGM, 9 May 1934; Producer: Lawrence Weingarten; Writers: sp, John Meehan; b/o story by Vina Delmar; Players: Joan Crawford, Gene Reynolds, Franchot Tone, Edward Arnold.

29. *Chained*, MGM, 1 Sept. 1934; Producer: Hunt Stromberg; Writers: sp, John Lee Mahin; b/o story by Edgar Selwyn; Players: Joan Crawford, Clark Gable, Otto Kruger.

30. *Ah, Wilderness!* MGM, 25 Nov. 1935; Producer: Hunt Stromberg; Writers: sp, Albert Hackett, Frances Goodrich; b/o play by Eugene O'Neill; Players: Wallace Beery, Lionel Barrymore, Aline MacMahon, Mickey Rooney.

31. *Anna Karenina*, MGM, 20 Aug. 1935; Producers: David O. Selznick/ Clarence Brown; Writers: sp, Clemence Dane, Salka Viertel, S.N. Behrman; b/o novel by Leo Tolstoy; Players: Greta Garbo, Fredric March, Freddie Bartholomew, Maureen O'Sullivan, May Robson, Basil Rathbone.

32. *Wife Versus Secretary*, MGM, 26 Feb. 1936; Producer: Hunt Stromberg; Writers: sp, Norman Krasna, Alice Duer Miller, John Lee Mahin; b/o novel *Office Wife* by Faith Baldwin; Players: Clark Gable, Myrna Loy, Jean Harlow, May Robson, James Stewart.

33. *The Gorgeous Hussy*, MGM, 1 Sept. 1936; Producer: Joseph L. Mankiewicz; Writers: sp, Ainsworth Morgan, Stephen Morehouse Avery; b/o novel by Samuel Hopkins Adams; Players: Joan Crawford, Robert Taylor, Lionel Barrymore, Franchot Tone, Melvyn Douglas, James Stewart.

34. *Conquest*, MGM, 26 Oct. 1937; Producer: Bernard H. Hyman; Writers: sp, Samuel Hoffenstein, Salka Viertel, S.N. Behrman; b/o novel *Pani Walenska* by Waclaw Gasiorowski and a dramatization by Helen Jerome; Players: Greta Garbo, Charles Boyer, Reginald Owen.

35. *Of Human Hearts*, MGM, 8 Feb. 1938; Producer: John W. Considine, Jr.; Writers: sp, Bradbury Foote; b/o short story "Benefits Forgot" by Honore Willsie Morrow; Players: James Stewart, Walter Huston, Beulah Bondi.

36. *Idiot's Delight*, MGM, 23 Jan. 1939; Producer: Hunt Stromberg; Writers: sp, Robert Sherwood; b/o play by Robert Sherwood; Players: Clark Gable, Norma Shearer, Edward Arnold.

37. *The Rains Came*, 20th Century-Fox, 15 Sept. 1939; Producer: Darryl Zanuck; Writers: sp, Phillip Dunne, Julien Josephson; b/o novel by Louis Bromfield; Players: Myrna Loy, Tyrone Power, George Brent.

38. *Edison, the Man*, MGM, 13 May 1940; Producer: John W. Considine, Jr.; Writers: sp, Talbot Jennings, Bradbury Foote; b/o story by Dore Schary, Hugo Butler; Players: Spencer Tracy, Rita Johnson, Lynne Overman, Charles Coburn.

39. *Come Live with Me*, MGM, 23 Jan. 1941; Producer: Clarence Brown; Writers: sp, Patterson McNutt; b/o story by Virginia Van Upp; Players: James Stewart, Hedy Lamarr, Ian Hunter.

40. *They Met in Bombay*, MGM, 25 June 1941; Producer: Hunt Stromberg; Writers: sp, Edwin Justus Mayer, Anita Loos, Leon Gordon; b/o story by John Kafka; Players: Rosalind Russell, Clark Gable, Peter Lorre.

41. *The Human Comedy*, MGM, 19 Mar. 1943; Producer: Clarence Brown; Writers: sp, Howard Estabrook; b/o play by William Saroyan; Players: Mickey Rooney, Jackie "Butch" Jenkins, James Craig, Marsha Hunt, Fay Bainter, Van Johnson.

42. *National Velvet*, MGM, 19 Dec. 1944, color; Producer: Pandro S. Berman; Writers: sp, Theodore Reeves, Helen Deutsch; b/o novel by Enid Bagnold; Players: Mickey Rooney, Elizabeth Taylor, Ann Revere.

43. *The White Cliffs of Dover*, MGM, 25 Apr. 1944; Producer: Sidney Franklin; Writers: sp, Claudine West, Jan Lustig, George Froeschel; b/o poem "The White Cliffs" by Alice Duer Miller; additional poetry by

Robert Nathan; Players: Irene Dunne, Alan Marshal, Roddy McDowell, Frank Morgan, Van Johnson, Elizabeth Taylor.

44. *The Yearling*, MGM, 20 Dec. 1946; Producer: Sidney Franklin; Writers: sp, Paul Osborn; b/o novel by Marjorie Kinnan Rawlings; Players: Gregory Peck, Jane Wyman, Claude Jarman, Jr.

45. *Song of Love*, MGM, 12 July 1947; Producer: Clarence Brown; Writers: sp, Ivan Tors, Irmgard Von Cube, Allen Vincent, Robert Ardrey; b/o play by Bernard Schubert, Mario Silva; Players: Katharine Hepburn, Paul Henreid, Robert Walker.

46. *Intruder in the Dust*, MGM, 27 Sept. 1949; Producers: Clarence Brown/Dore Schary; Writers: sp, Ben Maddow; b/o novel by William Faulkner; Players: David Brian, Claude Jarman, Jr., Juano Hernandez, Porter Hall, Elizabeth Patterson, Charles Kemper, Will Geer.

47. *To Please a Lady*, MGM, 28 Sept. 1950; Producer: Clarence Brown; Writers: sp, Barre Lyndon, Marge Decker; Players: Clark Gable, Barbara Stanwyck, Adolph Menjou.

48. *Angels in the Outfield*, MGM, 24 Aug. 1951; Producer: Clarence Brown; Writers: sp, Dorothy Kingsley, George Wells; b/o story by Richard Conlin; Players: Paul Douglas, Janet Leigh.

49. *It's a Big Country*, MGM, 16 Nov. 1951; Producer: Dore Schary; co-directed with Richard Thorpe, John Sturges, Charles Vidor, Don Weis, William A. Wellman, Don Hartman; Writers: sp, William Ludwig, Helen Deutsch, Ray Chordes, Isobel Lennart, Allen Rivkin, Dorothy Kingsley, Dore Schary, George Wells; Players: Ethel Barrymore, Gary Cooper, Van Johnson, Gene Kelly, Fredric March.

50. *When in Rome*, MGM, 27 Feb. 1952; Producer: Clarence Brown; Writers: sp, Charles Schnee, Dorothy Kingsley; b/o story "Roman Holiday" by Robert Buckner; Players: Paul Douglas, Van Johnson, Joseph Calleia.

51. *Plymouth Adventure*, MGM, 15 Oct. 1952, color; Producer: Dore Schary; Writers: sp, Helen Deutsch; b/o novel by Ernest Gebler; Players: Spencer Tracy, Gene Tierney, Van Johnson, Lloyd Bridges.

BEN MADDOW
BIBLIOGRAPHY AND
FILMOGRAPHY

BIBLIOGRAPHY

"Obsequy." *Poetry*, 38 (May 1931), 79. Poem.
"The City." *Poetry*, 60 (Jan. 1940), 169–75. Pseudonym, David Wolff. Poem.
 Harriet Monroe Prize for 1940.
"The Reconstruction of the Truth." *Arts and Architecture*, 61, No. 1 (Jan.
 1944), 20–21, 46. Essay.
"The Lilacs." *Mademoiselle* (April 1947), pp. 177, 298–302. Short story.
"The Wire." *Harper's Magazine* (Oct. 1947), pp. 63–68. Short story.
44 Gravel Street. Boston: Little, Brown, 1952.
"Elegy Upon a Certificate of Birth." *Poetry*, 85 (Jan. 1955), 194–95. Poem.
Gauntlet of Flowers. New World Writing *17*. Philadelphia: Lippincott, 1960.
 Novella.
"To Hell the Rabbis." *Kenyon Review*, 23 (Summer 1961), 448–59. Short
 story. Also anthologized in *Best American Short Stories 1962*. Ed. Martha
 Foley and David Burnett. Boston: Houghton, 1962.
"In a Cold Hotel." *Hudson Review*, 15 (Summer 1962), 169–96. Rpt. in *The
 Modern Image*. Ed. Frederick Morgan. New York: Norton, 1965. Prize
 stories 1963: O. Henry Awards.
"Sad Seduction of the Teddy Bear." *Hudson Review*, 16 (Autumn 1963),
 362–69. Short story.
"On the Square." *Hudson Review*, 16 (Autumn 1963), 369–74. Short story.
"Stamp Out Illiteracy, But Slowly." *Genesis West*, 3 (Winter 1965), 79–82.
"Psalm of Twelve Fridays." *Poetry*, 105 (March 1965), 355–57.
"In a Cold Hotel." *New Theatre in America*. New York: Dell, 1965. One-act
 play.
"The Wind Machine." *Harper's Magazine* (Aug. 1966), pp. 55–60.
The Great Right Horn of the Ram. New York: Samuel French, 1967. One-act
 play.
"You, Johann Sebastian Bach." *Hudson Review*, 20 (Autumn 1967), 389–
 416. Short story. Rpt. in *O. Henry Prize Stories*. Garden City, N.Y.: Double-
 day, 1969; *American Literary Anthology II*. New York: Random, 1969.
 Awarded $1,000 National Endowment for the Arts Prize, Washington,
 D.C.
"The Circumcision of James Buttonwood." *Playboy* (Dec. 1968), pp. 187,
 301–302, 304–308, 310. Short story.
Edward Weston: Fifty Years, An Illustrated Biography. Millerton, N.Y.: Aper-

ture, 1973. Nominated for National Book Award; awarded annual prize of Photographic Historical Society.

"Up from Zoar." *Playboy* (March 1975), pp. 72–74, 80, 184–88. Short story.

Faces: A History of Portrait Photography from 1820 to the Present. New York: Chanticleer Press, 1977.

A Sunday Between Wars. New York: Norton, in press.

A History of the Nude in Photography. New York: Harper, in press.

FILMOGRAPHY

Native Land, 1942. Co-screenplay. Pseudonym David Wolff.

The Man from Colorado, 1948. Co-screenwriter with Robert D. Andrews. Nominated by the Writers Guild for Best Screenplay.

Framed, 1948. Screenplay.

Intruder in the Dust, 1949. Screenplay. Nominated by the Writers Guild for Best Screenplay.

The Asphalt Jungle, 1950. Co-screenwriter with John Huston. Nominated by the Writers Guild and Motion Picture Academy for Best Screenplay.

The Stairs, 1953. Writer and director for the National Mental Health Association.

The Unforgiven, 1960. Co-screenwriter with John Huston.

The Savage Eye, 1960. Original story, screenplay, producer and director with Joseph Strick and Sidney Meyers. Venice, Edinburgh, Mannheim Film Festival Awards; Robert Flaherty Award.

Two Loves, 1961. Screenplay from novel *Spinster*.

The Balcony, 1963. Screenplay. Nominated by the Writers Guild for Best Screenplay. Cited Edinburgh Film Festival.

An Affair of the Skin, 1964. Screenplay and direction. Re-edited and retitled *Love As Disorder*.

The Chairman, 1969. Screenplay.

The Secret of Santa Vittoria, 1969. Screenplay with William Rose.

Storm of Strangers, 1970. Writer and director. First Prize San Francisco Film Festival; American Film Festival, Blue Ribbon; Venice Biennial Medal, 21st Festival; Melbourne Film Festival, Special Prize; Festival Dei Populi (Florence) Award; Edinburgh Festival; Atlanta International Film Festival, Gold Medal; Cine 1970, Golden Eagle Award.

INDEX

The text of *Faulkner's Intruder in the Dust: Novel into Film* was set into type on the Variable Input Phototypesetter in 10-point Baskerville with 2-point spacing between the lines. The book was designed by Jim Billingsley, composed by the Book Division of Moran Industries, Inc., Baton Rouge, Louisiana, printed offset by Thomson-Shore, Inc., Dexter, Michigan, and bound by John H. Dekker & Sons, Grand Rapids, Michigan. The paper is Patina, developed for extended shelf life by the S.D. Warren Company.

THE UNIVERSITY OF TENNESSEE PRESS : KNOXVILLE